Praise for previous books by Joan Freeman

"Joan Freeman is to be congratulated on a refreshing and original work which should be read by anyone who has the slightest interest in education, the psychology of abilities or even their fellow human beings."
Research Intelligence

"A highly enjoyable, readable, informative book, with a clear direct style, mercifully jargon-free and wholly unpretentious."
British Educational Research Association

"The field of education for the gifted and talented would be radically improved with more research of this calibre . . . I strongly suggest putting it on your reading list."
Roeper Review USA

"A book to be valued and should be read by all parents and teachers who care about their children."
Perspective

"Others may claim to have highlighted the needs of the most gifted school children, but it is Joan Freeman who has put it on the map and kept it there."
The Independent

"The integrity of the research shows through and the writing style makes this bedtime reading . . . there is no denying the foundations of erudition on which this book is written. Like the renowned psychiatrist Oliver Sacks a generation ago with his fascinating descriptions of extreme mental disorder, Freeman's book too has the potential similarly to draw a wide audience of readers into another field concerned with extreme dimensions of human activity. By simply making her work so accessible she merits similar acknowledgement and recognition."
British Journal of Educational Psychology

"Parents, teachers, gifted administrators and college professors will find Gifted Children Grown Up to be an invaluable addition to their book shelves."
Gifted and Talented International

"Your book is an excellent report and resource. I will use it a great deal. You write with clarity and down to earthness that I admire."
Professor John Feldhusen, Purdue University, USA

"This book is a fascinating read, accessible and with insights for educators, parents and the gifted. The findings and warnings in this book are of relevance, not only to those concerned with the education of gifted children."
The Psychology of Education Review

"a compelling read . . . making vivid links across time and across theory."
Educating Able Children

"Anyone interested in the education and development of gifted students will find a wealth of information in these pages."
High Ability Studies

Gifted Lives

This book reveals the dramatic stories of 20 outstandingly gifted people as they grew from early promise to maturity in Britain. Written by an award-winning psychologist who has meticulously recorded these intimate biographies over the last 35 years, this fascinating account reveals the frustrations and triumphs of her remarkable participants, and investigates why some fell by the wayside whilst others reached fame and fortune.

The individuals featured here possess a range of intellectual, social and emotional gifts, including mathematics, the arts, empathy and spirituality. As well as negotiating the basic trials of growing up, the particular abilities of these exceptional people often meant they were confronted with extra emotional challenges, such as over-anxious and pushy parents, teacher put-downs, social trip-wires, loss of fun time, boredom and bullying in school and conflicting life choices. Their stories illustrate how seemingly innocuous events such as skipping one or more school grades could have devastating life-long consequences, and allow the reader to ponder thought-provoking questions such as: Does having a brilliant mind help when you are ethnically different or suffering serious depression? How does a world-class pianist cope when repetitive strain injury strikes, or a young financier when he hits his first million?

Joan Freeman's interpretations of and insights into the twists and turns of the lives of these extraordinary people are captivating and deeply moving. She shows us that while fate played a large part in their successes, so did a personal outlook which could see and grab a fleeting chance, overcome great odds and put in the necessary hard work to lift childhood prodigy to greatness. Readers will identify with many of the intriguing aspects of these people's lives, and perhaps learn something about themselves too.

Professor Joan Freeman, **PhD**, is a Fellow of the British Psychological Society, which has also honoured her with a Lifetime Achievement Award for her work with the gifted and talented. She is Founding President of the European Council for High Ability. She has published 17 books, two government reports and many scholarly papers, and is invited to lecture around the world. She has a private psychology practice in London (www.joanfreeman.com).

Gifted Lives

What Happens When Gifted Children Grow Up?

Joan Freeman

Routledge
Taylor & Francis Group

LONDON AND NEW YORK

First published 2010
by Routledge
27 Church Road, Hove, East Sussex BN3 2FA

Simultaneously published in the USA and Canada
by Routledge
270 Madison Avenue, New York, NY 10016

Routledge is an imprint of the Taylor & Francis Group, an Informa business

Copyright © 2010 Psychology Press

Typeset in New Century Schoolbook by Garfield Morgan,
Swansea, West Glamorgan
Printed and bound in Great Britain by TJ International Ltd
Padstow, Cornwall
Cover design by Andrew Ward

This publication has been produced with paper manufactured to strict
environmental standards and with pulp derived from sustainable forests.

British Library Cataloguing in Publication Data
A catalogue record for this book is available from the British Library

Library of Congress Cataloging-in-Publication Data
Freeman, Joan, 1935-
  Gifted lives : what happens when gifted children grow up? Joan Freeman.
    p. cm.
  Includes bibliographical references and index.
  ISBN 978-0-415-47008-7 (hb) – ISBN 978-0-415-47009-4 (pb)
  1. Gifted persons–Great Britain–Case studies. 2. Gifted persons–Great
Britain–Longitudinal studies. 3. Gifted children–Great Britain–Longitudinal
studies. 4. Gifted children–Education–Great Britain–Case studies. 5. Gifted
children. I. Title.
  BF412.F74 2010
  305.9'089–dc22

                                                            2010006470

ISBN: 978-0-415-47008-7 (hbk)
ISBN: 978-0-415-47009-4 (pbk)

Contents

Acknowledgements

Life must be lived forward but can only be understood backward.

Søren Kierkegaard

Hundreds of people have given me their time and answered my showers of questions generously and openly since 1974. My debt to all of them is beyond simple thanks, but that is all I can say. In truth, for the people who have stuck it out with me over the years, my early strict objectiveness has rather fallen away. Although they don't all know each other, they all know me. I've become an unusual sort of friend to so many, popping up every few years on their doorsteps all over the country to ask, 'How're you doing?'

I sincerely thank all the people who've shared their experiences with me; not only those directly in the study, but also their parents, sometimes grandparents, husbands, wives and life partners, religious leaders, mentors and some of their friends.

Professionally, my investigations have been a personal journey. I've seen great changes in approach to the whole area of gifts and talents. At the start of my project, it was generally accepted that the gifted and talented were rare and often peculiar, but by 2010 that view has almost gone. The possibility of developing natural abilities to the highest levels is now seen as much more available to every child. It is no longer the preserve of a favoured few – a democratisation of the development of high-level potential.

My contribution to psychology has been to increase understanding of the development of gifted and talented individuals. It is for that I was given the Lifetime Achievement Award from the British Psychological Society by my professional colleagues. I thank them. And if indeed my research and writing have helped to bring about positive changes in people's lives, I am very proud.

In recent years, the British government has put educational programmes in place which were unthinkable when this research started. Many millions of pounds have gone into supporting the development of gifts and talents in schools. Not all the schemes have been successful, but the scene across the country is now much more positive for the potentially gifted and talented. The next step is to help the adults, the later developers, because this study has shown how vital it is to keep going after the school gates have closed.

This text is so highly condensed from my decades of information-gathering that, as an author, I fear at best over-simplification and at worst distortion. It's encouraging, though, that what I published in the three earlier books on this project was widely accepted by the people concerned. And where there has been any clash of our memories on what really happened, it has usually caused amusement all round. Names and places have been changed, unless those involved had no objections.

For helping me in this massive work, I especially thank Professor Gillian Parker and Della Alvarez. Many in the media have given me encouragement through their continued interest. Different TV productions have starred some of the participants and me. The popular Channel 4 series, *Child Genius*, organised by Leanne Klein, took up my idea of following-up another group of gifted and talented children. Thanks, too, to so many of my professional colleagues who have given me support, urged me to continue the research and write this book, especially Pieter Span, Bob Sternberg, Rena Subotnik, Harald Wagner, Detlef Rost, Ulrike Stedtniz, Diane Montgomery, Angela Mendonça, Zenita Guenther and Taisir Subhi. I thank all the Tower Education Group for their tolerance in waiting for me to work on our next report, notably Johanna Raffan. To supportive friends, Rosemary Friedman, Scarlett Epstein, Lucien Gubbay and John Maddox (in memoriam) – thank you.

Thank you to my endorsers, Louis Wolpert and Brenda Maddox. Putting your approval in print is committment indeed.

My sincere thanks to Leslie Gardner, my agent, who really cares for her clients. And to Becci Edmondson, my publishing editor, who has steered me carefully.

This study has taken a great deal of time and money. The work could not have been done without the financial support of the Calouste Gulbenkian Foundation (UK) and the Esmée Fairbairn Foundation in London, most especially Hilary Hodgson. She gave me encouragement, endless patience and a great deal of flexibility. I thank her most heartily.

The best reward for me has been the development of affectionate relationships with the wonderful people who have been with me on this project for so long. We have got to know each other pretty well. I believe our friendships will last even though the official project must come to an end. I wish every one a good and fruitful life.

To my family for putting up with disruption. And to Hugh – editor supreme and my dearest love.

Introduction

Although . . . the seeds of excellence must lie in individuals themselves, we cannot afford to be complacent. Society has a vital duty to provide the framework, the teaching and support, and even the incentive, to enable people to develop themselves and their abilities to their fullest possible potential.
Sebastian Coe (to Joan Freeman), Olympic gold medal runner and Chair of the Organising Committee for the London Olympic Games 2012

The lives of gifted people, their passions, beliefs, ambitions, joy and despair, make up the dramatic and sometimes startling life-stories in this book. I've known all of those involved since they were children in the mid-1970s, appearing in their lives every few years as the decades rolled on. I've tested and interviewed every one for very many hours. They are part of the longest intimate study of the gifted and talented in the world.

Far from the psychologist's office or the school classroom, out in the real world, I've been seeking to solve some of the mystery surrounding ideas and myths of giftedness. What are the gifted like? How do they interact with the rest of the world? Are they always successful? What makes them tick? How do they cope with the anguish that is so often a part of creative endeavour? How does it feel to have your brilliant insight scrutinised in the public eye? These vivid life-stories are almost novellas, and some could make a book or a play.

Each person in this book was measured as being at least in the top 0.2 per cent of the population in intelligence; some had intelligence too high to measure at all. But that is only a part of their make-up. Many are also gifted and talented in several areas. Each one featured has been chosen because their lives illustrate aspects of how it is to live with this astounding exceptionality, from childhood through the teenage years to maturity.

I am the psychological profiler, the detective, working to tease out reasons why people behave as they do in their particular circumstances. Among my qualifications as a psychologist, I am a counsellor. I also have a strong natural curiosity about people, which probably drew me into psychology in the first place. I've learned to question carefully, I hope with an open mind, to be sensitive in listening to replies and interpreting what I hear and see according to a variety of academic theories, as well as my own instinct.

Unlike a postal or e-mail questionnaire, to which people just jot down ticks and crosses or add a few words, my intimate style of personal exploration demands trust if it is to be worthwhile. Maybe some embellished a story or two, but if so I believe this was not significant in the bigger picture. Overall, in statistical terms, the trends and probabilities from the many hundreds of interviews were clear to see. The numbers are to be found in the three previous books on the study. But this fourth book is different. It gives just 20 portraits of the gifted people selected from the original sample of 210 who had spanned a very wide spectrum of abilities.

This has been no ordinary psychological study. As the decades passed, I've played much more of a part in most of the participants' lives than researchers usually do – something between a mother-confessor and a watchful god-fairy. I reappear at intervals with my tape-recorder and camera, noting what they have been up to – at least what they're prepared to tell me about. For some, I hope I've been a good friend, providing careers advice, writing references, as well as offering a relatively objective shoulder to cry on. For others, maybe I've been a nuisance. Some have been reticent to talk at difficult times of their lives, while others call me in to talk over their problems. Occasionally, I've felt I almost know them better than their own families.

For most, their true gifts and talents are far too high or too subtle to be scored by any tests. Some could do almost anything brilliantly, whether sport, music or philosophy, while others have stayed keenly focused on a single area, such as mathematics or music. It is entirely because of their gifts and talents that they've found themselves in challenging situations which the non-gifted would never experience.

Long studies

The great benefit of long studies is to see how children's behaviour develops, so that successful actions can be encouraged and bad ones dropped. Catch 22 is that such studies inevitably started way back when things were different, begging the question of how relevant the findings are today. There's no way round that one.

During a lifetime, gifts and talents may take many different forms, appear in quite unexpected situations and at different points. Some people reach old age before they start to shine, like Mary Wesley, the highly successful English writer, and the American Grandma Moses, who only began her world-famous paintings in her seventies. Neither had any special attention for their gifts as children. In this intimate investigation with two and occasionally three generations of a family, I could see how experiences and attitudes that were formed in gifted children threaded through their teenage lives into adulthood, affecting their success and happiness.

My own understanding of gifts and how they may or may not develop has gained immensely because the research went on for so long. In 1974, the youngest in my sample was just turned five and the oldest 14. Now, in 2010, writing at what I think is the end of this long study, it has acquired a historical aspect. As in all history, at any point in time the people involved cannot know what is going to happen; they are fixed in their time, as indeed I was at any time in the work. The novelist, L. P. Hartley wrote that, 'The past is a foreign country; they do things differently there.' But unlike a novelist or historian trying to piece the past together, I tape-recorded words at the time and took photographs and records – a time-capsule to hand.

Watching every life develop along its twists and turns and ups and downs, it struck me frequently and forcibly that had I stopped my investigations at the normal developmental times, usually at the end of one of the educational stages, the picture would have been quite different.

Only the gifted and talented can say how it is for them at the time. And telling it like it is, is not at all the same as remembering. Memory is well known as a slippery trickster. It can gloss over or exaggerate the bad times and the good. What is half-remembered cries out to have sense made of it, sometimes with a little fine-tuning. Two of the women, for example, had remembered university as the happiest time of their lives, though I'd recorded both of them at the time as soaked in tears. Sigmund Freud, in *Civilisation and its Discontents*, wrote that, 'nothing once formed in the mind could ever perish [. . .] everything survives in some way or another, and is capable under certain conditions of being brought to light again.' But he also presented the world with the ideas of repression and the distortions of memory.

Without a long-term perspective, expensive programmes for the gifted may not be justified. Although they are usually presented as providing an initial boost to children's achievement, it may be largely due to the Hawthorne effect, that is, to sheer attention and change. We do not know whether there is any measurable difference in long-term achievement in the children who attend courses for the gifted, either compared with children on any other courses or how long any possible benefits may last.

Growing up gifted

The essential message from this follow-up of gifted and talented children compared with the non-gifted is that they are normal people – but with one big difference – their extraordinary abilities. Unfortunately, other people may react negatively to their exceptionality, and in very different ways. Some of the gifted were exploited for adult glory, while others found their feelings of self-worth squashed for being 'too clever by half'. Too many had to cope with teacher put-downs in class. Does it make the teacher feel better, I wonder? To a sensitive child, it could take just a single traumatic remark or action to change their lives; this was the case for little Ady in Chapter 11, whose teacher dramatically tore up his sensitive poem to the glee of the watching class because it wasn't quite in line with what she'd set. Or it could be the slow grind of parental anxiety and pressure for success that wears down a child's natural enthusiasm, as it was for Margaret in Chapter 9.

Yet whatever obstacles the gifted faced as youngsters, these were as nothing compared to what they had to accomplish as adults to be seen as outstanding. The daily banal grind of earning a living was often the most powerful force in adulthood, which obliged many to push their gifts aside to pay the mortgage and feed a family.

Fate could be kind or cruel. But how each individual reacted to what they'd experienced depended very much on personal outlook. Many times across the decades, I've seen how two youngsters with the same high potential reacted quite differently to a similar obstacle in life. There were two youths, for instance, with very high school-leaving qualifications who faced the same challenge of gaining entry to Oxford University – both having already been turned down. One boy, together with his mother, took a train to the university and knocked on the doors of college after college demanding to be seen, until he managed to gain acceptance by one of them. The other boy's family and headteacher thought perhaps he had aimed too high and retreated without even trying.

Personality and intelligence are not the same thing, although they do get confused. Again and again, I could see how personality is a major player in what gifted people choose to do (or not to do) with their lives. Shakespeare said it in *Two Gentlemen of Verona* (Alexander 2006),

Some to the wars, to try their fortune there;
Some to discover islands far away;
Some to the studious universities.

(I. iii. 9–11)

So, what are gifts and talents?

Here, I've used the word 'gifted' to mean outstandingly high mental ability, and 'talented' to mean outstandingly high artistic ability, though the two overlap, and many in this book have both. Formal definitions of gifts and talents vary immensely, especially in different societies, so that no individual could fit into them all. Most people see 'gifted' children as being far in advance of their age-group at school, and the 'talented' as little virtuosi, bowing to acknowledge applause. But whereas the children do not make new contributions to their field of expertise, gifted and talented adults do.

From my long experience of hundreds of the gifted and talented, from toddlers to grandparents, I cannot accept that all babies are created equal in potential and that it's only environment that makes the differences between them. Not every child has the potential to compose like Mozart, even if they had his upbringing. Although circumstances certainly do make a difference to individuals, they can only influence the potential of what's there to be developed. In all the millennia of recorded human life, no-one has ever taken a child at random and purposely brought them to gifted level.

Descriptions of giftedness usually depend on what is being looked for, whether IQ scores, school marks, solving paper-and-pencil puzzles or creative work recognised by an expert. It is strange that gifts which are vital to the health of a society such as entrepreneurship, economics or people-management are rarely considered by schools. My view is inclusive and concerned with the psychology of giftedness and talent in its many manifestations. I am certain that in every country, there are children packed with potential who are never recognised in a formal educational setting, but who given the opportunity would grasp it and rise to great heights. Some in this book had to overcome heavy odds to shine, while others appeared to have it all made ready for them yet simply turned their faces away from golden opportunities.

This unique look at gifts and talents

When I started this investigation, I had no idea it would go on for so long. About every ten years or so, I believed it had come to an end – as I do now. But colleagues kept asking me what had happened to the children, so I got myself another grant and undertook another year of travelling about the country to catch up with them again.

Attitudes have changed. In the mid-1970s in the Western world, educational and social feelings were against distinguishing children by high-level potential, other than for dance and music. This view still holds here and there. Before my study, no evidence about gifts and talents had ever been carried out in a scientific way, that is with specifically controlled comparison groups. There were, though, plenty of anecdotes on the lines of, 'I once knew an amazing child who . . .', 'My friend's little girl . . .', 'The trouble with gifted children is . . .'.

Back then, I too used to think of gifted and talented children as rare creatures, bored stiff in a normal classroom. The popular image of a gifted child was of an old-fashioned boy with thick spectacles and painful emotional problems, guarding his sensitive soul from the uncaring world with barely a friend to talk to at his high level.

William Shakespeare pictured prince Hamlet that way, as an intellectual student deep into philosophy, whose emotional problems removed him from real life. He had plenty of intelligence, but when he was pulled out of university to attend to corruption and murder at court he could not act because he was 'sicklied o'er with the pale cast of thought'. Shakespeare himself had little time for dallying with ideas; he had plays to put on and money to earn. He seems to have had little patience for the gifted, not least, as he wrote in *Cymbeline*, 'Golden lads and girls all must,/ As chimney sweepers, come to dust.'

But my long involvement with truly gifted individuals in their daily lives has discovered a very different and much more complex picture than the stereotype of the strange gifted boy. I found friendly normal people with some exceptional abilities. But because of those abilities they had to deal with growing up in a world which sometimes sought to exploit them and sometimes stood too far back in awe to give them the support they needed.

This study has remained unique in research into gifts and talents in two ways. Firstly, the in-depth face-to-face interviews over 35 years have reached depths of understanding that no other such study of the gifted has ever done. Secondly, comparisons are vital for scientific evidence. By setting up matched comparison groups of the gifted and the non-gifted from the start, I was able to show their similarities and differences as they grew up. General population statistics are not sufficiently focused. If one only looks at the highly-achieving – as almost all writers on gifts and talents have done – there's no way of finding out whether or how they might differ from other individuals.

To begin with, I had to persuade 60 schools to help me, and 210 families and their 210 children to let me into their homes and tell me about their lives. At times I felt like a salesperson trying to get my foot into so many doors. On the road, my tools were the public pay phone (pre-mobile) by the roadside to check on appointments, rain-splattered maps (pre-satnav), my open-ended questionnaires and my camera (pre-digital). My little audio tape-recorder captured almost everything of our interactions, which were then keyed into my primitive Osborne 'transportable' computer. It had a tiny screen offering just a phrase or two, so that I had to scroll back and forth along each sentence to read it. Dogged determination (inbuilt) was essential to seek out each family in town and country, through rain, sunshine, snow and storm. It took over my life from time to time.

Objective measurement is essential to counter so many of the myths about gifted and talented children. I never took anyone's word, neither teacher nor parent, about whether a child was gifted and measured all 210 of the children individually on many standardised ability and personality tests to be quite sure. The deep questioning conversations I had in the comfort and familiarity of someone's home could produce quite different answers from those given when children were in the unnatural situation of facing a stranger questioning them across a table in an office.

Early on, I discovered that certain children get picked as gifted and talented in particular situations. In a school with an average ability level, for instance, teachers would point me to children who they saw as gifted, but who would have been below average in a high-powered school. Other children failed to get sufficient chances or encouragement to develop their natural gifts, found life frustrating and lowered their sights to what was expected of them.

Parents and teachers also made mistakes in identifying children as gifted when they were not. Kevin had taken it badly and suffered from childhood depression because he was not able to satisfy his dominant mother's view of him as a brilliant intellectual. Not unreasonably, he saw himself as a failure, both to her and as a human being. As an overweight 12 year old he spent a lot of his time in front of the television sometimes asleep, and I found it difficult to get him to relax with me and talk. He seemed to find it difficult to get his thoughts together. His single mother complained that his primary school had discriminated against him so that he did not get into her choice of an academic secondary school. She went to his primary school many times to try to change their minds. I agreed with the teachers, who had probably saved him from a life of everyday school humiliation until he was obliged to leave.

If I had stopped the research while Kevin was still at school, or even a few years later, I could have marked down his sad childhood as negative due to parental pressure. But within ten years of leaving school and home, the butterfly broke out of his chrysalis. As an adult with his own earnings, he was able to escape his dreary life. In his mid-forties he very cheerily runs a bar in the South of Spain with his wife and children. His life is crowded with friends and laughter, fun and sunshine. Gifted indeed.

What I have found

Any labelling of children does make a difference to their growing sense of who they are. In the first big statistical analyses of the vast data I'd collected by 1980, I found that the children whose parents had identified them as gifted had emotional problems far more frequently than identically gifted but unlabelled children. Thanks to the home visits and the long conversations, I was able to find out why – the children labelled by their parents as gifted were also far more likely to have troubled home backgrounds. This was not always so, but significantly more frequent for the labelled gifted children than any of the others.

No amount of brilliance in a child can provide a shield from emotional disturbance. Many of the labelling parents had blamed the child's gifts for behavioural problems, when the roots of the problems were buried in what was going on at home. Rachel Wallace, for example, (Chapter 1) had to cope with often being told she was a big problem to her parents because she was so gifted. Distress in the children's lives, such as warring parents, naturally caused them unhappiness as it would any child. Some of the gifted were grade-skipped in school, though this action, even by just a single year, does not imply that the child has a matching emotional maturity, and many did not. This educational jump can be successful in the short term, but in this longer view I have found it to cause mourning for lost childhoods right into middle age.

Baruch Spinoza, the seventeenth-century Dutch Jewish philosopher, wrote of 'the deep difficulty of excellence'. When I hear people say glibly that the gifted can look out for themselves and that, like cream, they will always rise to the top of the milk, I want to tell them how it really is – how tortuous the road to excellence can be, and how it depends on so many things whether anyone can keep their foothold and stay on it.

That precipitous path is beset by threats to excellence. No matter how high your potential when you are born, the big barriers of poverty and social disapproval can wreak havoc in your life. To reach success and happiness you need opportunities – generous, appropriate learning material, good teaching with consistent challenge, examples to follow, motivation for the long hours of practice and the personal courage to take a chance. There's no formula for producing a gifted child or a gifted adult, but we know that without high-quality material provision and consistent high-level teaching, potential gifts cannot be realised. This goes for all subjects – sciences, sports, arts – though I am less sure about business!

Potential high-flyers need to feel worthy of their gifts, to have a good self-concept, or they will not put in the energy and time to develop them to their highest levels. The amount of praise a child gets is cultural and so must be judged as appropriate. Too much praise falls like water off a duck's back and too little will not provide enough encouragement. Mental ill health, such as depression or anxiety, devastates gifted achievement. Those who have reached excellence with those illnesses have done so in spite of them, between bouts, or know constant struggles against the debility.

Individual personality, which is about 50 per cent inborn, has a big influence on the actions needed to realise gifts, including ambition, hard work, seeing and grabbing opportunity and so on. Some people prefer not to use their gifts. Fate can inspire or knock down, depending on how the person takes it. Some rise to a challenge and some go under.

Just a few of my sample rose to worldly fame and fortune. Without exception, no matter how glittering their early prospects, everyone who reached a high level had worked extremely hard for most of their lives to reach it. The vital spark has been encouragement throughout life's challenges and positive outlooks all round. The complexities, interactions and unexpected turns of these life-stories are all here in this book – the put-downs, the strivings, the doubts, disappointments and depression, the highs, the parents who pressed too hard, the myths, the unstoppable urge to create, conflicting career choices, and strokes of luck seen and taken – they are all here as part of the true drama of these gifted lives.

PART 1

Too many gifts

Now there are diversities of gifts but the same spirit.
I Corinthians, 12: 4

Some people have so many gifts and talents that they could shine brilliantly at any of them. But time is limited and decisions have to be made about which paths to follow, about what to do with all that bursting potential. In this first part, I've featured three people who epitomise what it's like to be torn between competing gifts and talents. Where Rachel managed to jump a huge chasm from one gift to another, Jeremy almost ruined his life by trying to follow two ways of life at the same time, and Andy drew on his many gifts and talents to save his life.

Being able to choose well from a range of enticing possible courses requires taking an overview of what one can do, as well as what is available, and making a stab at what may be suitable for one's future. Such life decisions are not easy for a teenager to take. It not only means taking a clear view of the situation, but also knowing oneself. I have also seen that following one's heart can be more fulfilling and satisfying than taking a cold look at what is on offer as a career. Fortunately, over and over again, I've found that the most intellectually gifted youngsters also had an advanced level of personal awareness, but if they were persuaded to go against their inclinations they could make career mistakes. Those mistakes could be costly, in terms of either getting back on the right track again or spending a lifetime doing something they did not much care for, even though their native abilities brought them achievement.

People who have a wide range of gifts often think differently. Most can handle a lot of information in many fields at the same time, most famously women, as I found. Gifted thinking is not just hard work, dealing with deep problems or being inspired by startling flashes of insight, it often means a big leap in mental efficiency, which means that the gifted can do more with what they have. The gifted can keep competing ideas and interpretations active within working memory till they sort out a way of co-ordinating them. One might say that they have the extra gift of doing their best for longer.

Professor John Geake, the Australian neurologist, coined the term 'fluid analogising' for a way of thinking which uses implicit comparisons. Good teachers use it a lot, as do intelligence tests, such as, 'Black is to white as day is to . . .?' The gifted are really good at fluid analogising where there's a variety of possibilities to be considered at the same time, whether consciously or not. A simple example would be, 'What is the London of America?' It could be Washington (the capital), New York (the biggest city) or Los Angeles (the centre of the film industry).

Young Norman Mailer, the writer, was multiply gifted and talented, and also spurred on by an ambitious and dominating mother. He graduated in aeronautical engineering from Harvard University, but his heart yearned for literature so that he devoured books and writing prolifically. He was a man packed with energy. Not only did he become a distinguished Man of Letters in the field he loved, he also managed to have six wives, nine biological children and an adopted son. He did not spend time examining his navel, wondering about what to do, but leapt enthusiastically from one temptation to another. His saving grace was an iron discipline for hard work because he cannot be said to have had a talent for good relationships with women.

Not all multiple gifts come at the same time, though. Childhood gifts are likely to come in rule-based fields like music, chess or mathematics, which use the manipulation of symbols in objective knowledge. However, as neither chess nor performing music are usually school subjects, early excellence in mathematics is the only one from which one could draw a straight line between excellence at school and high-level adult achievement. Teachers can envisage their best pupils making good in the world, which is a big reason why they are keen to encourage mathematical potential. Everyone has heard of computer nerds, eight year olds who pass examinations meant for 16 year olds, or children like Ruth Lawrence and Sufiah Yusof, who entered university very early to study mathematics. In other areas, children who perform above what is usual for their age are still performing as children. A ten-year-old painter cannot paint like an adult.

That style of progress is true for child prodigies who hit fame and appear in the media from time to time. It was also true for the three people in this part. Their childhood prodigiousness did not match their adult gifts. For these three, fate came along, changed their lives and gave a big tweak to the emphasis on their gifts.

Mailer's shift could only be one way, from the objective discipline of engineering to the high creativity of serious literature, because the latter demands maturity and life experiences. Although children can have first-hand experiences, they can miss the emotional understanding of the nuances and subtleties of adult human relationships. To be a major creative adult requires new ways of seeing events, innovation and rebelliousness in response to the way things are. As Einstein said, 'Any intelligent fool can make things bigger and more complex. It takes a touch of genius and a lot of courage to move in the opposite direction.'

As the three gifted and talented people in this part grew to maturity, Rachel was able to leave her prodigious maths behind and move on to deep spirituality. Jeremy made the decision to move from musical prodigy to medicine, but realised his mistake too late. Andy drew on his extraordinary multiple childhood gifts and talents to conquer constant life-threatening experiences.

1

Maths prodigy to saint

What will be on the exam paper when you die?
Rachel Wallace

At her funeral, Rachel's Church of England vicar announced that she had become 'sanctified'. He looked at the packed hall of mourners and told them,

Many people get cancer. Many people get terminal cancer. Not many people become holy along the way. The last few weeks and months before Rachel died were utterly amazing and extraordinary, full of light and peace, full of coincidences which were not coincidences and whose number just intensified as the end drew near.

Her adoring husband, Robert, then addressed the funeral congregation. He was calm and joyful, 'In her own particular and inimitable way, and retaining flaws and frailties, she had allowed herself to become a saint.' In the eyes of those who knew her, and for workers in Christianity, Rachel Wallace had become a saint, though she was never officially sanctified.

Those who grieved for her described the church service as more like a wedding than a funeral – the happiness and love they felt were so overwhelming. Rachel had chosen the hymns which they sang together with all their hearts, and nobody wanted to leave when it was over. Many stayed to tell the vicar inspiring stories of the spiritual woman they had known. Susan Sontag, discussing cancer in *Illness as Metaphor*, described how 'people with cancer find themselves being shunned by relatives and friends'. But not Rachel. Quite the opposite. During the last months of her dying, many people had made their way through her little wooden gate to knock on her cottage door. They came to pour out their troubles, seeking her blessing and its comfort.

Most Christians, in fact most believing people, see religious instructions as a moral code to live by. For most of her young life, that was how it had been for Rachel – obedience to a powerful view of Christianity directed by threats and promises – though even as a little child, she'd had serious doubts. Naturally, when she was in her early thirties and first heard from her doctors that she was terminally ill, she was angry and grieved terribly for her snatched-away beautiful life.

But just a few months before she died, while still feeling relatively well and pumped up by steroids, she quietly told me that she'd quite suddenly stopped fighting her approaching fate, her life-long anguish fell away and she accepted that her dying was more of a gain to her than a loss. She told me of her spiritual conviction that was so much deeper than merely getting in touch with her personal resources. Her vicar told me later that this change had been so sudden and intense, it was 'as though a spiritual hand-grenade had blown her into deep Christian belief'.

In her final months, Rachel was able to see life as a unity beyond her immediate awareness. She was on her way to a different place. She could take a wider, freer perspective, as though watching from afar what was happening to her. She knew, she said, that there was a larger plan and meaning to life, something beyond mortal existence, and this gave her joy, contentment and infinite compassion for humankind.

With that insight, Rachel prayed every day, long and silently. Sometimes she prayed with her vicar and sometimes with a dear friend, a nun in a nearby Catholic retreat. There she found emotional space and tranquility. Several times a week, for an hour or so, as her death approached, she and the nun would talk gently about daily life and God. Then Rachel would stay there by herself for an hour or two longer before snapping back into the life of a busy young mother. She'd pick her three children up from school, see to their food and their homework, bathe them, put them to bed and read them a bedtime story.

During those final months, Rachel knew peak experiences and spiritual rapture beyond her daily living and anything she'd known before. From the time of her transformation, those who knew her said they could see a physical difference. Even strangers passing by would stop in wonder when they looked at her. Although she looked very healthy, her vicar saw her differently. He told me that she seemed to have become 'diaphanous, almost transparent, as though a light were glowing through her'. Spiritually she glowed, sometimes she stunned those around by telling them what they needed to know before they knew it themselves. People wondered at her prescience: how she could be so sure. 'Holiness is within all of us,' her friend the nun told me, but 'for Rachel there was so little time.' She had to grasp hers with both hands, and soared to an extraordinary height of spirituality.

As her praying became more intense, she found she'd stopped asking for things and instead began listening. Her Christianity deepened and the darkness which had plagued her most of her life, the guilt, the feelings of unworthiness and fear of punishment, rolled away. She had totally surrendered herself to God, at one with Him. Her vicar explained to me quietly that it was her absolute surrender which had made it possible for her to take on the mantle of a saint.

Rachel slipped away as dawn was breaking.

Mathematical gifts and spiritual beliefs

Thirty years earlier, when Rachel was just nine years old, I'd taken the rattling underground train to a poor, grimy district of London to have a long talk with her mother. She was a small woman with a small voice, and was soberly dressed as befitted her obligations as a Church of England vicar's wife. Afterwards, she generously invited me to join the family at dinner. Rachel, her mother and father, her sister and I, bowed our heads over the table and her father thanked the Lord for what we were about to receive. There were lamb chops with gravy, mashed potatoes and green beans. For dessert, there were tinned peaches and ice cream. We talked together over the good food. Mrs Wallace's sincerity was unmistakable, as she explained what her Christianity meant to her and her family:

Christianity is the centre of our world. When I became a Christian, I'd been contemplating committing suicide – but after that, I knew there was a point to life. At the time, I was being prepared for confirmation and in the final class. We were all kneeling in church in separate pews, and the vicar said, 'I want you to just kneel down and try to realise that God is real.' I knelt down and was aware of Isaiah's vision of the Lord, high and mighty, sat on His throne within the temple. And I was aware – almost as a touch thing – of Christ kneeling beside me with His arms crossed, and I was aware of the Holy Spirit's presence all round me, and I just had such an overwhelming conviction that if I opened my eyes, I would see the Holy Trinity.

I was totally unprepared for the experience and totally surprised because ours wasn't the kind of church that believed in conversion. I didn't tell anyone. The following week I was confirmed. That's when we were to receive the Holy Spirit, and I went up trembling all over, terrified. The bishop put his hand on my head, 'Credo', and I had this total sensation of a warm glow coming into me; and peace and joy. I have shared this many times later with other Christians, and they've said that it was an authentic Christian experience of the Holy Spirit. It's never left me – I've never doubted there was a God, even in deep depression. He is the most important thing in life.

When I was twenty, I heard voices: God spoke to me just as if he was actually there. He said these words: 'I want you to go to Uganda.' I said, 'No, the Lord can't order me,' yet I finished up in Uganda seven years later. Lots of things have happened since then that I have known about and experienced which can't be explained any other way, except that it's God.

Rachel's parents' faith decided their lives. She was born in Uganda where they were working as Christian missionaries, returning to England when she was three months old. Her father then became a teacher at an evangelical Christian school, which Rachel also attended. He left that to become a vicar. At times, life was a financial struggle for the family.

I measured Rachel's intelligence when she was nine years old. Her mother was not a bit surprised to find her daughter's IQ so high that it was over the top of the scale. She harboured great ambitions for her. Rachel's exceptional mathematical ability, she told me, had startled everyone around since she was quite small. Rachel added:

> My mother was convinced that I was a child prodigy, took me off to a child psychologist who confirmed my brilliance. I heard her say, 'Shall we tell Rachel how special she is; shall we tell Rachel what her IQ is?' I hoped that it was my giftedness that had made me feel special.

Rachel's feats of achievement

The next time I met Rachel was as a young teenager. She still looked like the little girl I'd first met – slender and pale, with long fair hair and big trusting pale blue eyes. At all times, she did her earnest best to please, and that included me. She took great care in answering my questions and responding to the tests I gave her. I'd found her a very attractive girl, articulate and rather serious.

Her mother, though, did not see her as I did. She complained bitterly about Rachel's brilliance, which had brought her great suffering. Glancing up at me for corroboration, as though I, the expert, would know the truth of her experiences, she sighed heavily, 'It was *so* difficult to bring up a gifted child.'

Her mother had put little Rachel in an impossible position. The label of 'gifted' came with conflicting dual roles. In one role, little Rachel had to provide superb school achievement. In the other role, she had to demonstrate what her mother believed were the correct 'symptoms' of giftedness, notably to be without friends and to have emotional problems. Little Rachel juggled her confusing obligations, though at a cost to herself. As a brilliant achiever, she brought her mother pride, but as a typical gifted child with 'symptoms', she not only caused her mother distress, she also brought distress on herself.

In 1998, the UK government's Office for Standards in Education gave me the job of reporting all the international scientific research on gifted children. One big conclusion was that the expectation of emotional disturbance in gifted children was widespread across the Western world, but not in the Far East. But even in the West where by far the most research is done, almost all the evidence points to the gifted being better balanced and emotionally stronger than the non-gifted. Indeed, they need to be stronger if they are to continue to work at an exceptionally high level. In this deep study, I could see that the gifts of themselves were not the cause of emotional problems – they were always due to other people's reactions to this exceptionality.

Rachel's mother was explicit about her gifted daughter

She's obviously outstanding in her abilities and therefore she could never find her academic peer-group, except somewhere like Oxford or Cambridge. She often says she can't make friends with anybody round here, because there's no-one able to have a conversation at the intellectual's depth she needs. She's a very deep-thinking girl. She has told me that her mind thinks independently of her – it goes on racing and racing and racing, and you can't stop it; it's got a life of its own.

She says sometimes she hates herself with a deep anger. When she has a serious problem, she attacks herself, which is very difficult to handle. She scratches herself and makes herself bleed, and then this morning, she was banging herself. I wonder whether it stems actually from when she was very tiny and her arms and legs wouldn't do what her mind wanted them to do. She couldn't control the pencil and so on; she wanted to do things and couldn't.

We had an incident with her. It all happened in the middle of the night. First, she sat on the landing and threatened to throw herself downstairs. We tried to talk to her, to calm her down, and eventually she went outside into the garden, barefoot in her nightdress, sat down in the flower-bed and screamed. When Rachel screams she really can; she used to do it as a baby in her temper tantrums. She screamed about three times at the top of her voice, so much so that several sets of neighbours phoned the police thinking murder was happening, and three police vans arrived outside! One of the policemen talked to her; I don't know what he said, but eventually she came in, somewhat subdued and went to bed. It was obvious she'd been under enormous pressure.

It was not only Rachel who had emotional problems, though. Her mother was a very unhappy woman. Her own parents could not afford to send her to university, and most days she expressed regrets to her family about her blighted life. Rachel took the brunt of it, feeling guilty when her own good fortune was frequently pointed out, and insecure between the incompatible goals she'd been set of intellectual achievement and emotional failure. Intellectually she learned all the Bible stories like Jonah and the Whale, and the graphic details of the locusts, plagues and rivers of blood, but emotionally a black cloud was always hanging over her. She was aware that if she did not give her life to Jesus, without doubt terrible things would happen to her:

Mother used to say, 'The Lord is really in control in this house, isn't he darling?' It was like somebody taking over my life and freedom. It made me reactionary and I'd always play devil's advocate, being the baddie at every opportunity. In fact, mother thought I actually was a conduit for the Devil. When we were having a family row, she'd say, 'The devil always gets into this family through Rachel.'

At an early age, Rachel was a born scientist. She struggled to make sense of her situation and like many a bright child she tried out her mother's ideas in the real world:

When I was seven, I was bothered by a bee. Now, I thought, here's a chance to test the power of prayer. I screwed my eyes up and said, 'Please God, take this bee away', but nothing happened. So then, I prayed to the Devil, 'Please take it away', and sure enough, the bee disappeared. You can imagine that I was really scared by that. Mother's all-powerful God had done nothing, but my devil had. That left a deep mark. From then on, I was *not* convinced that God was on my side.

Yet both my parents told me of the minor miracles that had happened to them, so I didn't write God off totally. I felt He was there, but a rather impersonal figure. Hell and damnation were always there too, so you had to believe the right thing. If you were just pretending to believe, God was bound to see the subterfuge and it'd be a disaster. My mother was always very doom-laden: 'Your father is late, he's had an accident.' 'He has a lump on his ankle, is it cancer?' I became so frightened of the future.

Still, I never felt as if anything happened as a result of my nightly prayers, so God couldn't be real. Once, in church people were asked to go forward. Grandmother was praying for me to do it. Mother said she'd given her own life to the Lord years ago. I was like a possession traded between them, my holiness being a trophy for my mother. There'd be a big tick if I'd given my life to Jesus and a big cross if I hadn't, and if I didn't tell my friends about Jesus I'd go to hell. I always felt I was not doing enough. I prayed night after night that Jesus would come and live in my heart because I might die before the morning and then where would I go? I was petrified that nobody had ever loved me.

Precocious, hard-working Rachel sought sanctuary in her school-work. It was safe and she soared years ahead of her age-group. Her mother, without much money and with only a secondary education, was sometimes at her wit's end to know how to satisfy the elder of her two daughters. Jesus did help the family out, she told me, such as help with the shopping as well as spiritual sustenance, but not in fees for education.

Why did Rachel behave like that?

On the whole, Rachel bore the severe pressures of her mother's conflicting expectations valiantly, but in the end, dripping water will wear away the hardest granite, and the unrelenting pressure loaded on her almost every day since she was born had built up an emotional head of steam which had to burst out like a volcano from time to time. She had told me about it very clearly when she was nine. Many years later when she knew she did not have long to live, she was eloquent about how it was to live as a labelled gifted child:

> To be clever was really important. It gave me value. And now I think that's the most cack, convoluted, arse-about-face (if you'll excuse the expression) way of looking at the world. I say to my children, the most important thing is to be kind, so much more important than being a smarty pants. You can have your arm up in the air and answer the teacher's questions first, and it makes you feel good because you've answered something – why does it matter? I always thought I was a creative genius because I was told so many times as a child that I could do this, that and the other. But I'm not a creative genius at all.
>
> My mother even wrote a document about the trials and tribulations of bringing up a gifted child. She obviously saw herself as under attack from health visitors, from the doctor, from everywhere. She felt she was criticised for what she was doing or what her child was doing. It wasn't only my anti-social behaviour, she told them, it was about me being cleverer than other children. She said I could read by the time I was two and

a half, which I flatly refuse to believe. She said I was too clever to go to a normal school, so she coached me for the entrance exam for the evangelical school. It was such a puritanical place that for a while, the headmaster even banned drama because it was 'of the devil'.

Mother saw ordinary things that I was doing and called them extraordinary. But she didn't have any friends and no-one with children with whom to compare me. When I was rearranging the furniture, she called it imaginative creativity. Well, all children do imaginative play. That's normal childhood behaviour, nothing out of the ordinary. Perhaps when she was a child, her mother never allowed her to do those things.

Strangely, Rachel's younger sister was exempt from her mother's anguish and designs, though indeed her academic career was modest in comparison. It has often struck me during my many years of home visits to the families of identified gifted children, how it's often just one child in the family who is stereotyped as gifted while the others are left to grow up normally, even if sometimes in the shadow of the nominated 'gifted' one. I wonder whether this is a strange form of the 'battered child syndrome', where one child in a family is constantly singled out for extra distress and punishment as a trouble-maker – the cause of so much family strife – the cuckoo in the nest. It was certainly true in Rachel's family.

Jumping a class or three

Rachel also hit another hazard of being gifted – acceleration in school. She'd been grade-skipped by three years beyond her age-group. I heard a slight tremble in her voice, when she told me how it had been:

At six, I was in a class with nine year olds, rather pleased at my own cleverness. By the time I was in the third form, I started being in the top five of the class with alarming regularity. Scored 98 per cent in the maths exam. I was quite competitive. Came top in English too. It made me very unpopular; my classmates felt I needed to be taken down a peg or six.

I felt nobody could ever really like me because I'd learned at home that I was not very nice. I had absolutely no confidence at all. They would spend their time teasing me. Nine-year-old little girls are so cruel to younger girls. I was much smaller than them, of course, and would have done anything to have a friend. Although I could cope with the academic work very easily, emotionally I wasn't up to it. Maybe it was my fault and I was asking to be picked on. I was a weed at the edge of the playground.

She lowered her voice and spoke as though to herself,

Oh dear, oh dear. There were times when I was quite happy, but mostly I was really really miserable. I used to come home sometimes from school and be crying my eyes out, being so unhappy.

Rachel had found, like other gifted children, that being too scholarly can be a challenge. Of itself, a great bank of knowledge does not produce creativity or any other form of discovery, although it does provide the foundations. Emotion is the drive. Gifted children are sometimes stuffed to the gills with school-type learning for the sake of their parents' or the school's glory in examination success. The youngsters work hard to take in all that the teachers can give them, and give it back in brilliant examination results.

A body of extremely well-funded American research promotes the idea that acceleration is the schooling of choice for the gifted – though entirely unsupported by any kind of in-depth long follow-up. An Australian, Professor Miraca Gross, investigated 15 very high IQ children for some years. Their lives were bleak, she claims, because they had to suffer normal schooling. She found them to have 'moderate to severe levels of depression', not to mention 'loneliness, social isolation and bitter unhappiness' in the regular classroom. Their terrible lives, she concluded, were due to their giftedness, and the particular fault lay with the attitudes of her fellow Australians. Maybe gifted

Australians, such as Germaine Greer, Clive James, Cate Blanchett, Paul Hogan, Kylie Minogue and Barry Humphries, had to have extraordinary powers of resistance to the fate of Antipodean gifted children – 'boredom, deliberate under-achievement and lack of motivation'. However, as she made no comparisons of these 15 with any others down-under, it is difficult to tell whether the youngsters in her study were even representative of Australian high IQ children. Deeper personal investigation of their lives might have found out why they were so unhappy.

I don't know of any study on school acceleration other than mine which has taken such a deep psychological look at how this distortion of a child's normal learning progress has affected them as adults. It's as though the hurry-merchants feel that youth is truly wasted on the young, so they want to take it away from them. The sacrifice of precious childhood for early examination excellence is rarely a good bargain in the long run. The major result over the decades of my study has been left-over distress in adults, and sometimes ongoing anger which can lead to depression.

I'm a believer in education in its truest sense. I don't want to see little children bent over their books while the world calls outside; well, at least not all the time. I want them to discover what life is about by interacting, experimenting, dreaming, playing, making friends, daring – and learning from their mistakes. Childhood isn't only for children either. The pleasures and creativity of childhood are the basis of all great work. Take childhood away from children and not only is the adult diminished, the world pays the price.

Rachel, as an adult, still bore the emotional scars of her upbringing and her school acceleration:

I don't mind meeting strangers now, whereas at one time I would have sat in the corner of the room and not dared say anything. I have friendships that I feel sure would not disintegrate if I was around, but at the same time, there's always the lurking fear that underneath they don't really like me, they're only tolerating me. It's not rational. I suppose I'm still quite negative about myself.

In truth, I had an awful temper until I was about 20. I was quite stubborn and determined. Sometimes I found relief in walks with my father who knew a lot about plants and used to find some extraordinary mosses and lichens. I felt that he at least loved me for myself. One way of getting daddy to myself was music. He'd do music with me endlessly, because he loved it. Then I stopped because I was terribly afraid he was trying to make me into a professional musician and I knew I didn't want to be. So I closed that door.

When dad got that job as a vicar in working-class London, the house and everything around dragged us all down. Hideous carpet, a garden the size of a pocket handkerchief and a builder's yard at the back. It was a creepy house; I could feel a dark presence coming down the stairs. I had to get out. My relationship with my mother was so bad, I asked to be a boarder. She was miserable, exhausted, just coping.

Rachel had to prove herself over and over. The great school successes that she offered her family soon lost their value because there were always further goals. She was young, strong and passionate. Nothing seemed beyond her reach. Each new school was a seam to be mined for all it could give. Pressure to succeed can cripple the gifted with perfectionism. Alternatively, many learn that it is sometimes better for their popularity to keep their brainpower to themselves:

I went to the local comprehensive. Again, I was with people older than myself, and as always – no friends. I was 16 [two years early] when I took A-levels in physics, chemistry and maths. I only got three Bs and was furious with myself. I was always a perfectionist. People at the school spoke of Oxford and Cambridge in hushed tones, but how was I to get there? I wanted to study medicine, so I applied and got unconditional offers from Manchester and St Andrews. I turned them down. Being a doctor wasn't good enough for clever me – too much like being a plumber with human beings. I needed more challenge. Anyway, I was too young to start medicine.

In my arrogance, I went for physics, the hardest thing
I could do. God knows what possessed me! Why not
maths, where I had always got As? I thought I'd join the
space programme and build rockets. I applied to
Cambridge, to Trinity College, but they didn't want me. I
was unhappy and dissatisfied with myself and very, very
lonely.

So I stayed at school and demanded more and more of
my teachers. I did all the work they set me and asked for
more. They begged to be relieved of all the marking I
made them do. I did two years' work in six months. I
worked so hard that my teachers said they were up till
two in the morning marking what I did – much to my
parents' approval. Yet none of us felt I was fully
stretched. No teacher seemed to be good enough. One of
them asked me if I was ready for the possibility that I
might not get to Oxford, that it might not be God's will –
and I said my will was superior. I was right.

If I had stopped my research when Rachel had just left
school and at her peak (the time when most research on
gifted children stops), how worthwhile her school acceleration would have seemed. Her superhuman efforts had
brought her seven A-levels, as well as a scholarship to
Merton, a prestigious college of Oxford University. She'd
been granted a place in physics two years early, at 16.

Her family seemed satisfied at last. As far as they were
concerned, what she was learning did not seem important.
And her complete lack of friends or social skills were of no
consequence. She was a brilliant young woman, flushed
with astounding school success, the daughter of proud
parents accepting the glittering reward of being an undergraduate at one of the finest universities in the world. It
was to be her oyster and she was its pearl.

The dark presence on the stairs

In Rachel's second year at Oxford University, we caught
up again over tinkling teacups in the old Randolph Hotel.
My heart went out to her. She was in a sorry state, her

lovely face was grey with fatigue and distress, barely able to keep going. Since she'd arrived, she'd been in psychological shock.

For the first time in her life, Rachel had been thrown on her own resources, released from a life that had been severely controlled and without normal opportunities to learn to develop relationships. Firstly, it was her mother's insistence that she was too clever to talk to other children of her own age, and secondly, her three-year grade-skip that had cost her all her school-friends, both at the time and for the rest of her school life. There was always a nearby adult to tell her what to do, think and believe. Once alone, she floundered, exhausted, lost in an emotional vacuum. The trauma she was experiencing and its long aftermath were not to leave her until just a few months before she died, only 20 years later.

She had reached out for help from her personal physics tutor who told her brusquely, in what she described as 'a male Oxford manner', 'Miss Wallace, you have to pull yourself together.' She was a fresh young girl in an almost entirely male establishment, all of whom were at least two years older than she was. The university counselling service was not helpful, she felt. Nowhere to turn; neither home nor friends. All those superb school grades suddenly turned to dust. In just a few weeks, she had plunged from glory to despair. It masqueraded as boredom and overwhelming fatigue:

My ambition was to get to Oxford, but when I got here, everything fell flat. My brain went to sleep after about four weeks and it hasn't woken up since. I don't even go to lectures because I fall asleep in them. I've worked about five per cent of what I used to, and my tutors couldn't care less. My own tutor never even looks at my work. There are so many things I don't understand. I'm so lost. A lot of what my tutor does with me in the half an hour a week I have with him is Double Dutch to me. I don't know how to master it. I'd always found academic things easy, so this is a revelation and an unhappy one at that. I'm sliding into depression.

There are people here who are so much better than me that I could never have a hope of catching them up, and certainly not coming top. It seems a cheat to have to work hard to be third or fourth. The panicking becomes a way of life. I just go shopping, drink tea, read books, wander round the colleges – anything but work. Sometimes I can't think of anything I want to do, so I walk around for hours utterly bored. It also happens to me during the holidays, when I tend to be lazy. It might be different for people who have to pass their exams because there's something at the end of it, say medicine, and they want to be doctors. But when you go in on a fairly vague sort of course like physics and you don't know what you're going to do at the end, then it's much harder to keep yourself going.

I get so lonely. I do have one friend, but apart from her, nobody. Black depression is there. I just get days of it and I try to keep myself busy, but I'm really powerless to do anything. I think it's getting worse, but I don't want to leave university. I don't think about tomorrow, because tomorrow I'm just going to be in the same situation.

Rachel's life of emotional battering had left her totally inexperienced at making relationships on the way to becoming a mature adult. Along with her familiar home supports, she'd lost her motivation for hard work and with it her academic learning power. In her loneliness, confusion, immaturity and poor self-esteem she was as vulnerable as the weak little lamb trailing behind the flock, ready to be picked off by a wolf.

The wolf pounced

Out of the gloom, a chimera of blinding hot sun shot across Rachel's bleak horizon and she flung herself towards it with all the hope and trust in her naive young heart. But it quickly turned to cold black fog trailing destructive tendrils which spewed their poisons throughout the rest of her life. With long pauses, she told me the story as we wandered among the dreaming yellow stone spires:

I encountered Jerry and I fell for him completely, hook, line and sinker. All my time and energy went on him. He was the leader of the Christian Union. First he seduced me into bed and then decided he loved somebody else. Just like that. I was devastated.

There's no black hole like it; I was in the pit of despair. I was really his plaything. I lived and breathed him. He was a fourth-year classics student, who left at the end of my first year. But sometimes he came back and was able to have me when he wanted to. I was completely broken-hearted. I couldn't work, just walked round and round Oxford, and sat in the College garden sobbing. I did just enough work not to get sent down.

Everything was tainted with sexual sin. I felt that if God really loved me, He'd make Jerry love me and He wasn't doing that. I was obsessed with getting married; my parents had brought me up to think that's what you did. I couldn't imagine coping on my own because I had a desperate fear of life. If I were ill there'd be nobody to look after me, and I'd be lying in an attic with a bottle of sour milk. I was in a terror of not being able to exist.

When I went home, I couldn't tell my parents. They knew I was miserable. I sat on the kitchen floor sobbing. I felt absolutely lost; I didn't know who to talk to, what to do. Mother had told me that if I slept with anyone before marriage, no-one would ever want to marry me. So I'd nothing to look forward to, nowhere to go. I was absolutely beside myself.

The Christian concepts of forgiveness and restitution didn't figure largely in my mother's mind. If I said sorry for something to my father, it was over, but mother would keep up the recrimination for weeks. I couldn't imagine any future without Jerry. I went back to Oxford to try to pick up the pieces over endless mugs of coffee with my one girl friend, talking about God and what it all meant.

The way back from desolation was sluggish until Robert came into Rachel's life, the man who would become the

love of her life and her husband. At first she viewed him
with some apprehension. He came from another social
world; one she felt was far above her own. She didn't know
their ways:

It took me a long time to realise that he liked me, because
he was quite provocatively dismissive of the female sex.
And it was beyond the pale for him that I was a scientist
and a member of the Christian Union. I thought he was a
lunatic because he didn't believe that you could ask
Christ to live in your heart and you would be saved. We
debated that long and hard. He didn't believe in speaking
in tongues, which had happened to me one day, and it
had happened to mother when she was hanging out the
washing.

When he was living in London, he started writing me
letters and sometimes came up for weekends. One
Valentine's Day, chocolates appeared in my pigeon hole –
he'd come from London by train and gone all the way
back again just to leave them. I thought, 'Oh my word!'
He said, 'Let go of Jerry and all that and see what
happens.' Walking with him in the snow one night in
Magdalene College gardens, the moon was up, the stars
were out and I felt he was a very solid and reassuring
presence, which he has been ever since.

Yet if Jerry had walked through the door, I'd have
fallen into his arms again. I used to dream about him for
years and years. I'm not sure a thing like that ever leaves
you. All through my miserable twenties, I was trying to
get back the feeling I'd had for Jerry – but with Robert. I
was absolutely desperate for something I couldn't have.

I left Oxford at 21, having barely scraped a third-class
degree in physics – more than I deserved. There was one
paper I enjoyed and I'm sure that saved me because I
knew what they were talking about. The other six, so far
as I was concerned, were in a foreign language. Proud
and arrogant as I was in my ability to learn, there's
nothing worse than opening an exam paper and realising
that you don't have a clue, that there's only a quarter of
one question you can do. I'd let my parents down. I'd

failed. I'd lost any sense of direction. I didn't know what to do. I was frightened, but I don't really know what I was frightened of.

Still in a low state, burdened with dark feelings of failure and yearning for her lost passion, once again Rachel was alone, this time in the grown-up world of work. She took a job with the Ministry of Defence doing scientific analysis to support RAF activities. By an amazing coincidence, Robert worked there too. She told me about it much later:

When I was with other people, I made a show of being Robert's friend because I felt inferior to him and he made me look better. There were long stretches of time when I didn't see him, yet dreaded going to work in case I did. It went on for years. I'd made a mess of everything.

My anger was for God, because nothing was working out, because He didn't do me any good. I didn't have any direction. I didn't enjoy my job and I can't tell you how desperate I felt: time was ticking away. Somehow, we lurched over the threshold of getting engaged. I did love him, but I wasn't in love with him. All through the engagement, I had terrible nightmares that I'd married the wrong person, and I'd wake up in a sweat when I was supposed to be blissfully happy. I thought, 'What have I done?' I felt as if part of me was dying. I was totally confused and lost. I wanted someone to tell me what to do. We got married. I was the most reluctant bride there ever was. I felt I'd disobeyed God and that he'd never forgive me, so I couldn't even turn to Him.

Robert was too much for me. I used to sob every night before he came in to get the tension out of me. I did my best to do what I needed to do, but felt trapped, lost – and inferior. I used to hear him talking to his father on the phone when he wanted advice, but he never asked me about those things. I felt cut out of his life. I was married to him, but he didn't treat me as a partner in any sense. I couldn't compete with his family. His parents apologised a long time ago for putting their big feet in. He was their darling son and I wasn't what they'd wanted. His father in particular could be quite controlling. He didn't know me or seem to want to know me – just a vicar's daughter. We had a fair few shouting matches. I don't think anyone had ever shouted at him before, certainly not a woman. Now we are good friends.

Rachel persevered in being a good wife along the lines she'd been taught. She supported her husband as he climbed his career ladder. She knew her old enemies, fear and distress, only too well:

> For a long time, I felt terrified and constrained; a terrible mixture. I used to lie awake and think, 'I've got to get out of here, I can't bear this, I'm going to walk out of the door.' During the night, I'd get out of bed and sit at the foot of the stairs and get so exhausted. Then I'd go back and feel his reassuring presence asleep next to me and I'd know I couldn't do it. The touch of his leg on my foot and I'd feel I was back on solid ground again.
>
> I was too scared to tell him all this because he might find out that I'd felt the marriage was wrong. But when I was pregnant with Samuel, I suddenly felt for the first time that he really loved me. I had a real role to play, a role that mattered to Robert, in a way that nothing else I'd ever done had mattered. Samuel turned up 5½ years ago, then Isaac two years later and then Flora 15 months ago.

Conflicts resolved

When I went to see Rachel for the last time, in 2004, she was at home in a perfect English village. The sun was shining on the flowering pink clematis round her cottage door. Her terminal cancer had allowed her a good day so she'd picked me up at the station in her car. I could see immediately that she was very happy. Some extra weight from the steroids she was taking gave her a comforting motherly presence. She'd acquired spectacles perched on her nose and smiling pink cheeks. She made me feel very welcome. The despair and red-rimmed eyes I'd seen in her

Oxford days had been replaced by a Cheshire cat grin. While we were settling in her living room and the tea-cups tinkled again as they once had at the Randolph Hotel, her angelic blonde toddlers played at our feet until their nanny took them away and we could talk seriously. She was as honest and sincere as she had always been. She knew no other way:

I was 37 years old and my darling baby was just three months old. I was breastfeeding, and I felt a lump. The doctor told me I had cancer. But I couldn't believe it. I was so happy and feeling fit. They said sorry, that's it, just a matter of time. Maybe I'll have six months left to live, maybe four years. Maybe I'll be dead by Christmas, maybe by Easter. Life has a different reality when you know it isn't going to go on for very much longer. On a good day, I do believe in God; on a bad day, I think 'Oh no, no'. When I'm feeling as though I've made a mess of something or I've got cross with the children, I know it's not the end of everything. You just have to get up and keep going. When I ask, 'Why me?', the answer is, 'Well why not me?'

I was terrified of dying because there are issues in my life which I desperately wanted to be resolved before I died. But I've been trying for so many years without success. It had made me tired, exhausted and bad-tempered, unfulfilled because I was not at peace. The only thing I felt fulfilled about was the three children – they were the only really good thing I'd done in my whole life.

The load I've carried all these years was too much for anyone to bear. All that turbulence, it's had to come out. I knew God was there, but my first thought was, 'Yes, this cancer is killing me; this is my way out.' It was as if there was this large black hole inside of me which was unfulfilled, empty and never satisfied. There was always the underlying sense of guilt, giving me real physical nausea, that the marriage wasn't right. I used to look around the supermarket at all those things, all that food. The sweetest of foods couldn't mask the sour taste.

As the sunlight filtered through the cottage windows, we talked with great honesty for hours. We reminisced about our earlier times together. But slowly I became aware that although she was answering my questions, I was beginning to tell her about myself. Neither of us knew then that she was on the cusp of her abrupt change into a state of holiness. Not only physically, but spiritually, she was approaching the end of her struggle. Strange things had begun to happen. I could sense something but did not know what it was. She told me:

About a year ago, I was by myself on a train and I felt all the anguish leave me. It was like God reached down, taking all the bad out of my heart and putting something good there.

I'd gone to meet Robert. We had lunch, went to an art exhibition and walked in St James's Park, and I thought, 'This is marvellous.' I felt so blessed with all the care and love we'd had from the children, our family and friends. You take those things for granted and then you open your eyes and you can see that love and care everywhere. It was as if we'd just met each other, all the layers of resentment had gone and we could see each other without any baggage attached. We both knew that God had touched us in a most profound way, which I'd never believed possible. I suddenly felt free. I loved him completely, as if it had always been true, without all the other stuff.

God could cure this cancer. He could, but He probably won't. Why should He do it for me? Hundreds of thousands die every year from cancer, why should I be singled out to live? He often doesn't seem to heal people like that. The prayers said for me in the prayer group have helped me to live life very well over the last 18 months and I don't want it to stop or I'd feel the draught. It comforts me. I went to church and heard the story of Gethsemane and Jesus' words on the Cross – My God, why have you forsaken me? In my case, He hasn't . . . though it does feel like it sometimes.

There was a long silence and several fat tears ran down her cheeks. Then she smiled at me:

I'm not really interested in doctrine any more. Life is for living. God gives us so many good things that are so much more than we deserve. I often just stand at the window and breathe the air, feel the sun or the rain and say thank you.

I find it very hard leaving Robert; I can't imagine how lonely he'll be. He says I'm a very reassuring presence to him. I know he'll cope. I hope he finds a better wife next time. I wish for my children that they will grow up to be people of soft heart, kind, generous, thoughtful, and I hope they come to love God and be thankful for the gifts He gives them. I hope they find people to love and who love them. I want them to be free to enjoy life, not to try too hard and to be courageous and truthful.

I'm still in the midst of my days. It's hard knowing how to express the depth of sorrow I feel at leaving the children behind. I'd love to see them grow up and it's so hard to think of somebody else bringing them up. When they first told us it was terminal, Robert sobbed for a day and a half and I felt so sorry for him. The sobbing is still going on. I'd give everything to stay and pray for a miracle every day. I told Robert, 'I will love you forever.' I know that if I lived another 50 years, we'd still be together. I want to celebrate love whenever and wherever I see it. A mum with her children in the supermarket, a couple together, I think how beautiful. I feel so happy for them. It's enabled me to celebrate life and goodness unreservedly.

The cancer brought a salvation. If I'd had to think of another 30 years of slugging it out in my marriage the way it was and the alternative of our six months of real love – there's no choice! Dying's nothing to be afraid of. It's something to look forward to, and probably better than this. Or there's nothing, in which case it won't be able to hurt me. What's to be feared is between now and then, the terrible grieving for what I would like to have had in the future, which I won't have.

It just blows your mind if you think too hard about the world. It's like when you're doing maths and you're using power to the tenth over 26 or something – you just do it, but if you ever thought about what that number was, you would never stop. Things like quantum mechanics are just incredible, really incredible. All that maths that I studied – I can hardly remember how to integrate, just about how to differentiate. And why would I need to know? Does it help me every day? No. When I was young, I was stupid and arrogant. I thought I was tremendously clever, that I could do anything. And I discovered that I couldn't.

In the about 30 years I'd known Rachel, she'd told me so many times of her loneliness, and blamed herself. Her lifelong conflict between gifted intellect and gifted sensitivity was at times more like outright war. She'd missed the normal rough and tumble of picking up essential social skills which added to the poor self-esteem she'd learned at home. She did her best to fulfill her impossible dual task as an obedient Christian and a difficult gifted child, but she was up against supernatural forces.

The guilt and fear of punishment accumulated, encouraged by her mother's terrible accusation that Rachel was letting the Devil into the family. She could get angry with God, demand that He listen to her, ask favours of Him, pray for guidance and believe (most times) in His love. But here on earth, what she really needed was a pal or two of her own age with whom she could link arms, complain and dream, and giggle. As a teenager, there was no experimenting for ways to relate to boys, no practice, no flirtation, no friends to confide in. She was very determined that she did not want her children to live a life like hers:

If my children were clever, I would very definitely want to send them to a school where I knew they'd be catered for. I would pay fees and go without myself to give my children that. Or at least a school which had quite a lot of clever children, because then you get some sort of companionship, people to talk to of your own ability. I feel very strongly about that.

But then, I won't be here to see to it, will I?

Things were different long ago

Rachel had seen things very differently when she was a keen young gifted child, when she'd driven herself (and her teachers) to mental and physical exhaustion in the quest for her scholarship to Oxford University. Once there, her underdeveloped emotional maturity brought her years and years of anguish. Her disastrous love affair brought momentary exaltation, followed by years of mortification. Perhaps, as with other saints, it was the beginning of her holiness. By the time she had truly found her earthly life's goal, the happiness of family life, her life was at its end.

The extent to which people feel they can control the events in their lives has a profound effect on their behaviour. Two psychologists tackled the idea in the 1960s. Julian Rotter said that people who feel in control of their lives – with an 'internal locus of control' – are more successful than those who feel dependent on others – with an 'external locus of control'. Much later, Mark Seligman, at the University of Pennsylvania, called it 'learned helplessness'. This can be just in one area or produce a general feeling of being hopeless at most things. The best way round it is to build up awareness of successes. Start small and build up to bigger challenges to be overcome. Parents can do this for children, and teachers in the classroom can make their pupils feel better about their learning. Friends can do it for each other too. Praise is the key – not too much, by praising everything, and not too mean – but just right for the effort as well as the success.

Rachel fitted this idea perfectly. She'd never developed a sense of control over her own life because she'd discovered that whatever she did, it had little effect. All her control was 'external'; it mostly came through her family. The people she was trying to impress. Over and over again they told her what a failure she was in their eyes, and bitterly she felt it was all her own fault. But after many years of anguish, in her final months, she had become mistress of her own life. And how sweet it was.

Was it her impending death that brought calmness and saintliness on so suddenly? Her friend and mentor, the nun, was perfectly practical. She told me:

> Rachel knew that time was running out swiftly, so she had to grasp at God. It was now or never.

Just as she had once run hard towards gaining more school successes, she ran hard towards Jesus. After all, it takes energy, hard work and practice to become saintly, just as it does to develop other forms of giftedness or excellence.

Spiritual intelligence means being open to a kaleidoscope of ways of knowing which blur distinctions between the physical and psychic worlds. Truly spiritual people, as Rachel became, have special abilities to meditate and visualise different ways of being while tapping their own inner knowledge. Her spiritual gifts meant that she had an awareness of unity between herself and others, feeling herself part of the human community and the cosmos.

To crown her life, Rachel had managed to resolve her terrible conflicts. She had harnessed her gifted intelligence with her sensitive creative self to produce a feat of emotional strength, sustained by her early life of holy images and holy teaching. She'd known more of life than most, with experience and insights to call upon. This enabled her to move swiftly to an extraordinarily high level of understanding, both spiritual and mundane. Her path became clear and she moved without hesitation along it, in time to bring those around her into the glow of her holiness and love.

2

Spoilt for choice

To get ultimate happiness you have to go with your heart.

Jeremy Kramer

To be lost in a jungle of extreme potential, born with gifted abilities to do almost anything, your life choices can be overwhelming. Confusion starts in childhood, when so many sparkly temptations compete for attention. It's equally confusing to parents and teachers because gifted children often become passionate about an interest – which the adults assume points the way to their future careers – then suddenly the children reach satisfaction, drop the interest, and move on to the next. It could be planets, pre-historic creatures, the piano, sport, anything.

Alas, as the years go by, the freedom to change direction becomes more and more restricted. For teenagers, at a time when real-life decisions must be made, those with the potential to shine in many directions hold the winning cards to a variety of prizes. Which to choose? At 14, Jeremy Kramer could have chosen a life of science, maybe to change the world with his discoveries, or he could have been one of the world's great musicians bringing delight to international audiences. Whatever he chose would demand total dedication to get to the top. Without that utter commitment, the likelihood of his national or international status in any field would be slight. For a tender youth with little worldly experience, he faced a terrible life decision.

Jeremy was born packed with high-level potential. His family was loving and supportive, with enough money to provide all he needed. They lived in a fine suburban home in a big city. His father was a businessman and his mother a professional cellist in a chamber orchestra. I'd measured his intelligence as hitting the ceiling of the IQ scale, and his capacity for learning and thinking was truly exceptional from his earliest years.

Even at nursery-school, his mother told me, he was such a keen learner that, 'He'd demanded more teaching and less play.' At the same time, Jeremy was a musical prodigy. Already before he'd reached the age of five, he was faced with a conflicting mixture of temptations and obligations. Once he reached proper school, almost every teacher spotted his learning potential and urged him to follow their own subject area. As he'd emerged from babyhood, this tiny child had already been faced with what was to be his constant life challenge – a search for balance between his multiple pro- digiousness and an awareness of his emotional fragility.

The performing penguin

Jeremy's parents were ambitious for him, and were gener- ous in providing the teaching that would contribute to his progress. What proved more difficult to provide, though, was the rock-solid emotional support that their son needed. They had divorced when he was 15, his father moved out, and somehow it seemed that both parents' hopes and satisfactions became wrapped up in Jeremy the *wunder- kind*, rather than on his three younger siblings. From his earliest years, he had already taken up his role of fulfilling others' hopes and dreams.

As a psychologist and expert, I am often in the position of defending the state of giftedness from the charge of bringing children unhappiness. The myth of genius being akin to madness is widespread – anything from schizo- phrenia to autism. Yet all the scientific evidence shows that the gifted are much like other people in every respect, other than their ability to do something, or many things, at a far higher standard than most other people. My research has shown that having an intelligence level within, say, the top 2 per cent is not in any way conducive to mental disturbance. Quite the contrary. The lives of almost all gifted people are enviable in their abilities and strength. But when things go wrong, if a child wants to be awkward, how much more effective he can be if he is also gifted.

For Jeremy, the roots of his future dreadful emotional problems gave the impression of being related to his giftedness. Yet for him, as for many gifted people who are emotionally distressed, it was not his gifts that were to blame. The build-up to his adult emotional instability had two roots. The first was his innate predisposition to it – as it would be to anyone of any ability. The second came from the way that the important people in his life treated him because of his gifts. His life was directed in ways which suited the adults, rather than what was right for this sensitive small boy.

From nursery-school onwards, he felt that he was undergoing a non-stop trial by performance. Even at primary school, he was strangely astute and aware that adult pressure on him to perform outstandingly was affecting him emotionally. He made his first big life decision. With only his few childhood years of experience to guide him, he purposefully put his feelings aside to get on with whatever task he had been set. By his early teens, he was better able to tell me about what had happened:

My being seen as gifted has produced awful deficiencies in me. I was emotionally scarred by being made to perform. All the time it was, 'Look what Jeremy can do.' I could do almost anything on demand, but I used to feel like a performing penguin. I was only using 40 per cent of myself, the other 60 per cent which could have given me creative pleasure just never developed. All my performances took on a compulsive edge, becoming defences to hide from the fear of being found out as being *less* than average. You can go on like that in education until someone asks for originality.

On the one hand, I clung to the applause and admiration which gave me a false confidence, but my personality problems ran alongside and were never noticed. I never felt gifted as a person. I had to detach myself emotionally to do it. I felt like a robot. But a robot can't appreciate a work of art; he can only get good results.

It didn't take long for me to associate my gifts with negative emotions. I was pleased to make other people feel I was a gifted person, but I was terrified in case I was asked to do anything original. Creativity was a blank. I didn't dare try it. I never played a piece that I hadn't been told how to play by my teacher. My playing wasn't from me; it was just regurgitation of something someone else had created. In all my life, I have never once bought a record to listen to.

I've never read a book for pleasure. I just can't do it. I have to re-read lines. By the time I've finished a sentence, I've forgotten the beginning. All I can cope with are really low-level books. At primary school, I won all the reading prizes because I could read the words perfectly. My spelling was immaculate. But when they asked me to tell the meaning of the words I'd just read, I couldn't. It was mechanical reading. I'm really very stunted in that area. All the damage had been done by the time I was seven.

Jeremy's problem with reading was strangely typical of autism as described by Professor Uta Frith, a world authority on autism, at University College London, in her sharp book, *Autism*. She writes that, although a highly intelligent autistic child can learn to read all by himself 'yet he doesn't understand what he reads'. But autism could be crossed off as Jeremy's problem because he clearly did understand what he read when he needed to. He read with perfect understanding to pass all his examinations with flying colours throughout his long education, not least working through very high-level intellectual arguments as part of his medical and specialist psychiatry qualifications.

What really got to Jeremy was being a 'performing penguin', as he called it. I suspect that he semi-consciously set up an intellectual block as part of a rebellion against the role he'd been given. It was as though he was prepared to read out loud when they wanted him to, but he dug in his heels at paying more attention to understanding what he was reading. How could he have known as a four year old that his attempts to preserve his individuality were against his better interests? As the years went by, this kind of heel-digging-in seemed to become a habit, part of his armoury to protect his sense of self. And every time he used it, it worked against his better interests.

The big decision

While a full-time school-boy, in the evenings and at week-ends from the age of seven to 18, Jeremy was also a student at the grown-up Royal Northern College of Music in Manchester. Every year, he had to take an audition to stay there. By 15, he had completed every grade-course in trumpet, piano and theory, finishing with a full flush of Grade A music distinctions, plus an A-level in music. All that remained for him was the college leaving diploma, normally taken by 21 year olds.

That's when he faced his first key dilemma, the fork in his vocational route. While the music college strongly encouraged him to aim for the concert platform, at school he shone in science and was strongly encouraged to study medicine. There was a time dimension too. Music practice, and the coming and going from music college, took great amounts of his time. If he spent yet more hours on his musical life, he would have less time for science at school. No day could be long enough for the work this boy had to do. Nor could either route ever be entirely satisfactory, because while doing one he could always hear the siren call of the other.

In this study, it often appeared to be the high-pressured academic schools like Jeremy's which were the least flexible. Their aim for the future lives of their high-flyers was usually limited to which university they might go to, a matter which the subject teachers usually took care of. There was an assumption that their bright pupils did not need any other career advice. Such major life decisions were often made on the basis of school marks rather than individual inclinations or deeper personal guidance.

Understandably, the wide variety of possible career routes for multiple-gifted youngsters, like Jeremy, can confuse the keenest careers guidance professional. One gifted girl shrugged her shoulders as she said of her careers officer: 'He came to school and said I could probably do anything!' Another was underwhelmed by the technology: 'I got a computer printout which was supposed to select the ideal job. It said, "Cut off after 80, 127 remaining". I was supposed to select four, but there wasn't much point when I was suitable in attitude and qualifications for all of them.' During his months of agony in choosing what life-path to follow, Jeremy came to see me to talk it over a few times. It was never satisfactory because his confusion was so great, and all the arguments had been worked over hundreds of times until he could no longer see the wood for the trees. He did not blame anyone but himself for his career decisions:

> No-one else could have helped me choose between music and medicine. I spent hours and hours and hours thinking it over. Someone would say, 'I think you should do music for this reason,' and I'd reply, 'Well, those are just the reasons I shouldn't do it,' and I wouldn't get anywhere. I'd covered every single aspect of why I should or shouldn't have done each one.
>
> Eventually, I came to the conclusion I'd be better off doing medicine. Firstly, I could do it and still do a lot of music, but I can't do music and do any medicine. Secondly, while I was at music college I saw a lot of brilliant musicians who didn't have a job. Thirdly, it was the music students themselves. For a lot of them it was all they could do, and they weren't always very bright. I didn't think I could stand three years' solid study and socialising with people like that. I need a bit of intellectual input.

A life in medicine

In his second year at his London medical school, I found Jeremy still happy with his choice. His intellectual reasoning to study medicine and play music as an amateur seemed to have worked. He had already directed the university Christmas music concert, giving it his all, rather as another gifted musician, Jocelyn, did (described in Chapter 8) when she too tried to combine science and music. But whereas Jocelyn could not bestride those two powerful horses as a university student, Jeremy had spent years developing perfect control. He told me he could switch his learning procedures off and on at will:

> I didn't go to a lecture for seven weeks, because I was preparing for the concert 14 hours a day. The staff objected to some extent, but they said that so long as I passed my exams, it would be OK.

It took a few years for that early euphoria to fade. He could not play enough music to keep him satisfied, and his anticipated intellectual discussions with his fellow medical students turned out to be similar to his earlier impression of music students. They lived the lives of students – more interested in beer and discos than what he saw as the finer things of life. Strangely, too, although he came from a non-orthodox home, being Jewish he began to keep kosher in his food. Living in his simple room in a large student block in London's sleazy district of Soho, he had not set himself an easy task. It defined him, but it also distanced him from many of his fellows. His mother understood this at the time:

> He sometimes feels alienated. His personality is different, his interests are different. The artist in him is very quiet and sensitive. It's also his insecurity and his own high standards. When he does something right, it never ceases to amaze him.
>
> At school, he truanted quite a lot, and continued the habit at university. Nobody seemed to have bothered him about it at either place. The Latin teacher at school, whose lessons he always missed, chose to disregard it, possibly because neither of them liked each other. Still, he knew that Jeremy would come out with an A, and of course he did.

Like so many gifted youngsters, notably boys, Jeremy was competitive from a very early age. He looked for challenge wherever he could get it. As he progressed through the school system, he'd experimented with different ways to get the best from his teachers and his world. Over the years, he had consciously devised a self-challenging approach to his school-work, along with an excellent repertoire of personal learning strategies. By the time he was a medical student, he had mastery of those, and told me how he achieved his excellent grades:

When I was younger, I thrived on competition with friends, but now I do it for myself. I set myself an aim and have to achieve it. Even during the day, I'll find my own little challenges. Like, I can just go for a game of snooker, not because it's nice and relaxing, but sometimes, it's, 'Right, I'm going to beat this guy, and I'm going to really go for it, get the best score I've ever done.'

I've got exams in three or four weeks, and I'm being quite honest when I say that I haven't opened a book all year. I like to feel the pressure, to build up some anxiety, so I know that if I don't start now I'm definitely going to fail. It's the challenge of doing that. I'm fully dedicated to working at this point, and only at this point. For my first year exams, I only started revising two days before. My method is to cram for a couple of weeks, doing 24 hours a day, and not sleep for a few nights. Everything seems to go in at that point, so I must be able to absorb the stuff.

I can do this last-minute stuff, because I understand the principles, so I understand the subject before I even start working for it. If I were totally lost, then I'd really start worrying. A lot of students sit in their room with a book and slog away at details, but if you test them on the principles, like something that they're supposed to deduce, then they fall down. That's something that I can get right and they won't. I'm only learning the details at the last minute, and I find that a lot of them stay with me. Even now, I remember a lot of last year's work, which I'd only learnt in a few days, where other people I know have forgotten it.

It's important for me to spend a very large period of time each day on my own thinking and sorting out what I've been doing. I need that thinking time to be productive. Even if it's three o'clock in the morning when I get to bed, although I might be very tired, I'll probably stay up another two hours just thinking.

I feel very different from the others. My experiences have been different. I don't accept things without thinking and I've always tried to be truthful which means I don't always agree with others. I've never been part of a group, but I have a lot of acquaintances. I just don't think there are people around that I could spend all my time with. I can feel really happy most of the time, but it's just every so often that bad feelings hit me.

Control and pressure had become Jeremy's familiar companions since nursery school. That habit of mind extended to his relationships – no girlfriends for him while he was studying hard – a rare sacrifice for the other young people in my study. The majority of the gifted young people enjoyed perfectly normal relationships with friends of both sexes. Many a girl could have fallen for Jeremy, who was tall, dark and handsome and with an attractive personality. He smiled while he talked to me and looked sincerely into my eyes. It was neither for lack of opportunity nor masculine know-how that he made that decision. Yet it proved to be one more distancing from his fellow students. He said, 'I suppose I've never met a girl who is quite irresistible. I get all I need in life from my friends of both sexes – apart from physical pleasure of course.'

If I had stopped our contact then, when Jeremy was still a young student, I could have given him a tick for success – the culmination of many correct life decisions. He was reasonably content and cheerful, highly competent, looking forward to qualifying as a doctor, aiming to spend the rest of his working life helping ill people. Yet, I made a note at the time that it would be difficult for him to find a girl who could meet all his needs – to be beautiful, intelligent, musical, scientific, lively and sexy. I could see him becoming a very good doctor. I hoped he wouldn't become arrogant with it. He never did.

Ten years later, though, how different his life looked. Jeremy's views were to change radically as he entered adulthood. On his own, away from home, he'd begun to recognise the deep negative effects of his early role as a gifted child and how it had affected his learning right through to his medical finals:

> I'm good at sequences, at being tested. But as to knowledge of the world, that was always missing. To make up, I used to read encyclopaedias and the *Guinness Book of Records*. I over-used my memory and the left side of my brain, instead of using my imagination. The way I used to work – that last-minute swotting, was maladaptive behaviour.
>
> I could only work in fear. Only the fear of failure made me work in the end. How I got those great results as a student was to do a detailed survey of which questions were likely to turn up. Then I'd put all my energy into them. So I could make a brilliant response to, say, three questions on embryology but know nothing much else about embryology, whereas others would know more about embryology and get lower marks than me.

The deep pain of mental illness

In his late-thirties, I visited Jeremy, who was living in a couple of rooms he rented at his mother's home. He had a separate entrance, which eased their rocky relationship. I found him in the grip of bipolar mental illness, bounced mercilessly between cold clinical depression and the fire of mania. My visit coincided with a depressive phase. He was very talkative, but at the same time with little hope on his desolate horizon. His father paid for his psychotherapy, and he was taking two types of anti-depressants, though he felt that none of it seemed to do much good.

He believed that the unrelenting pressure throughout his life to demonstrate gifted achievement had traumatised him. It was, he felt, a life directed by others, who had ordered it in such fine detail that he had never developed his own intrinsic motivation, his own will. His malign past, the years of other people's control, was finally breaking him down. It had come to him strongly when he'd felt himself trapped as a young hospital doctor. Yet another controlling system – and one too many. The fragile light he'd been seeking, ownership of his own life, had once more slipped from sight. But in his manic phase, he had been working as a doctor by day, revising for exams and playing music in clubs late into the night. His constricted hospital life was merely the catalyst; he knew it had started long before:

Looking back, I can see that, even as a young child, I was prone to morbid, depressive, obsessive thoughts, often asking myself, 'Why am I so unhappy?' I think I'd actually lived most of my life in a state of mild sub-clinical depression. I've considered death and suicide since I was seven, so I was astonished to discover when I grew older that it was considered a mental illness. I was always serious, asking questions and analysing. My personality predisposed me to a depressive type of illness in later life. I've been asleep for years.

A lot of my life, I've been frustrated because I was lacking a sense of who I really was. My array of abilities turned my childhood into a set of achievements along other people's parameters. The exams, the high marks, the wonderful music performances, none of that impressed me. I thought I was achieving very little. But I would have had an even greater sense of failure in not achieving, not being applauded. Deep down, those successes were just second-rate. There was a higher level of happiness which I saw in other children, which came from knowing what they wanted and fulfilling that. My achievements just led to more achievements. Part of me wasn't being nourished really deep down.

I'd really have enjoyed the typical hedonistic pleasures of being a child. Every Saturday, as I went to music college, what I really wanted to do was watch television with my friends. I had five days a week school with the expectation of high grades all the time. The sixth

day was music college, and on the seventh it was Hebrew
classes, typical for Jewish children, especially boys.
That's seven days a week education. Sometimes I just
wanted to do nothing, allowing some shoots of my own to
burst through. But that was not for me.

Early on, I knew how my emotional state had been
badly affected by all that repression. So I was my own
psychiatrist. When I was 16, at school we were asked to
write down what we thought we were going to be. The
two most obvious lines were something academic or music
– but I wrote psychiatrist. I was such an analytical
person, hypersensitive to people to try and find what
makes them happy. I believe I was temperamentally an
observer when I was a baby. Mother said I just used to
look around, didn't use to make any noise at all, just sit
and watch, and watch, and watch, and watch. So I used to
take in a phenomenal amount of information and not
necessarily give out very much.

Nowadays, people see me as the doctor who left
medicine to become a musician. Medicine was nearly
right for me. Within me, there's a very, very cerebral
logical thinker and a very caring person. It was a really
valuable education, but it didn't take me closer to the
place I was looking for. I did about 13 years as a medical
student and a doctor. The moment I made the medical
switch from physical to psychological, I was so much
happier. I'd thought I'd found my niche within medicine. I
was good at it. Reports from my superiors were full of
praise. I knew I was getting closer to where I was
supposed to be, but after a while, I realised I still wasn't
satisfied.

I narrowed it down further, working in psycho-
dynamic psychotherapy. I came with a wealth of
information from what I'd done naturally in childhood,
and to my amazement found it was all written down –
exactly what I had thought all my life. It justified a lot of
my thought processes and ideas. I started having
psychotherapy myself while I was training, killing two
birds with one stone. I still see the therapist every couple
of weeks.

The great reverse

Just before his final qualifications, Jeremy walked out on his career in medicine. He had become a fine, respected and much-needed child psychiatrist, and it was infuriating to all who knew him. Why did he not stick it out just that little bit longer to finish what he had started? Experimental work by the great psychologist Kurt Lewin in 1940s America offers a clue to Jeremy's sudden departure. Lewin described how tensions within life circumstances create forces which cause people to act. His proposal of a Force Field in life was taken up in George Lucas' 1977 film, *Star Wars*, as a metaphysical power – 'May the force be with you'.

As for Jeremy, when someone is confined as the way out comes into view, the force to reach it becomes very much stronger and can be irresistible. That's why jailbreaks happen far more frequently just before the sentence is complete than midway through it. It's as if the prisoner can smell the freedom and no longer resist the urge to escape. In Lewin's terms, Jeremy's timing made sense. Just as he was about to break through into a more senior position with much greater freedom to direct his own life, he took his chance and leapt over the restraining wall:

I'd been institutionalised until I was 30. I went straight from school to medical school, straight into hospital and the National Health Service, straight through to psychiatry. I was a breakdown waiting to happen. I'd actually had my first episode of mania a year before I left. It is strange to say, but I almost needed to have a depression, to collapse and then put the pieces back together again in a better way. I became ill to rise from the mental ashes. I went over the top. I was doing ridiculous things, but deliberately.

Within work, I looked like a rather brilliant child psychiatrist. The patients didn't suffer, so I was never pulled up. Then the depressions came again, ten times worse; proper psychotic depressions. I couldn't function. When I was manic, I had an abnormal strength, so it was in my next manic period that I resigned. I never regretted it. I've never looked back. No excuses.

I couldn't leave in cold blood. I took two weeks off work and went to the Glastonbury rock festival. I took a minute dose of LSD, the only time in my life. I'd always thought it was dangerous, and it was. Problem was, I was already depressed. I became acutely psychotically paranoid. [His mother had told me, 'He went to Glastonbury and never came back!']

Within 24 hours, everything was wonderful. I'd finally found the answer to all my problems. There was a calm and a peace within me that I'd never found before. All sorts of tensions and problems just vanished. I listened to music, I heard a new depth and realised why I loved it. It was possibly one of the most fantastic moments of my life. I wouldn't trade it ever again. Problem is that when you're high, you inevitably swing low, and highs never last as long as the lows. The lows could last a year, characterised by being in bed all day every day, wanting to commit suicide all day every day. I lay there, working out how I'm going to do it, when I'm going to do it, realising how useless I was as a person, how stupid I'd been throughout my whole life, how there was no future. That depression would be with me for a year. A year lost.

It took seven years to end. I finally have a sense of being in the right place at the right time.

One in four people of the UK population were diagnosed with some form of mental illness in 2009. Though I have not statistically analysed the proportion of mental illness in my whole sample of gifted people, it seems to me that they suffered far less than the national figure indicates. Sigmund Freud wrote that, 'the trend to self-destruction is present to a certain degree in very many more human beings than those in whom it is carried out', though he did not work out any statistics to back his statement. Jeremy certainly understood Hamlet's more poetic words: 'How weary, stale, flat and unprofitable/ Seem to me all the uses of this world!' Jeremy toyed with the idea of ending his life, but he did not.

The life of a musician

Nearly 15 years on, Jeremy still lives with the consequences of his 'escape' from medicine and his bipolar
disorder. But the deep pain of his illness has long gone. He
continues to help his many friends with their problems as
an ex-psychiatrist. He was very good at it, after all.

His life is his music business, which he's built up with
non-stop work since then. Over the years, he worked
through his bipolarity by playing every night – excitedly
when he's in an upswing, and more safely and with less
enjoyment in a downswing. His standing is excellent as a
piano musician and singer. Sometimes he plays the trumpet, but he has become well known as a piano vocalist and is
in demand seven nights a week. He sings smooth accessible
jazz, blues and soul, accompanying himself on the piano.
He is part of a very large agency which provides musicians
for restaurants, parties, weddings and corporate functions.
He has lots of friends and makes good money. Medicine
has doubtless lost an excellent clinician. But Jeremy is
much happier:

> I've survived, I'm stable. I'm still quite competitive and I
> still need to achieve. I have something to give. I'd really
> like to open my own venue. Put my name to it. I want to
> stay a musician. So I've found the answer to that.
>   I feel I've been given something more than other
> people, so I owe it to the world to give back in a spiritual
> sense, to produce something worthy. So far, I've been too
> messed up. It's been a long journey for me to get to
> clarity. If I can find what that very thing is, I'd like to use
> it. Money hasn't bothered me at all. I look at some of my
> friends and see they are so hung up about money. I have
> a hunger for success in something. The money will come.
> My success is to find happiness, and find where I belong. I
> haven't got time to choose the wrong thing again.
>   Many close friends love me being a musician.
> Actually, a lot of people in normal jobs really wish they
> could have done what I've done. Once, they had a passion
> for something they wanted to do. They've got a house and

a wife and kids, and I certainly wouldn't knock that either, but they would have loved to have done this sort of thing. They're very proud of me. I'm their interesting and special friend. I'm not ready yet for all the dinner parties, and staying in the house and watching telly or having babies. I don't think I've ever been ready for it.

Because Jeremy plays every night of the week, it causes problems with girlfriends. He's confident that someday, he will find someone who can live with his nightly absences. For the time being, though, he feels he's never been happier. And he still feels gifted in a very different way:

> I am perceptually gifted. My life's been a sort of experiment; myself as a guinea pig. I have an ability to synthesise vast amounts of information and perspectives from it to help me in the listening role of psychotherapy. I could take on people's perspectives. But I also have the ability to cut off and duck back at will. But seven years of mood swings was a bit long and has left me impatient: I haven't got time to waste. Thank God I learned the piano. Now I'm making a career out of it.

A 'bipolar' life

So much of Jeremy's psychological life had been dominated by ongoing and severe two-way tensions. These were not only between his gifts, but also in his bipolar illness between mania and depression. William Shakespeare's question was also his – 'Tell me where is Fancy bred,/ [. . .] in the heart or in the head?' (*Merchant of Venice*). Jeremy chose his career and life-path intellectually and rationally through his head, though perhaps he should have listened to his heart.

His depression had started early. In children, it is more than sadness; it distorts their emotional development. At least 2 per cent of all children under 12 struggles with significant depression, and by the teenage years, the figure rises to 5 per cent – that's at least one depressed child in every classroom. Like Jeremy, more than half of all adults who develop depression say they can look back and pin-point their early symptoms before the age of 20. Early attention and treatment can alleviate later problems.

Bipolar illness comes later in life and both its depressive and manic phases bring delusion. In the pain and despair of depression, sufferers feel the world would be better without them and may turn to suicide. In mania, people feel wonderful, have boundless energy and live in the moment. But the drugs which control mania also flatten all emotional feeling, so people tend to stop taking them, preferring to have their familiar human feelings, even though they are distressed by them.

Kay Redfield Jamison is a world expert on bipolar disorder and Professor of Psychiatry at Johns Hopkins School of Medicine, USA. In her influential 1995 auto-biography, *An Unquiet Mind: A Memoir of Moods and Madness*, she wrote about her own bipolar illness, and even though it drove her to attempt suicide, she felt she would miss it if she lost it. Jamison believes it appears more frequently in artistic and high-achieving families, such as that of the poet Lord Byron. But the most recent research indicates that, whereas an up-and-down personality is conducive to creativity, serious bipolar illness kills it.

Depression too is claimed to be found more frequently among creative people. The trouble is that it's almost as widespread as the common cold, and among all levels of ability and creativity. For example, Virginia Woolf's well-known struggle with severe depression throughout most of her life is often associated with her brilliance. But Hermione Lee, in her immensely detailed biography, *Virginia Woolf*, found that not only is there no evidence for this assumed connection, but whenever Virginia became ill her creativity stopped. Virginia Woolf, like Jeremy Kramer, was a sane woman with bouts of madness. But unlike him, she went over the edge: her suicide marked the end of her creativity.

Jeremy had suffered from pressure to perform at a high level from a very early age. His days were packed with lessons. He soon discovered that his achievement was a way of pleasing his parents and teachers for their love and admiration. Granted, he had the required gifts, but he also had the untapped potential to splash around with paints, run around with arms stuck out pretending to be an aeroplane, imagine funny stories and talk to his teddy. All through his life, he felt that his creativity had been squeezed out of him. As an adult musician, that loss was his tragedy. He told me with a sad face:

> I can't even play jazz: I just learn it. My improvising skills are pretty poor. I've never gone to the piano to play for pleasure, always to impress someone. The pleasure was in the applause, not the doing. In fact, I don't know how to create pleasure for myself. I even find it difficult to choose new clothes in a shop. My long-time girlfriend tries to help, but she fails.

Normal kind parents quite rightly want to do the best for their children and to develop their potential into accomplishment. But some press too hard and are called 'pushy parents', others 'helicopter parents' because they can't resist hovering over all aspects of their offsprings' lives. There may be deep underlying psychological reasons, such as wanting to control their children or concern for them as their financial investments. Parents may also use their children as surrogates for their own ambitions, getting them to chase the success they never enjoyed.

Every loving parent walks this delicate tightrope, especially those whose children have gifted and talented potential. A big part of the problem lies in a lack of true communication, especially when the problem of too much pressure is not recognised. Teenagers can be resentful about their parents' high aspirations for them, and feel their complaints are brushed aside – Jeremy was far from unique in feeling like a 'performing penguin'. But similarly, teenagers are not always willing to talk openly to their parents about their hopes and fears. School counsellors can be helpful, though not many understand how it is to be gifted.

There were other gifted children in my study who had experienced pressure like Jeremy. Some are here in this book. Each had learned to deal with it in their own way and managed to adapt to their circumstances. Some simply brushed it off, and others took it to heart. But adaptation which is appropriate in childhood circumstances can be inappropriate and harmful later. Even in his mid-forties Jeremy still recognises his deeply ingrained habit of seeking approval by achievement. As he would doubtless agree, being aware of a psychological problem is halfway to dealing with it.

3

Stark odds

I was just really brilliant – shit hot.

Andy Armistead

If ever a boy was bursting with potential, it was Andy Armistead. It wasn't just his top of the range intelligence, but his superb performances in everything – music, sport, mathematics – almost everything he did. In his early teens, he sang in his town choir and played in the Manchester Youth Orchestra, as well as excelling at tennis and other sports. I remember him at 17, his pale grey eyes, long dark lashes and a mouth which curled easily into friendly smiles. Each time I visited him at his home, after hours of lively conversation he treated me to wonderful piano perform-ances of Beethoven, *con brio*, fingers skimming surely over the keyboard. What a treat for me. He was dark-skinned and thick-set like his African father, though his brother and two sisters were slender, pale and white-blonde.

The family lived in a spacious red-brick house built about 1900. Although Andy was preparing for important exams when he was 15, and so many anxious parents of gifted children had refused to let me even talk to their children at such a time, his mother was easy. The family welcomed me warmly into the living room, a cheerful com-fortable place with a decidedly lived-in look. It was a place, as the poet Robert Frost put it, 'When you have to go there, they have to take you in.' It was home as a place to be, rather than home as a place to grow up and leave. I stepped

over the kids' discarded trainers while Andy cleared a space
for me on the sofa. I sank back and relaxed. The piano was
open and ready.

Andy and his mother were good for each other. All his
life she'd given him unquestioning emotional and intellectual support, as well as an exceptionally long rein of freedom to be himself. She told me how her family had risen
swiftly in the world – 'Three generations out of the work-
house.' Her winning a place at the free selective grammar
school had enabled her to rise to a university Master's
degree. And now there was Andy, with the potential to turn
everything he touched into gold. But as the story unfolded
over the years, his life did not turn out anything like
expected. Instead, faced with constant life-threatening
menace of Shakespearean magnitude, he was able to draw
on the power of his kaleidoscopic gifts and the love of
his family in extraordinary ways to save his life over and
over again.

From the beginning, Andy's mother had not found him
an easy child. He'd seemed to her to fit one of the stereo-
types of the gifted child – the wild and uncontrollable
model – so, she'd joined the National Association for Gifted
Children. For his part, he'd had a few big parental changes
to adapt to. His mother told me how it had been:

> From about the age of three he was very difficult,
> tremendously aggressive; it was dreadful if he was
> crossed. The child psychologist said he was just very
> frustrated; she thought that was the way gifted children
> would be. But he was living in a household that was
> offering him books, music, theatre visits, stately homes,
> swimming, tennis, people who talk and are lively. It's
> more likely that it was because our marriage was going
> downhill and I'd been trying to keep him quiet, avoiding
> the issues which were more between his father and him
> than with me. He certainly got better once we were
> divorced.
>
> Now [at 15] he's just argumentative, mostly about
> what he considers to be my very untidy and illogical
> mind. He has no false modesty at all about his. I end up

shouting at him that he's overbearing, arrogant etc, etc. But I don't think it's as much to do with adolescence as to do with him and me. He said that he was living in a nest full of feminists and would report us to the social services for maltreating him – not valuing his male personality!

It's not only the supreme self-confidence and his brightness that makes him different; it's also the fact that he's black, half-caste as it were. And also in the past year, he's decided that he's gay – and his is a very macho, male school. When he first told me, my reaction was, 'Don't be so silly, of course you're not.' But it's OK now; it isn't a problem to me anymore, though I am anxious about the AIDS thing and the exploitation of young people. You'd think it would be quite a load, with his colour and his sexual preference, but in fact, he hasn't presented me with that problem at all lately. He's perfectly happy.

Andy understood the emotional tangles his mother and two fathers had struggled with, and the extra efforts his mother had made to make up for any fall-out emotional disturbance to her four children. He thought perhaps they'd all emerged stronger from the changing family situations, even though his mother alone bore the burden of guilt for the turbulence in their lives. The fathers did not seem to be a part of that.

Even at the age of ten, when I'd first met him, Andy had a lively imagination and a sweet feeling for his world. He had a reasoned way of thinking and expressing himself, which was to stand him in good stead as the terrifying years went by:

> I'd like to have seen England as it was before the forests were cut down, a totally forested country; it would have been absolutely incredibly beautiful. But I don't think I'd like to live there as myself, as I am now, in the past, because I wouldn't fit, you see.

Andy at school

When Andy was 13, his second (adoptive) father left the family, taking his financial support with him. Andy's mum then became a single mother coping with four children at school as well as her own full-time local authority job. The money dried up. Andy was suddenly removed from his excellent private school where he was happy and doing well, and dropped into a tough all-boys comprehensive. It was a terrible shock to him. Although he handled his many differences from his new school-mates with as much skill and sophistication as a young teenager could muster, his multiple gifts and talents could not protect him. As his school years went by, he seemed to me to become more disillusioned and a touch of bitterness had crept into his soul. But by 17, he had carefully worked out ways of using his intellectual gifts to protect his inner self from the constant threats to his sense of well-being. He was able to present me with his old cheerful optimistic view of life:

I'm not very black, so sometimes people don't notice, and their reaction is a surprise because I'm coloured when everyone else in my family is white: it is a bit weird. It's not a nice position to be in, half-caste; I get the whole range of insults that go with it. Going through life as somebody who's very good at things but coloured, I've had to build up defences. But I'm difficult to hurt emotionally.

I've learned to isolate myself mentally from anything that might hurt me; I just sort of close the door. My music is a useful emotional outlet, and it's also something that I gain emotion from, so it's an input as well. I can please myself quite easily playing the piano, and if I'm angry, it'll help me to control myself and bring myself round.

When I play the piano, like with Mozart's Piano Concerto Number 21, I can completely lose myself. I used to stay on after school to play the piano. Once, I got so carried away that by the time I'd reached the front door there were enough alarm bells going to waken the dead. I was in a quandary then whether to stay and wait for the caretakers to come and shout at me for not leaving – although really they should have cleared me out – but in the end, I climbed out a window and ran away.

My home is free. If I bring somebody back to this house, a friend or a lover, they always say, 'Isn't your house amazing, there are so few restrictions?' Even at a younger age where there were more, my mother was very 'loose' and let us do what we thought was best. We're all fairly bright and intelligent and trustworthy, and she trusts us. There's a really nice atmosphere here.

I simply asked Andy what gave him pleasure, and he gave me full measure in his reply:

What gives me pleasure? You ready for this? Have you got any more tape? Playing the piano, playing the recorder, playing the clarinet, talking to people, reading books, learning new things, experiencing new things, playing tennis, playing badminton, playing squash, playing rugby when I get the chance, playing table tennis. Going to new places in my personal and everyday life, seeing new sides to people that you didn't know were there before. Everything; everything's something new; there's nothing that I dislike. Watching the leaves on the trees shake about, watching a fly trying to get to the bottom of a flower – just literally anything, because everything has its own relevance, so it's always interesting. Even if I was to go to jail for doing something that I didn't do, that wouldn't be bad, because it would be another experience, another new thing to be interested in, new people around you, and such things.

It wasn't only the high-level intellectual environment and constant encouragement to shine in his private school that Andy had lost, but the assumption that the world was his oyster. At the comprehensive, he found most boys not only much less intelligent than him but also more socially disadvantaged and not very articulate. From day one, he'd either had to adapt quickly or be ground down. He tried to put a positive spin on what had happened to him by viewing his experiences as educational, but at times it got to him:

The kids had some myths about the private school, where people wear funny green blazers and they're all clever. Then on top of that, my mum couldn't afford the new uniform, so I ended up in my first days in my posh green blazer, whereas they all wore black. So I was this odd little person in bright green. I could do stuff really easily, so I spent a lot of my time just middling and trying not to attract too much attention.

I'd come from a school where all these very clever people were busy passing exams. Now I was greeted with, 'Go back to your posh school' and things like that. And if I ever answered a question in class, I'd get ostracised for it. It was very difficult. In self-preservation, I had to try to fade into the background and be grey. I did that to a certain extent by under-performing in end-of-year exams, things like that.

Absolutely every single time in PE – without fail – there was one boy who kicked me in the groin with his boots. Pretty much every break-time, I used to get bullied in some way, shape or form until the music teacher allowed me to stay in the hall and play the piano.

Some of the people at school, they make you think that you're just a turd on the sideboard because you're middle-class. To stay sane, I had to make myself an average person. So I refused to be on any sports teams or school productions, and I even held back on the academic side. But towards the end, when I was in the sixth form, there was a smaller, much more enlightened group who started to accept me. One of the bad things that comes out of holding back on the reins is that I found it very very difficult to let go again. I did the minimum of work, because I was already at the top.

For me, the experience of the comprehensive is of being really just utterly bullied and having people really try to break me in some way, trying to stop me being who I am. I tried my best to ignore it. I thought, 'You do what you want to and think what you want to; it doesn't bother me. I'm going to continue doing what I want and I'll do it in my way.' That fight is definitely from my mum. I'm indebted to her for life for being sure of myself, knowing myself, really knowing myself. Really asserting that and saying, well, 'This is me, and if you have a problem with that – tough.'

The experience is what it is, and you either learn from it or you don't. I gained a very strong sense of self-knowledge through my troubles at school. And also gained some understanding of the reasons why other people do things, how they perceived me. In a sense, it's a very freeing experience. It allows you to be yourself without constantly trying to pander to some other person's expectations of you, or trying to fit into some sort of role that people expect of you. I hated it that the teachers thought I was underachieving, because I knew I was educating myself extremely well.

It was a two-way problem for Andy's teachers too, who found themselves colliding with his carefully constructed and at times barbed psychological barriers to hurt. They did not find him easy and most did not appreciate him:

They'd write sarcastic things in my report like, 'His loud and flamboyant personality is perhaps justified in his results' – they'd never say, 'Well done.' I might have been an abominable person if I'd stayed at the other school, but I certainly would have had better exam results. Fortunately, they didn't accelerate me. It would only have made things worse. When I was about 16, I started to play truant quite a lot. Often, it was just from the classroom. I'd go to the school library and read Bertrand Russell's philosophy, really interesting stuff. Or I'd go home and play the piano. Mum would find about it from time to time.

One of the routes for gifted children in difficult school circumstances is to become the class clown, which Andy did very well. He had a mischievous sense of humour, which was particularly difficult for the careers teacher. Being in a socially uninspiring environment, his limited objective was to get the school-leavers into jobs, any jobs. But this awkward boy had a very different kind of ambition, and Andy treated him to a little of his special teasing:

The careers teacher told me, 'Look, they want 50 bus drivers – here's the form.' I laughed at him. When I told him I wanted to go to university he asked, 'Have you considered other options?' 'Well,' I said, 'I'd thought of being a toilet attendant; you know, work up from the bottom, start as a loo brush,' and he said, 'That's glamorous!' Truthfully, I'd really like to become an actor, but I want to go to university first, so I chose a course which I knew I was going to enjoy, and which had a fairly low workload. You should have seen the careers people's faces when I told them I was going to university to do Honours Philosophy.

In spite of the bleak school buildings and the unwelcome atmosphere, Andy's mind bubbled with fun and challenge. He lifted the boredom of his daily school life by playing intellectual cat and mouse games with his teachers:

With a new teacher, I just have so much fun because they don't expect it. I run circles round them and do the most terrible things. I'll give you a juicy example. In the lesson one afternoon, I did a perfect act of the despondent person, completely down and slumping around, and I'm usually very cheerful and bright. The teacher sent me out of the classroom and asked my friend what was the matter, and he said, 'I think something is amiss, he's not been right all day.' She came out and asked me, 'What's wrong, Andrew?'

'It's personal.'

'Is it your girlfriend?'

'Yes! She's pregnant,' and I promptly burst into tears and flung myself on her. She wrapped her arms round me and said, 'Oh Andrew, Oh Andrew. Dear oh dear!'

For the next two weeks, I was smothered in sheets and leaflets about what to do. Then, I just couldn't stand it any longer, because I had to keep a fairly straight face every time I saw her in a lesson, so I told her that it was a false alarm. She was great about it; she just laughed and gave me As for all the essays I'd done!

Andy was a square peg in a round hole – a gifted pupil in a school geared to a much lower level of education than he needed. No attempt was made to offer him any form of special provision, and no teacher took him aside for extra lessons or organised visits. There was not even a grouping of the brighter pupils for special interests. He was even subject to put-downs from those who were employed to help him reach his potential. He adapted by lowering his marks and his profile to fit in. Andy was fortunate in his educationally rich home life and in his sturdy personality, but at school he was on his own so he took his education into his own hands:

The syllabus bored me to tears. Really, really bored me. My goal was much more to educate myself, rather than to learn what was required of me, which is why I read everything and read widely. I don't think I ever scored less than 90 per cent in one of my multiple-choice exams. And nobody else even came close to that. I started reading Bertrand Russell when I was 13, and on to his proof of mathematics when I was 17.

I used to find it very frustrating that there wasn't anyone at school that I could really sit down and talk to, but I had to accept it. I refused to conform, to get drawn into conversations where the limit is sex. Homosexual people are just ordinary people. Being good at a lot of things seems to be disturbing to other people, though I did sometimes play down 'me' in the introduction into a new group, making myself less obtrusive than I really am.

Still, I'm glad I can do things. I like being able to sit back and ignore lessons and then do the work. I know now that I do understand things faster than other people. I can grasp things faster, and as a result I'm usually idling when they're working hard.

Andy at university

There was a downside, though, to that scholarly idleness – Andy didn't gain the necessary points to get in to university. Our boy had to use his initiative. Andy discovered that the philosophy professor at Birmingham University was a specialist in abstract logic. He phoned him and asked cheerily, 'Can I come please?' The answer was 'Yes'. But the young student was soon disillusioned:

I'd gone with all sorts of expectations of peer excellence. I'd expected university to be a creative place where people really thought in depth about knowledge and learning. I'd wanted to study the logic that drives pure maths and number theory, but I found that it wasn't what it was about. The others on the course were learning stuff by rote, and not really gaining knowledge or understanding of the deep-lying concepts. The examinations dominated what they did.

They were doing just enough, exactly what I'd hoped to be getting away from. My essays were written purely for myself. I did very, very little research. University was too easy. I didn't have to do excellent work to get a good grade, just fairly basic stuff. It wasn't what I'd expected it to be.

I always go for the concept. I learn the concept and then I will think for myself. I will give an opinion and I'll write what I think. Of course, in a subject as old as philosophy, somebody has already thought of whatever I wrote. I used to get essays back with lines all over the place, saying, 'Quote the reference.' But you know, that was actually my own thought I'd written.

I used to take this problem up with my tutor. He seemed to think I'd copied up what I'd put in my essays, but I didn't. I sat there and thought it. I played my own game, not their game. I did what I wanted because I'm me and I know what I want. I know what my goals are, and I know what I want to achieve, and as long as I'm achieving those things, that's fine. I don't need peer validation, and I don't need to have some professor sit there and say, 'Yes, you're jolly good at philosophy.' I knew I was good at philosophy. Even so, I got a 2:1 in my first year and a 2:2 in the second year. But then . . .

Into the maelstrom

At school, Andy'd had a sexual relationship with an older man. In his first year at university, his lover died of AIDS, one of the first in the UK. The man's family had refused to allow Andy to see him when he was dying, spitting venom at him in the hospital corridor. Andy knew in his bones that he was positive; 'I knew what I did with him.' Certainty came with a medical test when he was 19 and new at university.

At that time, the world was angry and frightened about AIDS. Its virus had not yet been defined. Sufferers were shunned so as not to infect others. Nobody knew who had caught it, who was carrying it or how long the virus took to show itself. Those who were diagnosed as positive were unsure of their prognosis or the privacy of their test results. People Andy had known were dead within six months of appearing ill. The gay community was in a panic. When men met in gay bars, if one partner had died of the disease his survivor's drinking glass would be broken. His friends knew that Andy's 'other half' had died. He reckoned he might manage to live until he was 20. His future was shattered and the study of academic philosophy began to seem irrelevant.

Still, he threw himself into his work and completed not only the required third-year thesis in his second year, but two extra ones, gaining excellent grades on all of them. Academically, he came to life: 'The three theses were good stuff. I got to sit with my tutor regularly and really talk through ideas, which was great.'

All very well, but Andy's immediate choice was how to spend his final months of life. Jumping through the university hoops would have been such a chunk out of his remaining time: six months to the exams, another month to wait for the results, and then a piece of paper. No. It was too high a price in time out of what he had left to him. He left university without a degree.

Andy was thrown into great distress, lonely and without help. Fortunately, he had already learned how to use his gifted intelligence to his benefit. Now, he quite consciously thought out coping strategies to control his mounting anxiety . . . and protect his physical immunity – his life. He returned to live with his mother, but didn't tell her of his illness: 'The last thing I wanted was that every time I walked in the door my mum would look at me with that look. The few people who'd known about it at university would look every time they saw me with a mixture of pity, sorrow and fear.' His mother did not understand why he had left university so close to the end of his course. She could not understand his personal world. Few could. He described it:

Think of a community where people are dying quite regularly and you've only just found out that it's something connected to sexual contact, but you don't know what. You don't know if it's oral sex or just touching.

So much of my school life was spent being ostracised, so I didn't have much in the way of a social life there, like going out with my classmates. I wanted to be openly gay, to see what it's like walking hand in hand with somebody, or kissing on a park bench. Or how about a dinner party where all the invited guests are gay and you talk about gay things in a gay context.

Mum would have been absolutely distraught, 'You're dying, you're dying, you're dying', every time I had a cold, every time I sneezed. I didn't want to be exposed to that too much, because I knew that that would upset my equilibrium and pull me down. It was surprisingly easy to keep my secret. I lived just for each day. I couldn't start a proper career or even stay on my course because surely I was going to be terribly ill, then . . . dead in two months. I needed to maximise the time I had, to get away from home and all the caring people. I absconded; just upped and went. No goodbye. No note. I just disappeared. I didn't want the concern and the questions. I didn't want to see the look in people's eyes.

I went to London and picked up old contacts. I worked as a media salesperson and earned a fortune because I was ever so good at it. I progressed very, very rapidly. You get advancement if you're good and I knew I was good.

Of course, mum and the entire family were frantic. Then it became very difficult to get in touch and say, 'Hi, I'm fine, don't worry about it', because then there would be all the 'why' questions again. I had the test when I was already a year beyond my expected death and found I was on the borderline of being diagnosed with AIDS. I could expect up to two more years of life. More than I'd expected, but very hard to face. Time galloped. Soon I was diagnosed with full-blown AIDS and given six months to live – and lucky if I lived that long. I went on working, earning lots of money . . . and called mum. Lots of emotional stuff. I expected to die at 22.

Then this new wonder drug, AZT, appeared. It killed white blood cells in the bone marrow. They were giving me very, very high doses with God-awful side effects, leaving me no quality of life. But it wasn't proven to be effective, so I decided to have my remaining six months with better quality of life, to live how I wanted to live.

But, oh dear – I fell in love – got swept off my feet. And I lived with him for a few wonderful years. I refused to see a doctor, just living on precious borrowed time. There really was urgency and I wanted to see the world. We went to Amsterdam for its vibrant gay scene.

One summer's day, I flew to Amsterdam to see Andy. The fatherly driver of my taxi from Schipol airport was concerned at leaving me in a somewhat desolate area. We both smiled with relief when we heard a cheery 'hello' from Andy leaning out of an upstairs window. He ran down from his apartment to give me a big hug and welcome me in. My remembered picture of Andy as a youth was way out of date. Now he'd grown a man's muscular body decorated with strange and magnificent twisting tattoos climbing up his smooth brown arms from his wrists to his shoulders. His smile starting under his wide moustache still took over his whole face. The apartment was airy, simple and elegant as befitting the life-styles of its two dedicated IT inhabitants. I found it exciting that Andy, in spite of his illness, had been riding high, using his gifts and talents to the full.

Andy was working for Hewlett Packard, a big computer company, and had swiftly risen to building up the customer-support operation at global level, until –

Suddenly I got really sick; my intestines almost stopped working. I couldn't even walk up the stairs. I'd refused medication before, so I hadn't developed resistances to a new treatment, and it saved me. It was really, very, very close . . . very, very close . . . doctors not looking you in the eye, kind of close. The pictures that they used to show – skin and bones. It was horrible, horrible, horrible.

Back at work the responsibility increased and the stress was making me ill. I had 20 large-scale projects and about 50 small-scale projects, all of them reporting to me. I managed the business integration, process design, doing much of the IT specification for it, working with the telecom guys, etc, etc. I adored it, loved it to bits. I was good at it. I literally designed an entirely new process management and documentation methodology for the organisational structures that I built, which has become an HP standard. As indeed has the project management training that I designed. I also designed and gave the technical training. HP actually produced a white paper document on matrix organisations and networking organisations, which was derived from another organisational document that I drew up . . . stuff like that.

I was just really brilliant – shit hot. The support operation itself was 25,000 people worldwide. So, it's like being given this huge toy, this huge wonderful magnificent complex detailed fabulous toy to play with. You get to decide what it does and how it's going to look, to mould it into shape and to create stuff, to be innovative and daring and take the ideas and make them really happen in real life. Just so much fun. I can't describe how much fun it is.

Then it struck again. I was desperately ill for seven months. My old flame moved off and I fell in love anew, this time with J. Blinded love! I had to think I had a future. Hadn't had one since I was 19. Quite a novel idea. With the new medications, I was not quite so much in fear of dying the next day. Nobody in my state had lived that long – nobody. I'm one of the longest survivors I know of.

Yet again, Andy's adult life had been almost wiped out before it had begun. Having survived the bullying at school and made it through to university, there was little future – just weeks. Low-grade fevers and feeling 'God-awful' dogged his waking hours. Dry retching stomach problems were added to the side effects from the drugs. He came to a stop. Fortunately, Dutch social security is generous. One doctor told him, 'You were supposed to be dead a long time ago.' But on he went into a romantic dream:

J. and I married as a registered partnership in Amsterdam. We did it in a big way in a beautiful very old building, with champagne in the gardens afterwards, and then everybody was loaded into a tourist boat for a canal tour through Amsterdam. In the centre there's a square with big trees overhanging an old white wooden church, which has been transformed into a restaurant. The reception with the dinner was outside on the terrace with the gorgeous summer sun baffling through the big trees' leaves. We had a professional wedding cake with a beautiful sculpture made of marzipan of two nude men entwined in each other's arms. The family and work friends were there. Then a big party in the evening in a big disco at Amsterdam zoo. We danced out on the terrace with pink flamingos around us.

But the stress of my illness on J. was heavy, so we came back to England where we were more at home. I'm still grieving for the life and work that was perfect for me and my talents. Oh, what could have been. My future was snatched away from me again. You can't get used to that. Every day was like my last. It makes you appreciate things so very much more.

Andy started all over again. After passing two completely
new science A levels in eight months, he was accepted for a
physiotherapy degree in England. I wrote him a reference
saying, in effect, that he would be as brilliant at operating
a warm human body as an ivory keyboard. He wanted to
specialise in neurology and pain management. Alas, J.,
Andy told me, had suffered a midlife crisis, said some
terrible things, and they'd split up, though they are still
good friends. Andy cannot be other than himself, inventive
and funny, but he has softened. He has acquired wisdom.
He has plenty to offer:

> I find that I am looked on more as a wise friend who
> knows a great deal and whose opinion is usually worth
> asking. It's the combination of a great deal of experience
> and deep general knowledge allied with an
> understanding of the human condition and how people
> work. I suspect that the knowledge and insight that I
> have always had is probably more easily dealt with when
> packaged in an older body than when packaged in the
> body of a young upstart [grin].

The disease never lets up on Andy. His many doctors have
given up predicting. He could not finish the physiotherapy
course because he became too ill, and says optimistically
that he is simply taking a year off. It became difficult
for him to work because of growing dystonia producing
tremors in his hands and feet, spreading with horribly
painful cramp-like spasms to the bigger muscles, plus the
devastating infections, such as three bouts of pneumonia
in 2008, and the horrible side effects of the treatments.
Sometimes he drops things and has difficulty holding his
cutlery. He can manage a keyboard with care, but no more
Beethoven.
     Andy lives as a close loving family with his sister and
her three-year-old (gifted) son in a town by the sea. He and
his mother are in contact most days. There are blissful days
when he feels well, cycles to his local beach, head held high
in the sunshine, and can imagine a future. He says he has
'a wonderful life'. He has learned 'to relativise', as he calls it

– to take a long perspective and see small troubles for what they are. Wisdom indeed.

In the spring of 2009 Andy and I spent a few happy hours catching up. He has become a chubby, jolly man, all crinkly smiles through his bearded face and plenty of chuckles. He talks readily about his afflictions, taking his customary positive attitude towards their increasing dominance in his life. He deals with them as they come. He feels that his life is as good as it can be and is glad of it.

Virus versus gifts

Had this research finished at the end of Andy's school career it would have been easy for me to conclude with great confidence – in line with almost all the lobbying for gifted children – that his schooling had been inappropriate and boring and consequently he would suffer lifelong under-achievement. Indeed, his comprehensive school seemed almost to make an effort to cut back this tall poppy, this superbly brilliant youth, to the size of other children. Not only did they fail him educationally, but also socially, in spite of one or two exceptional teachers.

Either no-one at the school saw the bullying he endured every school day, or did not care enough to intervene. It was not his gifts which brought the bullying, but his difference from the others. Coming from a posh school, he had a middle-class use of language and expectations, added to belonging neither to the blacks nor the whites. His gifts and talents were his salvation, providing him with resources to counter and escape his daily torment.

Andy's dramatic life shows how it is possible to use gifts and talents in ways which have never been recognised or written about by researchers. Just as Andy did, others can use their intellectual powers in a conscious and positive way to ward off daily threats. Andy also has a strong character which enabled him to educate himself with what he had to hand. Alone, he took advantage of the school's modest facilities to design and expand his education. He used his regular truanting as a means to improve himself.

The school library was his sanctuary from the classroom. He'd begun to blossom at university.

In the flower of his youth, fate threw him in cruel, painful twists into the maelstrom of life-threatening disease. All day and every day, the spectre of his imminent death seeped through his waking life and his dreams. His stark choice was to protect himself or die. Saul Bellow put his dilemma beautifully, saying, 'Death is the dark backing a mirror needs if we are to see anything.' The dark backing did indeed make Andy see clearly, and drawing on his strengths, he shifted his exceptional talents into a new self-protective mode. His gifts and his talents were his life-line.

Quite extraordinarily, he became his own psychotherapist. His intellectual control of his emotions became near to professional – a self-invented, self-applied version of Cognitive Behavioural Therapy (CBT) developed by Aaron Beck in the 1960s – although Andy had never heard of it. In this increasingly popular therapy, patients are helped to get cognitive control of negative emotions, and to deal with harmful thoughts and expectations to ward off destructive behaviour. It works on the premise that it's not merely the events in your life which cause you harm, damage also comes from the way you perceive things and how you act because of that. It's a two-way process; what you do affects your thoughts and feelings and they affect what you do. So, instead of delving around in your murky history for toxic events in the old way of psychotherapy, the CBT method moves straight into finding practical ways to improve your state of mind right now.

No-one helped Andy, though. He found a way of surviving by consciously changing his thinking, emotions and behaviour – a remarkable feat in his time of immediate threat. It was how he'd protected his sense of self at school, and again at university when he'd devised theories in philosophy which his tutor assumed he'd copied from texts as the other students did. Andy's defence against death was unquestionably an extremely high level of intellectual achievement.

But even Andy could not escape the terrible anxiety which was his daily companion for more than 20 years.

What would he leave behind? Would those he loved remember him for long? He wanted so much to breathe and live. To wake up every day not knowing if your life would end in weeks, months or years brought stress as intolerable for Andy as it doubtless is for a multiple murderer on death row, though in Andy's case it was all for a love affair when he was 17.

Sure enough it got him down, but it did not tip him into depression. His combination of gifted intelligence and sturdy personality brought him immense psychological resilience, and has undoubtedly given him many more years of life. That gift of resilience is what helps someone across barriers and out of situations that could destroy them (as when Anna, the concert pianist, lost the use of her arms; see Chapter 8). No-one taught Andy how to do it.

There is considerable evidence that the gifted can use their abilities to reduce their vulnerability to a variety of risks. He purposely cut himself off emotionally when he was being tormented, putting the bullies' taunts and kicks into perspective. Yet he also had the control to fully experience the wide range of his emotions in other safer situations. He is a highly sensitive person, who recognises only too well the mismatch between his intellectual potential and the education he was offered at school – yet quite spontaneously he told me he was grateful he had not been accelerated. In that school, he'd reckoned, jumping a class or two would have made him even more attractive to the bigger bullies and the dripping sarcasm of the teachers.

There are rich lessons here for all children. If they could be helped to become more aware of their thought processes and learning strategies, they could not only widen their thinking repertoire, but also improve their ability to know when to select and apply different approaches and actions – to go for the best strategies in a situation. Context is vital in making such decisions: a good performance in one context may be poor in another. And as Andy found, a good performance can also be seen as rocking the boat and has to be stopped. It's the adaptable thinkers, the ones with open minds like Andy's, who can be most successful in a wide variety of contexts – to act responsibly and creatively.

Robert Sternberg in the USA has a theory – 'Successful Intelligence'. It fits Andy perfectly. The successful person, Sternberg says, needs three kinds of abilities – analytical, creative and practical – in any area of endeavour. Abilities being a kind of expertise. Successful musicians, for example, use Sternberg's three abilities in this way: they use analytical abilities (to read a sheet of music), creative abilities (to make something special of it) and practical abilities (to perform perfectly to please their audiences).

Could Andy have survived as one of the longest living victims of AIDS without being gifted and talented? I doubt it. His is an extreme example of how a multiply gifted person could self-administer his emotional and intellectual functioning to preserve his sanity and indeed his life over and over again. Brilliant scholarly grades would not have saved Andy's life – but his gifts did.

PART 2

A dominant gift

> A man can only do one thing well; if he tries his hand at
> several, he will fail to make his mark in any of them.
> Plato, *The Republic*

Some gifted and talented people can experience an
unquenchable desire for just one discipline which dominates their lives to the exclusion of almost all else, sometimes from early childhood. The people featured in Part 2
are like that. John's life has been dominated by music, the
two Davids' by their fine art, Selma has always been
empathetic and caring, Gary has had a gift for integrity all
his life, and Anna and Jocelyn are ultimate musicians.

Each unitary gift requires a lifetime of dedication to
reach a standard which can be seen as outstanding in adulthood, certainly if it is to be recognised at a level of genius.
John Milton, the seventeenth-century poet, for example, was
so studious as a boy that he recalled on his twelfth birthday,
'scarcely ever did I leave my studies for my bed before the
hour of midnight' – laying the foundation for his vast erudition – and maybe his eventual blindness.

But too much formal education can ruin the delicate
flower of creativity. Irving Berlin, towards the end of his
life, considered, 'I've not done badly for a poor immigrant
boy who can't read music.' Asked what effect a more
sophisticated musical education would have had on his
talent, he shot back – 'Ruin it!'

Perhaps the best description of what it is like to throw
oneself into another realm of work and consciousness

beyond what other people can do was written by Franz Kafka in his diary of 23 September 1912:

> This story 'The Judgment', I wrote at one sitting during the night of the 22nd–23rd, from 10 o'clock at night to six in the morning. I was hardly able to pull my legs from under the desk; they had got so stiff from sitting. The fearful strain and joy, how the story developed before me, as if I were advancing over water. Several times during this night, I heaved my own weight on my back. How everything can be said, how for everything, for the strangest fancies, there waits a great fire in which they perish and rise up again. How it turned blue outside the window. A wagon rolled by. Two men walked across the bridge. At two, I looked at the clock for the last time. As the maid walked through the ante-room for the first time, I wrote the last sentence.

The individuals in this part did not reach Kafka's world fame, but they'd often known that total loss of consciousness which happens in truly creative endeavour. Mihaly Csíkszentmihályi, Professor of Psychology at Claremont Graduate University, describes the state of flow in his book, *Flow: The Psychology of Optimal Experience*. It's a creativity which is released when you have absolute concentration and absorption in what you are doing. It's when you exercise your skills to the utmost and it brings with it a wonderful feeling of fulfillment and happiness. For flow to work, there has to be a balance between the difficulty of the task and the person's skill. If the task is too easy or too difficult, then flow simply will not happen.

In this part, flow is unmistakably there in Anna's intense musical practice, the fine-art of the two Davids, Suzanne's immersion in the minds of others, and Gary dedicatedly working his way into grand finance. But it was not so for Jocelyn, who in spite of her immense childhood gifts and talents, could not manage a state of flow in adulthood. She was too easily sidetracked, lost her determination and concentration, and so never reached the level of success of the others.

4

Opera star

Opera is the ultimate art form.

John Daszak

John Daszak's powerful tenor voice soared over the upturned faces of the packed audience at the Royal Opera House, Covent Garden, London. There was neither a shuffle nor a cough. No-one had sung Benjamin Britten's dramatic *Peter Grimes* better. The music critics gave him rave reviews. *The Guardian* newspaper, for example, wrote that he has 'the voice of a beautifully flawed hero. He has an abundant theatrical imagination; his acting is alive and present, cool and composed . . . it is his skilful negotiation of this balance that has lent his recent roles, including Pierre in the ENO's (English National Opera's) recent staging of Prokofiev's epic *War and Peace*, such vigour and weight. Which is also why he is increasingly in demand by directors.'

John's most contentious leading role was in Verdi's *A Masked Ball* – unlike anything that Verdi could have imagined in the eighteenth century. Directed by the Catalan, Calixto Bieito, it involved vivid onstage sex and a lot of drug-taking. The critics loathed it, using phrases such as, 'a crude anti-musical farrago', 'a coke-fuelled fellatio fest' and 'a new nadir in vulgar abuse of a master-piece'. News of first-night audience booing made the papers, and the company's general director was called to account for his decision to hire Bieito. The cast were on the point of rebellion, not least because of the opening scene, which involved male singers (including John) sitting on toilets, and another in which the chorus are called on to give a Nazi salute. John shrugged his shoulders when I asked him about it, and took a broad philosophical approach to the performance:

> It's about the conflict between duty and pleasure; about the fact that those who have responsibilities may also have outrageous desires. Opera is an art form that combines so many different elements – music, drama, design – that it's very hard to please everyone. It should be about questioning things, not reinforcing our existing opinions. I don't take much notice of reviews, but I'm human. It's not nice if you don't feel that what you're doing is being appreciated. But when somebody says something great about me, I tend not to believe them.

A mother's faith

As a toddler, John was plucked from obscurity by his mother. She was a strong and determined woman who knew her own mind. In 1984, she'd told me:

> John definitely has a presence – a sort of aura. It was definitely proven by the time he was two and a half that he was musically gifted. My husband proved it in as much as he tested him. First of all by the fact that he went to the piano and would sit there for over an hour, which is good at that age; concentrate and sit there. Not plonk, plonk, plonking, or banging, but picking out little notes, not definite tunes, but obviously a tune was in his mind. It was even obvious to me who's tone deaf.
>
> When he was between three and a half to four and hadn't yet started school, he used to carry around a small book about musical instruments; he'd point to the violin and say that he wanted one. We had a violin on the top of the wardrobe, which someone had given to us. One day when I was cleaning upstairs, I got it down for him, and he was absolutely thrilled trying to get tunes out of it. My

husband felt that we ought to try and encourage this, and to that end, we asked a local violin teacher, but she refused to teach him, saying that he was much too young. We were at our wit's end because it was getting increasingly obvious that he wanted it very much and was obviously able to do something. So I phoned up Chetham's School of Music and asked them could they recommend a violin teacher who would take on a very young child. They did, and he started having lessons just before he was six.

Even though he passed the audition for Chetham's at six years old, the Education Authority said they wouldn't pay till a year later. So he had to wait. I'd like to say that Mozart was composing at four, but if he'd have come under our Local Education Authority he wouldn't have been acknowledged. It was a desperate thing for us to pay for these private lessons at the time, and also to get him to his lessons. We didn't have a car, and I had to take him on a bus and a train, and I had two other young children. But we managed, and he went on from strength to strength. That year, after he'd been refused entrance, he entered various competitions and just wiped the board at all the local festivals. Eventually, he started there at seven.

Mrs Daszak had absolute faith in John. She had something about her, like the mother of Nathan Milstein, the brilliant Russian violinist born early in the twentieth century in Odessa. Nathan was a rather quarrelsome boy, so his mother decided to teach him the violin to keep him busy. He proved to be good at it, and soon, just like John, was sent to a special music school. He made great progress, and by the age of 12, was accepted by the best teacher at the St. Petersburg Conservatory. His devoted mother took him to live there, leaving her husband and six other children, staying nearly two years. They fled back under Communism when the family faced financial ruin and hunger. By then, fortunately, the young genius was able to earn enough money to keep them all. Just in time, in 1939 as World War II was about to start and he was in his early twenties, his success and its influence enabled them all to emigrate to America, then London. He had become a world star.

John Daszak is a big, easy-going man who loves his mother dearly and is proud of her personal achievements. As a boy, though, he readily agreed with her that because he was so clever he didn't have to exert himself academically, and consequently didn't do well in his school work. She knew from my testing that his IQ was within the top 2 per cent, so he had more than adequate potential for whatever he might need. One warm evening, when John was nine years old, Mrs Daszak and I were standing at her front door saying goodbye. As I turned down the steps she called after me, 'John's singing in a concert on Friday, wouldn't you like to come so that you could then say you'd heard him sing before he was famous?' She was right and I was sorry I didn't hear him then.

Mothers and fathers seem to have different biases in their promotion of gifts and talents in children. Mothers go more for the arts. There were strong mothers behind famous artistes such as Noël Coward, Joan Collins and Elizabeth Taylor. Fathers seem to guide their children towards the more rule-bound activities, such as chess, or sport, such as the father of the Williams tennis sisters. Steffi Graf's father started coaching her in tennis when she was three and continued to dominate her life until she rebelled as an adult. It was his father who enabled Lewis Hamilton, the racing prodigy, to reach stardom. And the same for Tiger Woods, the golfer. Of course, many fathers and mothers push hard on their children who are not able to live out their parents' dreams. The burden on the child can be devastating. They have effectively been set up to a life of failure, and that can also be at the expense of other children in the family who miss out on their parents' support.

Like Nathan Milstein, John's scholarship to Chetham's at the age of seven was to study the violin. But whereas Mrs Milstein was absolutely right, Mrs Daszak was not quite as accurate. John had to give up the violin at 12 because he simply wasn't good enough. The school let him stay to try different instruments and a wide range of music. He switched to singing. When his voice broke, he worked on repertoire and learning new languages. It was clear, he said, 'I'm not one of these who had a natural voice from an early age, a wunderkind. It was something I had to work on.' Indeed, singing tuition and practice were to dominate much of the rest of his life. But quite unknown to him, somewhere in his genes John did have a musically talented and courageous family background. His talent had not, after all, come out of the blue.

John not only had a powerful mother, but his father, Bogdan Daszak, had lived a life of exceptional bravery and determination. He had managed the extraordinary feat of reaching England from the Ukraine during World War II. When he was about 16, in March 1944, the Germans had occupied his country. They captured him by going round the villages threatening to shoot the families unless the sons joined the German army. At that time, the boys hated the Russians even more, and so were half-willing to join the Germans who were fighting the Russians. But since the Russians had by then become allies of the British, the boys became enemies of the British. Many who had been badly treated, ran off and escaped. Bogdan, though, was an educated town boy, not a peasant like the others, so he was used for paperwork in a camp.

One day, he too escaped under a hail of heavy fighting, fleeing into the nearby mountains, where he lived for days without food. For the rest of his life he was determined there would be food on his family's table, no matter what. He experienced horrors and hunger, and was eventually taken as a prisoner of war by the British. He could not know whether his family was alive, nor could he try to contact them because he knew that if someone found out he was alive, they would torture his family. In fact, Bogdan's father was tortured, though who knows whether it was by the Germans or the Russians.

About 40 years later, in the mid-1980s, a friend spotted the name Zenon Daszak in a magazine and told Bogdan, who was thrilled to find his long-lost brother alive. Zenon, he said, was always practising the violin, though he'd preferred football himself, and he used to laugh at his brother's devotion. Zenon had become head of music at the conservatoire in Lvov in the Ukraine, their home town, and had played in the Bolshoi orchestra.

Lvov at that time was under Soviet rule and it was forbidden for a Westerner to openly contact someone there. Bogdan, though, managed to pass his brother a secret message, along with his childhood pet name, something that no-one else would know. They met in 1989 in Munich during the beer festival, where Zenon was adjudicating at an international string competition. This had to be in secret, shaking off the KGB. Zenon had named one son Bogdan. Another of his sons, Uri, had become a well-known viola player. Both brothers died in their sixties and John no longer has contact with Zenon's family. It had been particularly important to Bogdan that his family became totally British. He forbade them from visiting the Ukraine.

John's route to stardom

John was accepted for Chetham's School through a rigorous examination by experts in musical talent. There was nothing his mother could have done to influence that. The teachers there select young children, not all of whom will have had access to the best teachers or facilities. This means that the selectors sometimes have to take a stab at who they sense in their bones will become a great talent in the right circumstances.

The psychologist Dr Rena Subotnik worked for many years with students at the prestigious Julliard School in New York. She describes how the Auditions Committee selects from extremely competent young musicians, most of whom have trained hard all their lives, usually in specialist schools such as Chetham's, and often with considerable private tuition in addition. They look for applicants who can get the most from tuition but at the same time keep the vital spark of their individual talent alive. Dr Subotnik found that to make it to the top, a highly talented performer not only had to be expertly taught and to practise all hours, they must also have charisma, a stage presence, be passionately in love with their music, and be able to communicate that to an audience.

John's progress to the front of the professional opera stage demanded many years of unstinting training and practice. His motivation was his own desire to succeed, as well as his mother's encouragement. Motivation is about why people do things. It can be external, as when individuals are forced into doing something, or intrinsic, when it comes from the individual's personal force. The intrinsic kind is by far the more powerful. It's part of our feelings of self, learned and developed through interactions with the world. That sense of self largely determines what we want to learn, how we go about learning it and whether we persist.

The Americans, Allen and Adele Gottfried, produced the idea that one can even be gifted in motivation. They see the motivationally gifted as individuals who work to an extreme in their striving and determination to fulfil their desires. It starts, they say, in childhood, and increases strongly in the teenage years. It is seen in great belief in oneself, what one is determined to do, which supports them across the inevitable hurdles.

As an adult, John Daszak told me, *con brio*, how he revelled in his talent and the opportunities it had given him:

I enjoy music. I enjoy performance. I even enjoy the research side of it, finding out about operas, looking into characters. It doesn't feel like work. It's like that for a lot of comedians, actors, TV personalities. People often ask us to do things for nothing, which I do sometimes. If someone asked me to do a role for very little money and I was free, I would do it. Wouldn't matter if it was for charity or not for charity.

Straight from school I went to the Guildhall School of Music and Drama in London. It was a severely disciplined place, producing cerebral song-singers, as opposed to theatrical dramatic opera singers. They don't let you perform in your first year; you must work on what they set you. For the first year, all I did was work on lieder and phrases from lieder. Well, at Chetham's we'd done shows and concerts and choir and orchestra, lots of extracurricular activity, and suddenly I wasn't allowed to do any of that. It was boring and I felt chained.

After two years of that and the awful social life, and I was seriously thinking about giving up singing altogether. I changed to the Royal Northern College of Music in Manchester because they've got a good vocal side and a reputation for producing opera singers. It was warmer, bigger, more exciting and more fun. You can get your friends together and put on a show. It's got more space, more practice rooms and a better social life. I stayed for five years, partly funded by grants and different sorts of scholarships – considerably more money than I made in my first professional year.

Italy next for nine months; to the Academia d'Arte Lirica (Academy of Lyric Art). It was in a beautiful little old building in a very small old walled town, near Ancona on the Adriatic Riviera. Within three months, I was fairly fluent in Italian, and once I could speak I could ease myself into the culture and the Italian use of the voice. No-one in England had mentioned caressing the voice or about breathing and the way one actually supports the voice. It's totally different to say caress the music, don't bash it, inhale your voice, don't vomit it out. Immediately you understand that it's something that you're trying to treat well rather than just make a big noise with. I had one lovely teacher who'd stood me in front of a mirror, opened her mouth, and said open your mouth like that . . . so . . . and opened her mouth very wide, and I'd open my mouth and it wouldn't be as wide as hers.

We sang simple music to start with, like old Italian songs. You could tell immediately when you were doing something wrong because it was such a simple sound. In England, at 18, everyone's trying to sing Puccini arias and Verdi arias but of course, the people that originally sang Verdi and Puccini were brought up on Italian songs. There's a whole progression that one should really go through before bashing away at Verdi and Puccini. It's not as simple as going into a room, getting the music and screaming your way through something. There's a whole culture around this with a lot more that one has to understand and feel. Italian opera is about standing there and delivering the sound in an aria then walking off stage. Unfortunately my voice proved not to be suited to Italian singing.

Opera is the ultimate art form: it involves every art. There's painting in the sets, art, design, music, language, prose and so on. It's the combination of everything. It's a perfect, perfect art form. If I were to do Rudolfo in *La Boheme*, the Duke in *Rigoletto* or *La Traviata*, I would make it more interesting with my interpretation of the characters. There's no difference between what I do and what an actor does: it's just that I do it while I'm singing.

Some people have a fantastic voice, but unfortunately you get them on stage and they can't do anything, or they're thinking so much about what they're doing vocally, that there is no real performance going on. You can see them blanking in the eyes with another perfect note coming up. When you get just two or three people in the same cast who enjoy performing and commit themselves 110 per cent, it's altogether different. I was playing Pierre in *War and Peace*, by Prokofiev, an epic piece. It was just such fun to be in.

The professional stage

I got my first break with the English National Opera, rehearsing and being on standby for a major part singing Števa in *Jenufa*, a Janácek opera, which suited me perfectly because it's quite dramatic. Števa's a bit of a cad. He's going to inherit the whole estate, and his half brother doesn't inherit. He treats Jenufa very badly and is always getting drunk and going with local women. And he buys himself out of the army. I enjoyed doing it; it was a part that I'd already understudied at Glyndebourne when I was in the chorus a couple of years earlier. That's often a first step, the chorus at Glyndebourne. From that they offered me mostly small roles, but gradually over time it built up, and now I do major roles, like Pierre in *War and Peace*.

The Times critic wrote of that production: 'Perhaps the greatest triumph is John Daszak as Pierre, a role that can seem underwritten, but not when sung and acted with such fervour and insight.'

> They asked me to be a full-time company artist, but I didn't have to accept something which might not be right for me. In fact, I've got too much work at the moment. I can get too detached from the reality of life that I need to spend time with my wife, Jacqueline Miura, who is a mezzo-soprano, and our two children. Sometimes it's really hard work. I come home sweating because I've been running around in the production, or climbing up something or throwing myself around, totally committed to it all.

The life of a successful professional musician is extremely hard. Travel is almost as much a part of the job as the music. John's life was organised for years ahead without flexibility for unexpected life events. Audiences pay for their tickets and naturally expect the artiste to turn up. Living the life of an operatic tenor demands an iron will and sacrifice, so that John's work schedule and his home life were often in conflict. He and his first wife, also a singer, divorced after nine years because of those demands on his time and energy. Work for a musician is where there are offers, and they don't usually appear on the doorstep. He was often on stage at night and sometimes out of the country for months to study without earning or spending time looking for sponsorship. The name of the game is dedication. Professional to his toes, John told me:

> In 1996 I was in Milan warming up for the semi-final of an important competition in about half an hour when my mother phoned to say, 'Your father's died of a heart attack.' I thought it was going to throw me, but it didn't at all. I just got on with it.
> Right now I've got work for the next few years all over Europe. I've been asked to La Scala again. I got offered a job in Santa Fe, but I chose not to go because my wife was heavily pregnant and with complications. I felt bad at letting them down, and it was good of them to let me off

the contract. I want a settled home life for our children. They do suffer if we go away for a long time. If you've got children and a family, it's just not good. Last year I was away nearly nine months.

I have to earn money and fees vary. If I do a big role at short notice the payment jumps up. I can stand in at short notice for quite tricky things. I can focus on it no matter what's going on around me. Although it's better to learn it over a long period and really let it soak in. Financially it's better to be on the road, though I have bigger overheads. Fees in Europe are much better than in Britain, because of better sponsorship for the arts. My wife and I sometimes clash. She was singing all the Chopin songs at the Edinburgh Festival in performances with the San Francisco Ballet. They were dancing to the songs. She was away for about a week while I was rehearsing here for a big performance. We were desperate for help.

Some singers simply stand on stage and sing. John's *forte* is the drama he brings to the role:

Sometimes when I do a role and the audience gives me a great ovation, it feels like it's been worthwhile. But you can tear your heart out and if the audience doesn't give you a great ovation I feel drained and depressed. Sometimes it's just because of the unattractive character I'm playing. I quite often play very strange characters, people who've gone crazy or who kill themselves at the end. Or I might be in a weird production by an *avant garde* director. In that way I've been creative in that I've created a new ground for something. But I don't feel particularly creative. When I'm in my roles I feel content, as though it's something I'm meant to do. Not in any sort of great destiny or fate sort of way, just that I fit in, I'm having fun doing it, and I feel that I'm quite good at doing it.

It's very difficult to sing and be emotional. Feeling emotion doesn't mean you give a good performance. You have to play the part. You can be thinking about the washing up or the shopping, but you make stage gestures or movements or something to make people think you've just given the most emotional performance in the world. There are actors who can just turn it on, and use all the tricks in the book, and make themselves look fantastic, or desperate, or pathetic, and it's simply to do with how they are performing, their acting technique. You know if an audience is responding to you and sense if they're listening and suffering with you. Even with an audience of a couple of thousand you can actually sense it.

Now that I'm freelance, I'm always auditioning. You have to make sure your career moves forward, that there's something for the future. From the age of seven I've been trained to be a musician – nothing else. It gives me a feeling of what I'm destined to do. But what if I don't get offered work, what would I do? I can't even be a builder; I don't know the first thing about putting anything up.

At the end of our time together, John gave me a wonderful recitation, talking and singing for an appreciative and amazed audience of one. I wish I could reproduce the magnificent sound from my tape-recorder.

Northern people like me are more successful in singing. Probably far more singers come from working-class northern areas or working-class Welsh areas because they speak in the up and downs of musicalities, the natural sort of warmth of the language. The open vowels of the north of England – o, a, e – project the voice very well. They're more like Italian vowels, ah, eh, in and o. If you come from the south of England and you're always forming your vowels as diphthongs, and mixing vowels together, it's very difficult to find the right way of projecting that sound.

Obviously accent doesn't come into it when you're blowing down a trumpet. There are very few French singers, so that's got to be language based. They're great talkers, the French; they sit around in groups pontificating all night long. The Italians of course have had a tradition of singing, because their language is so open and outward. But Italian has got quite a small vocabulary compared to English, so they have to do a lot more with their hands and bodies. They have to add to their words by demonstrating their intentions in what they're saying. In Italian you can ask a question or make a statement with voice inflection, so even speaking involves the production of sound. In English you can say exactly what you mean in a monotonous way without using hands at all. You can make yourself perfectly understood using the correct vocabulary and without moving a muscle.

John has won many competitions and been awarded several prestigious scholarships. Audiences have heard him around the world singing operas and recitals, and he is booked for years ahead.

Bringing on artistic talent

What makes one child choose the medium of sound and another words or paint to channel their feelings and achievements? Do the arts of singing and painting flow from the same source or have they different springs? Both my own and others' research has shown that general artistic ability does indeed come from the same broad source, but the form the surge takes is to a large extent directed by circumstances.

As soon as a baby opens its eyes, and probably before then, its senses have begun to be directed by its environment. Small children accept what they are aware of as normal. As each baby develops, some senses become dominant and refined to the extent that what the child learns to perceive becomes their personal truth. Musical talent can be detected as early as two when little ones start to understand some parts of pieces or songs and move in response to the music. Most children can sing well in tune and pitch, and keep a steady beat by the age of five or six. The highly talented start earlier and are usually brought up in musical homes.

A mother in my study, a piano teacher, told me how she had purposely and successfully pushed the sense of music in her daughter. Her reasoning was quite explicit. Her daughter, she felt, was neither intellectually gifted nor did she have a sufficiently strong personality to get on in the world, but she did have some talent for music. The best her mother could do for her was to get her into music college, to give her a profession, probably in an orchestra, and a good living, as well as a ready source of friends and colleagues. The mother was right and the daughter did indeed take her place in an orchestra.

The ability to play music is a recognised route to a successful life. In Victorian times, a middle-class girl who could play and sing sweetly in company was in a prime position to find a husband. The earliest example of progress through music is the biblical David, who was able to advance through his music from the life of a shepherd into the service of King Saul. The text records that, 'whenever the evil spirit came upon Saul, David would take the kinnor and play it for him; Saul would feel better and the evil spirit would leave him' (I Samuel 16: 23). Even when he himself became king, David's pleasure was in music. Later in his life, we see him at the centre of the dancing and music as the Ark of the Covenant is brought to Jerusalem.

Three thousand (or so) years later, in England's green and pleasant land, the music teacher explained how she set about getting musical advancement for her daughter:

> Jacqueline du Pré's mother did precisely the same with her as I did with my daughter. She sang with her and tapped rhythms out, frequently and regularly. This is how music starts, and any child, I reckon, could have done what mine have done, if they'd started in the same way.
>
> She was always on my knee when I was teaching the piano, so she soaked up a lot of music. I usually have serious music on the radio at the same time every day. Both girls came in for musical bombardment one way or another. I teach a lot of bright children and I reckon that if I can catch them early enough, and with parental help,

they do exceedingly well. The average child I teach, say
from the age of five, can get into the [specialist] music
school in five years.

It was that early music training that got my daughter
into the music school, because she was able to sing well in
tune. She had a good ear. She could recognise rhythms.
She could distinguish high and low notes, intervals, etc.
It's the aural side that's very important at an early age,
not the practical side, which is a skill only developed over
many years – unless, like Yehudi Menuhin, they start off
with it.

If they are not taught well, when they become
teenagers they seem to fall apart. They don't know what
on earth to do and they have to start all over again
because it doesn't come naturally any more. Somebody
with a gift for something doesn't think about it, he just
does it, and then if somebody else says, 'How on earth do
you do it?', it can sometimes kill it for them stone dead.
They stop doing it because they start to think about it.

There are very few people who are tone deaf. It's
simply that that part of the brain hasn't been encouraged
at a young age. The difference between the talented
children I've taught and the ones that aren't talented is
that they find it easy, and so they just charge ahead.
They're doing all the right balances and everything
naturally, whereas with the other ones, you're
continually saying, 'Balances . . . gently raise this,
lower that.'

Aesthetic perception begins with pattern recognition – the
extraction of figure from ground – such as the theme in an
orchestrated piece of music. The music teacher's daughter
had plenty of that. But young children have frustrating
'production problems' in using their developing perception
creatively. They may know what they want their production to sound like or look like, but haven't yet learned the
advanced skills and expertise to produce a real work of art.
It is particularly frustrating for very young pianists like
her, whose hands are not big enough to span an octave.
They have to make a little skip in the sound – de um – to

try to press both keys together. But they can hear that it doesn't sound right. It can be especially distressing for the highly talented, who need extra emotional support while they are struggling.

Nothing in life is heard or seen in isolation, so that the circumstances in which children develop their senses define their perception of even the simplest line drawings or sounds. Formal education is not, of course, the only way to develop talent. One has only to look at art in unschooled societies to see that. What is more, people who think visually can encounter particular problems in the normally structured classroom because their learning style is not compatible with that of the instruction. That is probably why visual thinkers, such as Edison and Churchill, did badly at school. Picasso hated school for the little time he was there and never really learned to read and write properly, or so he claimed.

Zoltán Kodály, the Hungarian composer of the opera *Háry János*, collected his country's folk music. From there, he devised a set of principles for music education, which his wise government implemented in all Hungarian primary schools. He believed passionately that every person is capable of learning music. He was right. His prescriptions have enabled all Hungarian children to sing. Yet, so many children and adults in the rest of the world still claim that they cannot sing. But singing sweetly for pleasure is not at all the same as the high-level, finely-honed, professional talent like John Daszak's.

All the long-term studies of talent development, including this one, have shown the strong effects of family attitudes, as indeed have biographies. Parents, like the music teacher, model and teach the value of the arts, usually taking part themselves, for as always, parenting too is an art. They have fun singing with their children and taking them to concerts and art galleries. But too much pushing by parents can also be misplaced, and can cause terrible feelings of failure in the child who can't reach their hoped-for high standards.

When parents truly believe that it is possible for their children to be talented, it goes a long way to making that belief real. They provide the early teaching, the materials the children need to learn with, and the feel for the art in an enjoyable atmosphere. But they also organise lessons and demand a high level of practice at home and in their school or city orchestra. They offer commitment and the time for their children to practise. Although some talent is part of everyone's everyday life, it cannot reach the level of being outstanding without help, whatever the individual's potential. Everyone needs the basic material to reach artistic excellence – you cannot play a violin to a high level without the instrument, without good teaching, without plenty of practice and without emotional support. All this usually starts at home.

John knows well that his success is in large part due to the close emotional support from home as well as his mother's superhuman efforts to get teaching for him. He is grateful, and yet . . . he does wonder at times:

I never thought of myself as gifted. I thought I was just at a music school, rather than a school for musically gifted. People say it's a wonderful gift; I thought it was just something that had been developed in me because I'd shown an interest in it. But I always felt I'd missed out on the scientific side. I was good at maths and I was interested in logical things. I might be even more gifted for something which I never developed. I see music as a language and maths as a language as well. In the end, you either know that language or you don't.

5

Two Davids and the goliath of art

I love going for walks, hearing birds in the countryside and around the village. You can be at a drawing board all day and into the night if you're not careful.

David Quinn

I love designing for people who have a very specific interest in design and their personal environment – and a budget to indulge it.

David Baker

These are the stories of two men called David who are both artists and who faced the intimidating mountain of making it in the world of art. Since when they were small, both had shown great potential in art, went on to develop it through school, and have grown up to become successful artists in very different ways. David Quinn is a wildlife artist who makes exquisite fine-detailed drawings and paintings of the natural world he loves. His work is widely published all over the world. David Baker is an architect who designs interiors, 3-D places in which people live and work. Their approaches to their artistry tie in with their personalities. The wildlife artist has infinite patience to watch and draw with his extraordinary skills of quiet, precise observation. The architect is outgoing; he has generous empathy and interaction with human clients with whom he brainstorms.

Though both had plenty of love and emotional support at home, the most important difference was the financial support each boy could depend on. Although the future wildlife artist had enough for his basic needs, he could not call on any extra help, and had to get scholarships and grants where he could. Fortunately, his city, Salford, provided an excellent free educational ladder which offered him a route different from his father's life of toil in a factory. It was very different for the future architect, though. His solid middle-class parents provided him with a private education and whatever financial help he needed to develop his career. What's more, his father was a professional art historian who was a fine role-model and mentor to his son.

Crucially, in their secondary schools, each boy found a dedicated art teacher who gave generously of his time at the end of the day's work, to inspire and launch their talented protégés into their careers. I hope the two teachers know what they have accomplished. As well as their names, the Davids also share a burning desire to practise their art, as well as to make a stable income from it for their families.

The lives of these two talented men show how different real life is from the racy image of the artist. The stereotype of the Bohemian artist with loose morals shown in the behaviour of, for example, Pablo Picasso, Augustus John, Jackson Pollock or Lucian Freud seems rather more acceptable because they are artists than it might be in an accountant.

Artistic talent

When children are recognised as talented in fine art, they are seen to have developed their natural ability to a recognisable level which few others of their age-group have reached. Professor Ellen Winner, of Boston College, is precise: 'The core ability of the visually artistic child is a visual-spatial-motor precocity that makes it possible to capture the contour of three-dimensional objects on a two-dimensional surface.'

This very early precocity soon becomes a habitual way of seeing and searching the world. As with music, art begins with pattern recognition, especially the ability to extract a figure from its surroundings. In music, talented little ones can distinguish a theme from its background of notes. One of the earliest signs of musical talent is when a toddler can sing back songs, often before they can speak. But there the two arts divide. Even as children, talented fine artists are aware of dimensions of space, colour and textures which are not noticed by other people. Memory in either of these spheres of talent can be outstanding. The sooner the open mind and supple fingers of a young child begin to practise the skills of any art, the more their perception and techniques can be refined.

Everything we are aware of is processed and interpreted by our minds. Even in a baby, images enter the eyes to be interpreted by the brain. As the infant gains more experience and some language, these too add to the shaping and interpretation of images. And what we see we mostly remember. It may be short term, just the immediate impression kept for a few minutes, so that the first items of a sequence are more easily remembered than later ones, or long term, which requires more effort. Most children choose the simplest and easiest route – the short term. The talented, though, are more likely to enjoy the challenge of complexity and keep images in their memory longer.

In chaotic homes, children are often less practised at discriminating complex sights and sounds because their attention is constantly diverted. They do less well in tests of discrimination between images, and find it much more difficult to describe what they see. Artistic talent, though, can find its way out later in life. A well-known example of late development is Grandma Moses, the American folk painter, who blossomed in her seventies and became a world figure until she died at 101. Vincent van Gogh did not even take up painting until he was an adult, though in truth his paintings did not sell well until after he died, which is rather a long time to wait.

A child prodigy is an extremely advanced child, usually under the age of ten, who is able to perform at an adult level in a specific skill. The child, though, does not make headroads into new creative ideas in the way that adults do because they do not have the experience. One current child prodigy in Iowa, Akiane, a 12-year-old girl, has been producing highly accomplished and popular paintings since she was about five. They are not, though, great works of art, which push back any frontiers.

Pablo Picasso, according to John Richardson his biographer, destroyed almost all his childhood efforts because he did not like them. His father, an artist who virtually gave his life to tutoring his son, removed him from school before he had learned to read properly. Young Pablo had the run of his father's studio and received his devoted art teaching day after day, and as an adult explained clearly how it was for him:

> Contrary to what sometimes happens in music, miracle children do not exist in painting. What might be taken for a precocious genius is the *genius of childhood*. When the child grows up it will disappear without trace. . . . As for me, I didn't have this genius. I outgrew the period of that marvellous vision very rapidly. At that boy's age, I was making drawings that were completely academic. Their precision, their exactitude frightens me. My father was a professor of drawing, and it was probably he who pushed me prematurely in that direction.

Many art-school teachers see work from their best pupils as good as some of what still survives of Picasso's childhood efforts. But while still a boy, he began to soar above his father's ability. By nine, he had produced his first outstanding painting, and by 11, soon after entering adult art college, he was on the way to international recognition. As a young man, he was in a superbly advanced position, ready to take his place in the forefront of world art. His father's sacrifice of his own career and his absolute faith in his son's genius was justified.

Neither of the two Davids living in the North West of England in the 1970s could have been described as artistic prodigies in the same class as Picasso. But I'd measured them in primary school and found them outstanding on the art tests I'd devised. My tests (constructed with the advice of experts) were based on both drawing and aesthetic judgement. The differences in the boys' individual art styles were apparent then, and began to emerge more strongly as they grew into their teens. The potential wildlife artist began to draw seriously, and the potential architect was investigating buildings and art galleries.

David Quinn

David, the wildlife artist, was very alone in his art. A sensitive boy in a working-class family, he had neither example nor daily teaching remotely like Pablo Picasso's, nor family money, like David, the future architect. Being without any artistic contacts, money to buy teaching help or materials, or a strong demanding personality, his life as a professional artist did not look promising. Yet even by the age of seven in a normal state school without any specialist provision, he'd distinguished himself enough for his class-teacher to show me his paintings with pride. They seemed wonderful to me too. I verified our opinions with a panel of professional artists. I showed them armfuls of paintings collected from many children, and they all picked out David's as outstanding.

His exquisite talent seems to have emerged without precedent in his family. Neither of his parents nor any of his four brothers and sisters showed the slightest inclination for art, whether in practice or appreciation. His parents were kind and accepting. They never questioned his choice of art as a career, though it was quite foreign to them. There was nobody with whom he could share his enthusiasm. Even as a small boy, his joy was drawing and so it has remained.

But he lived in Salford, a gritty industrial town, not Renaissance Florence. Earlier research I'd done in the city's primary schools had found great enthusiasm for music, notably in terms of brass bands. The city was extremely generous to little musicians. There were school orchestras, guitar clubs, the city children's orchestra and virtually free loan of musical instruments for all primary school children. But there was no official recognition of an exceptional drawing talent like David's, nor was he offered any special provision; not so much as a paintbrush. His father, though, did everything he could to support his son. Leaning on his easel, many years later, David, the wildlife artist, told me of the great support his parents had given him:

> My talent is something that was always there. My parents were fantastic. My dad used to bring home lots of waste paper from where he worked in a packaging factory. He'd bring home reel-ends, stuff that would have been thrown out. So there was always paper there for me to draw on. I've still got some of it now, more than 20 years later. I'll never get through it all. Dad worked on a slitting machine, a huge, huge machine where reels of paper would fly round at high speed. And he would cut them to correct widths. Then they would go to be printed or waxed for product wrapping and various other things.
>
> Until I was about 12, I only used pencils and it was really exciting when once he came home with some thick black pens and I started drawing with those. That really stood me in good stead, even recently, because I've been specialising in ink drawings. Now I use technical pens and various inks and pencils. I did get some oil paints when I was about 13, though Dad thought I was quite young to get something like that. In my teen years, I started to use watercolours, gouache or poster paints and oils. I was quite diverse in the materials I used. So I did quite well.

Thanks to the eleven-plus examination across the UK at that time, which selected bright children for a more academic education, the bright little future wildlife artist won his free place at Salford Grammar School for Boys. Within a year, he knew that he would devote the rest of his life to drawing. Fate, once again, threw him a life-line:

> The school had very good studios, so when everyone else had gone I used to stay behind to enjoy myself. The art teacher would let me use the best materials. He was a kind of mentor to me. He painted fantastic scenery for the school plays, and I really was impressed by him because he would paint in front of everybody while we were

working. I got lots of encouragement from him and the other art teachers.

As a young teenager, he took a Saturday job with a sign writer who owned an art shop. Writing signs was a highly skilled job and it gave him practice in graphic design and lettering. He worked hard and did well at school, eventually leaving Manchester Polytechnic with a first-class honours degree in graphic design, specialising in illustration. But without contacts or any strings to pull, he hit a brick wall. It hurt him then and it hurts him still:

> The first thing I did was to go to London, round all the agents that I could find who used artists with the kind of work I did. It was fruitless. I've had such bad experiences I've never used an agent since.

David Baker

One lovely autumn day when the leaves lay thickly around their nice, red-brick suburban home, I went to see the Baker family. Mr Baker was a university art historian who loved to share with his young son his own delight in nineteenth-century art and architecture. They often went together to marvel at the rich variety of Victorian buildings and art collections in their city of Manchester. Every day, through his work and interests, Mr Baker encouraged the young boy to share his pleasure in the lines and the spirit of architecture. He found a very willing apprentice. David, the future architect, saw his father as someone to be proud of, and also someone who he could strive to be like. By the time he was a teenager, he too had learned to love what he saw around him, which nourished his creative potential. He expressed it at the time:

> I like Manchester a lot, going sketching and looking at it. Sometimes I go into the City Art Gallery or the Whitworth Art Gallery and look round for inspiration. I really get a kick out of looking at things like the

pre-Raphaelite paintings: Jane Morris is just incredible, and William Morris, Andy Warhol too, and other artists; they really move me.

My painting does a lot for me. Compared with my peers at school, it's the best – that's what the teacher said. My art work is original; I'm well into Fauvism; I like colour and I know I've got an ability. I do get a big kick at having spent my time creatively and developed a skill. I'm aware of beauty all the time. Just walking down the road sometimes, or looking out of my window.

There's so much here at home – you don't really have to look very far to be moved artistically in here. Just look at the flowers, or the graphics on the record player, not that they're very good, but look at that carving. I'm not wild about the television – I think I'd take that away.

Boredom at school

At the age of 17, though, his father told me with some distress that he and David's mother were having an 'interesting' time with him. He'd been at a private academic boys' school, but in spite of his extremely high intelligence had found it utterly boring. After much anguished discussion, they moved him out of the private system to a free all-comers comprehensive school. Although he was still bored with the regular curriculum, he found wonderful opportunities in art. He'd landed in the right place.

Leo Tolstoy called boredom, 'The desire for desires'. Some claim that gifted children suffer from it more than other children. It's a fact, though, that almost all children are bored in school at some point, and very many are turned off school learning altogether by it. Bored children are to be found in the streets during school hours, demonstrating with their feet how they feel. And they are rarely gifted. When they do turn up at school, they don't learn as well as they could.

In this long research of mine, I found that the parents of the gifted who claimed that their children were bored at school had far more emotional problems at home than the parents of the other children, and at a highly significant statistical level. Interestingly, there could be a distinct difference between the parents' and the children's ideas about school boredom. The complaints of boredom generally came from the parents: the gifted children themselves rarely complained of it.

Two major reasons for the children's boredom emerged. The first was because of the problems at home which caused them psychological disturbance so that they found it hard to concentrate and take pleasure in their learning. The second reason was that they thought differently from the way the school expected them to. Like the future architect, many were creative and had great difficulty in shutting down their lively minds to fit in with the school regime. So often, the talents they had to offer in terms of quirky thinking and fresh approaches to a subject were brushed aside in favour of more paperwork and memorising.

Once free of his first school's high-level academic coercion and straight-laced curriculum, the future architect, in a less pressurised school, was fired to work harder and to move on to more interesting learning. Sir Michael Rutter, Professor of Developmental Psychopathology at the Institute of Psychiatry, discovered more than half a century ago that a school's ethos is not only measurable, it also has a significant effect on its pupils' achievements. David, the future architect, suddenly found happiness at his comprehensive school with a different and kinder ethos and looked forward to going there every day. Like the wildlife artist, fate (and sensitive parents) had presented him with what he needed:

> I could stay and paint until 9 o'clock at night in the art studio. Teachers would be there and I could get an hour of someone's teaching. I really enjoyed developing a portfolio of paintings. That's what got me into architecture school, rather than my A-level results, which were poor. I've always had great draughting skills and a really clear interest in architecture and painting.

The future architect was not only artistically gifted, but I'd measured him as intellectually gifted too. Like Andy in Chapter 3, only some of his teachers enjoyed his ready wit and intellectual games, so often a feature of gifted youngsters:

> The English teacher sometimes only understands what I mean three hours after – and by that time I can't remember what we were talking about. Once, I suddenly turned on the banks because they were investing in all the evil countries. That's evil invested in evil, which all seemed very relevant to *The Duchess of Malfi*. But the teacher didn't understand at all why suddenly I'd gone onto banks. I had to explain that Barclays was investing in South Africa and Lloyds in Argentina and then she understood.

Time out

Truanting also played a positive creative role in the potential young architect's life. He used it to good purpose, discussing and writing poetry, thinking about the world and appreciating art with his fellow truants. But he also did his school work:

> If I'd worked really hard in the morning, I'd sometimes take afternoons off with a couple of friends, and they'd just mark me absent. We didn't get drunk or play football. We used to write poetry quite a lot, and we'd read to each other. Say, if we'd done *The Wasteland* by T. S. Eliot in the morning, we'd have great fun in the afternoons, spending ages in the park with a bottle of wine, talking about it and eating oranges. We'd also talk about politics and the lumpen proletariat and things like that.
>
> I was learning more at the time in a different way about life and society, and was beginning to think about things like injustice, and the way human beings were, what people wanted, and why they behaved as they did. Then, towards the end of that summer, everybody had to have a long interview with the deputy head about school attendance and my cavalier attitude to registration had to stop. So then I stayed at school all the time. You could

> say that I took a new direction in life, and I've even
> started gardening on a Sunday morning – money-wise,
> being Seamus Heaney [the poet] wears thin.

I have to admit to sympathy with Baker. It had been a long-term habit of mine to remove myself from school from time to time throughout all the years I was obliged to attend. I discovered many ways to convince teachers that I was on official business elsewhere. At my selective girls' grammar school I would perhaps be 'visiting the dentist', if questioned outside. Many times I just took the odd lesson off if I felt like it or hadn't done my homework. Sometimes, I would plead a headache, and spend a pleasant hour or two absorbed in a book in the sick-room. In that little room, lying on the bed's flowered cotton coverlet, with the window open over the tennis courts, was much better than having my mind commandeered in lessons in which I had no interest. Did it do my academic career any harm? Probably. But I rather enjoyed having that occasional control over my own life.

Yet truancy is bad news for most truants and is not to be recommended in general. On any given day in the UK, there will be about 70,000 youngsters out of school – about 4 per cent of the school population. They do less well in life, are less healthy and more likely to end up divorced and as criminals. Nearly three quarters of young offenders have truanted regularly. Truancy costs money through extra costs in education, health and crime. Economists have somehow calculated that this is about £800m a year. And it is going up.

But truancy may not be as devastating for the gifted who can learn so much more swiftly than others in the class. Because it was so in-depth, this investigation was able to show that taking an occasional lesson off, or sometimes a day or two, was fairly common. Even Albert Einstein used to do it. Peter Smith in his book *Einstein* quotes him, 'Some lectures I followed with intense interest. Otherwise, I skipped many and studied the masters of theoretical physics with religious dedication at home.' When you have the capacity to fly intellectually, perhaps you don't need to attend every single school lesson. Sometimes too much didactic teaching consumes the energy and space that a young gifted mind needs to follow up independent and creative thought.

Certainly, many of the gifted youngsters, even if they didn't absent themselves physically, complained about the dreariness of being told what to think and learn in every lesson. Having a curious mind trapped for hours in a dull classroom calls for relief. Mental escape from class is also a form of truanting. Is there any schoolchild who has never daydreamed?

There is also a kind of semi-official time away from lessons in flexible schools. Teachers are trusted sufficiently to recognise the need for the gifted to have responsible time on their own. They can offer their high-achieving pupils library time to catch up on work, or reflective time to consider their work more deeply. Bright youngsters really appreciate the privilege and use it productively.

The three times problem

There is one mental escape strategy which only the gifted are capable of managing. It is their reaction to what I've called the 'three times problem'. I came across this procedure so many times across my years of study of the way gifted people think, that I identified it. It is usually devised and refined while sitting in a school class, but it also works for many in daily life.

It is a truism that most teachers are repetitive in a particular way, which in general is justified in getting information across. They have a way of presenting their lesson points in these three ways:

This is what I am going to tell you . . .
This is what I am telling you . . .
This is what I have just told you . . .

What happens is that each gifted student quite independently takes steps to avoid listening to it again and again. Quick learners, who take in the information at the first telling, develop a technique of mentally switching off at the second and third repetitions. This gives them a brief few moments to follow their own thoughts – to opt out of the situation – a very personal invisible absence from class. It is not the same as daydreaming, in which you drift away into a fantasy of your own. It is a specific technique designed to keep them learning and yet relieve the boredom of the repetitions.

The honourable aim is to switch listening on again for the next new point. The technique involves considerable perceptual skill to be aware of when that is about to come up – like voice changes, pauses and upcoming questions. The problem is that this mental technique has to become well practised before it runs smoothly. Until then, the gifted may miss parts of the lesson build-up. Teachers find it confusing. That's when they look bewildered at a student who is supposed to be a bright learner but who has missed a step in the explanation, and add a fourth statement to the list above – 'But that's what I've just told you!'

As with all habits, this one tends to persist because so often in adult life the same repetitions set off that well-honed reflex. In normal conversation, people often repeat what they say to emphasise points or to be sure that the listener has caught their drift. This means that even as adults the gifted may again cut off their attention while waiting through the next two (or more) repetitions. It has a downside, though. They can get into the habit of not listening carefully to what other people say, apparently distracted by their own thoughts – the absent-minded professor syndrome.

Being creative

As the two boys grew into their teens, their outlooks and behaviour began to fork at an even sharper angle. Though both were exceptionally sensitive, the would-be architect was more passionate and felt free to give vent to his emotions. His parents told me he would 'rant for over two hours in his articulate way', and cry openly when things upset him, such as a play on television. His prickly, uncomfortable relationship with his fellows in his mixed-ability school was not helped by his 'arty' style of dressing, for which he was sneered at with some derogative terms as a homosexual – and the barbs stung sharply.

He was a great talker, keen to say how it was for him and finding comfort, he said, in telling me. One winter's night I recorded his every word till nearly two in the morning. David, the potential architect, was explicit about his roller-coaster emotions, and closer to the image of a creative personality that people expect:

I think more deeply than a lot of people, and I feel more than they do. It's as though I had a depth of feeling that has to be used up, though I wish it wasn't like that, because I feel too strongly over people and things. Sometimes I cry or feel incredibly happy over just one thing. I'm far too sensitive because it results in self-pity – a waste of time. Loneliness brings on really deep depression almost immediately, even though there might be people all around me, and even while I'm talking to somebody. Half the time when I'm sad I'm enjoying it. It's genuine, though. Perhaps it's a desperate need for a rest, because when I'm ready, somebody can say something that pulls me right out of it and makes me very, very happy, and very active.

Anger is easier; it generally comes out. At home, I can shout and scream, and cry and cry, and really just get it out. Then I'm tired. But life carries on, and I've not changed anything. I just say, 'Sorry' and I'm annoyed with myself for getting angry.

I feel very, very different to the people who sit in the school common-room. I'll come in after I've had so much fun looking at things, sketching and talking, and they'll say, 'Oh, he must be drunk.' Well, that's partly our school, and it's because I'm so much happier than them, and they don't seem to be able to visualise happiness through thinking and friendship very much. While people grow up it's essential that sexes are mixed. Essential. It's so sickening listening to the attitudes of boys who are in an all-boys environment. They're so narrow-minded. A lot of my friends are girls, and I find that a bit worrying. You question your identity as a male if you fit in with females. One of my teachers calls me, 'a decadent namby-pamby boy'.

I usually laugh it off as a joke, being labelled 'queer', but it's also an insult, and because I've not fitted in sexually sometimes. I'm not prepared to get off with girls just because it's the 'done thing'. You should be what you are, and I do find some gay men incredibly attractive; not that I'm wildly mad about them sexually. I think they're so sweet and loving and they've got so much, though some of them are degenerate. Gay women are butch and absolutely great. But sometimes two men making love turns my stomach up and I realise it's not natural. But it's always a good thing if you can find love and it doesn't matter about male or female.

Adult life

There is still truth in the old image of the struggling artist starving in a garret. Making a living from pencil and paint is very hard indeed. It was so, even in glamorous Vienna or Paris at the turn of the twentieth century, unless you became a fashionable painter like Gustav Klimt who could depend on money from his portraits to keep his more adventurous work going. There have been times in history, such as the Renaissance in Italy or the Golden Age in Holland, when talented artists could mix with others striving like themselves in an atmosphere where the visual arts were not just acceptable but also keenly sought after. When the air is full of promise and challenge, there is an excitement, a possibility that things will turn around, that a rich patron will discover and support you. An artistic community is vital. Whether fellow artists give each other mutual support or stab each other in the back, being creative in isolation is the most difficult of all.

But isolation was the wildlife artist's lot. In my mind's eye, he will always be a gentle, sweet-faced, modest man of slender build, diligently bent over his drawing board in his terraced house in a small Cheshire town in the North of

England. From the outside, it was no different from the others, but inside he'd made it light, simple and elegant in an artistic way.

He had begun his career with low-paid or unpaid work. It took constant courage because there was neither a clear career path nor a specific goal he could aim for. He had to summon all the internal discipline he could manage to keep going in the way he knew was right for him:

> I started with general wildlife stuff, doing illustrations for all kinds of things. Calendars, jigsaw puzzles, books, magazines and newsletters. Anything I could find. Then I specialised in birds, watching them and studying them through my drawings. It gave me an insight into the birds and their identification that a lot of other birders perhaps wouldn't have. Studying something in order to understand it, to draw it, means you have to be extremely observant, and I found that I could contribute a lot to the knowledge of bird identification. Then I started to get papers published in bird journals. Most of it was unpaid.
>
> It used to make me laugh when I saw what the national average wage is because I don't think I achieved even that until I was 40. I've been supported by my wife, especially during the years when she worked in the bank. She knows how to manage money better than I do.

All creative artists have times of despair on the way up, and even when they get there. Sometimes it's difficult to separate personality and luck because an outgoing person is better prepared to seize a passing chance that an inward-looking person might not see or feel too inhibited to go for. In his modesty, the wildlife artist spent a lot of time hoping for a break, and doing what he could in his low-profile way to make it happen. Growing up in his community, his efforts were intensely isolating; no-one helped him to prepare for the cut-throat world of professional art. His paintings were his personal investigation.

Money was always a problem, and when it dried up in his mid-thirties and no-one seemed to be interested in the work he was offering, he knew despair. Yet all the time he went on giving his life to his work. His sweet nature and naivety gave him no warning or protection against being taken advantage of. Financially, things were bleak, so when a fine-sounding offer came he did not question it. It turned out to be a cruel experience which knocked his confidence badly, a situation which many a creative soul can recognise:

> I received an exciting invitation for a major work of illustration. It took me a year of research, making drawings and sample plates. None of it was paid in advance. When the contract arrived, it was extremely disappointing so I had to pull out. I hid my depression. I would go to bed when my wife went to work in the morning, I wouldn't answer the phone, didn't want to go out of the house. I was quite ashamed.

Yet once again in his life, fate lifted him and set him on his path again. His kind, generous father died, and even in death helped his son by leaving him a small sum of money. It was enough to buy materials and pay for a trip to the States. From then on, strangely, jobs offers started to appear, and have multiplied ever since.

David Quinn in his forties has become well known as a wildlife artist, with some prestigious awards to his name. *British Birds* magazine honoured him with the 1987 Bird Illustrator of the Year. They wrote in announcing this honour, 'He is one of the leading wildlife artists in the country . . . we are lucky to have him.' Since then, his work has appeared in important publications, including the *Helm Identification Guides* series, the *National Geographic Field Guide to the Birds of North America* and the *Handbook of the Birds of the World, Volume II*. In 2007, he published *Mammals of Cheshire*. He's even discovered some rare birds himself:

> My award with *British Birds* coincided with a boom in the hobby of bird watching. All of a sudden, publishers were bringing out books of all kinds of bird families from round the world. My big break was a bird migration

poster for the National Geographic Society which reaches a huge audience in America and abroad. In fact, most of my contacts now are in America. Their market's so big and my kind of work is given higher regard. I'm working on an American field guide right now. I'll draw anything, though. I don't see a difference between drawing, painting a landscape or a tree, and painting a bird. You have to see the thing and know how to paint it.

I love going for walks, hearing birds in the countryside and around the village. One of the reasons we moved here to Cheshire was that I could have that kind of experience every day. You can be at a drawing board all day and into the night if you're not careful. Because of my bird background, I notice everything that sings and everything that flies past.

His bad times are over

How different the lives of David, the architect, and David, the wildlife artist. During the years of the wildlife artist's lonely struggle, the architect had shot swiftly upwards. He began by working for two rival big-name designer-architects (one after the other), both hard drivers. Although he didn't like either of them, they'd given him wide experience and travel all over the world. By his early twenties he had acquired a sharp sophisticated view of life. According to his father, it cannot have been easy to employ his son in a junior position because of his swiftly gained experience and learning. It resulted in a few bumpy years when he got fired a couple of times. But his work in Hong Kong and Miami, and on a big hotel project on Broadway, New York, made him a lot of money. He'd earned enough to return to the smart West End of London and set up his own flourishing practice. In his thirties, with a wife and a baby, he was a happy successful artist:

I specialise in hotel design, restaurant design, and residential and lifestyle projects. It's about lifestyle. My clients are often connected with hotel projects or the music industry and that kind of thing, with a significant budget which is spent on finishes and furnishings. There's too much work coming in, so I choose the most appropriate jobs, as well as some consultancy work within the design industry.

I get paid for my opinions. People who want them don't just want a chat; they want something concrete and tangible that will give value to whatever they're doing. I love designing for people who have a specific interest in design and their personal environment – and a budget to indulge it. I find all of it extremely exhausting and demanding. Each individual has different aspirations and a different business so I'm pursuing projects simultaneously with very different agendas. Mostly it's with people who are creative, who have tastes, interests, objects, history collections, and want to find something new that's also an extension of their professional life. I develop it and bring a lot to it.

I've had about ten years' continuous experience in the design industry, with travel and outside interests. I started by working for other people, so I learned what they do and how they approach problems, how their imagination operates and how they make things work. In corporate jobs, it's understanding structures and agendas that aren't made clear in commission. That's what my real use and value is, why I'm employed – and paid so well.

Insight

Insight springs from the heady stir of past and present experience, and like all artists, the architect's insight often shows him the way. Insight involves the whole self, emotion, personality and intellect, reacting to a mix of the familiar and the unfamiliar. It's a daily kind of magic which is still largely a mystery, but treasured and sought after by all. It's like a fairy gift; as soon as you try to examine it – it simply vanishes. Maybe that's why there's been so little scientific progress in understanding it.

That vital spark often comes at times of relaxation or during easy familiar action. One late summer afternoon,

Isaac Newton invented the theory of gravity (it is said) when he observed an apple falling from the tree he was lazing under. Archimedes was lolling in his bath when he discovered that his body mass displaced an equal amount of water, famously crying out 'Eureka' at this discovery of how to measure the volume of a strangely shaped object. The story goes that James Watt was sitting quietly by the fire watching how the steam from the boiling water lifted his mother's kettle lid, when he had the insight that the power of steam could move even heavier things, and maybe he could devise a way to use it for traction instead of horse power. Poincaré, the great mathematician, was getting on a bus when he had a major insight, after which he concluded that logic alone could create nothing new. Millions of other insights have been responsible for practically every innovative human creation to date.

Insight is not only the gift of creative people, though. It is a common everyday experience, varying from hunches, educated guesses, or doing what you feel to be right, to the great Eureka experiences. It's like the spark of electricity which ignites the lightening in a storm, a short-circuit to the painful slog of step-by-step logical thinking which would not have got you there at all. You just know it's right.

The 'flash' of insight can also burst after some mild anxiety, and after it happens, confidence releases the tension. It can be measured by changes in skin response, heart rate and respiration. It produces a delicious feeling of satisfaction, and sometimes even a heightened sense of euphoria – a psychological reward which encourages a more intuitive way of thinking. So, the more insight is used, the more frequent and the better it becomes. Alternatively, when it is squashed, as when schoolchildren are forced to think in straight lines, the less easy it is to think intuitively.

To be an artist calls for tenacity in exploring light and colour and combinations of shapes and styles in the search for aesthetic satisfaction. Western education, though, encourages the more linear, rule-bound, left side of the brain to the detriment of the more creative right side from where insights originate.

Since he'd been a boy at school, the architect had learned to trust his insight which he had spent many of his childhood years developing:

I have an intuitive intelligence which I can rely on to take me towards a solution for a problem. After working in the usual way, I stop and then ideas suddenly come to me. Starting a new project, I collect all the information and just put it to one side, so it's kind of around. Then after a few days, my mind has passively chewed over it for a bit and I'm ready to start. If I start designing straight away, I might miss exciting insights.

I do everything. At the moment, I've got about four things going of different sizes. I'm involved in the refurbishment of Buxton Crescent, a big Georgian building in Derbyshire. It's been derelict for about 12 years. Apart from all the other consultants you can imagine working on it, there are financial and professional ones too, and it pools a big team. The job is to refurbish the natural thermal baths [built 1851–1853] and build a spa and a 90-room hotel. It sits above the natural spa water source. [It opened in 2004.] Another one is for a guy who owns an international china and glassware retail business based in London. He's bought a fantastic house which is less than ten years old. It's a beautiful modernist building. I'm refurbishing that in its entirety, everything to commissioning art work and buying furniture. I truly enjoy working with him. I'm also doing a fun neighbourhood restaurant in north London, and a private home just outside London, a beautiful Art Deco, 1930s, fabulous house. Just the sort of design I love.

The reason for me doing all of these things – a hotel or a restaurant or someone's house or whatever – is that I'm not simply making a series of economic decisions. I'm creating an environment that is tangible. As soon as I open the door and walk in to a new project, I'm on a spiritual journey. I'm immediately aware and affected by the circumstances that surround me. As a designer, I manipulate those – much more interesting than what's going on in the big offices, public spaces or housing. I find it entirely consuming – intellectually, academically, emotionally, spiritually and artistically.

The flowering of talent

The expression of creative talent is always personal. The processes involved, though, are much the same as those of ordinary, everyday decisions. In forming a work of art, every creative person makes judgements about values and can synchronise their knowledge and feelings in their work. In the arts, emotion counts: what you feel to be right can be as valid as any consciously learned skills. The fount of the arts is sensitivity, and its development is through experience and through the heart. It's a fragile flower.

We humans are talented in visual aesthetics. As infants we take great pleasure in gesturing; within a couple of years we enjoy making marks on paper and playing at making pictures. Higher-level artistry can develop at any age; though youth is an asset, it is not a prerequisite. Many retired adults turn to painting pictures. Nor does a person have to be in a particularly good psychological state to discover their artistic talent, as any art therapist knows.

Creative ideas contain the seeds of change, of fresh ways of looking at things. To be seen as such, creativity must also have relevance, rather than flash in the pan, though it may take years for work to be seen as original and valuable. An invitation to be creative is not an invitation to be pointlessly deviant. To be truly effective, all aspects of creativity need an above-average level of intellectual ability. It demands an enhanced awareness which can be focused and changed into symbolic form. At the beginning of art for a little child, a circle becomes a symbol for an apple and a little line out of the top is its stalk. Once a mark is placed on paper, it sets up relations with other marks as a likeness to an object, such as a ball, tree stump or pebble, and a possible scene. When the balance between psychological safety and freedom is right, then the child is able to take creative risks in experimenting, failing and trying again.

A frightened child under pressure to be a high achiever at school dare not take the risk of making mistakes or failing in a task. In my private practice, I see some highly gifted children who find it very difficult to draw like most children of that age. A really tense child might, for example, only feel able to use a corner of the paper to draw a tiny picture, and with such pressure that the pencil lead breaks. They inevitably tell me as they go along that they are no good at drawing.

Sometimes, in my private practice, I use a test called the Kinetic Family Drawings in which a child's view of family relationships can be portrayed and interpreted in quite complex ways. For example, children who are pressured and repressed find it almost impossible to draw a picture of themselves. They may 'forget' to draw themselves in the picture of the family or cover their drawing of themselves with scribble. If I do manage to persuade them to make an image of themselves, their portrayal is unlikely to have a relationship with the image of any other family member on the page, such as playing ball or dancing together. This test offers a way for the therapist to actually see the child's sense of self in the picture.

Anti-creative classrooms still exist in their many thousands, particularly in less-developed parts of the world. The teaching is authoritarian and takes little notice of pupils as individual learners, other than making efforts to mould them into the desired form. A non-creative teacher is devoted to discipline and the processing of information. Such classrooms, often dominated by religion, are places where the students' memory is highly valued and independent thinking and questioning are not encouraged. The creative classroom, on the other hand, gives pupils psychological permission to experiment and to fail; thinking is valued more than memory and children are given respect as individuals. A creative teacher is a facilitator, an agent of change, not the authority with the right answer.

Conformity and repression are the enemies of creative activity, but they are very good at promoting high achievement in school exams. The successful academic is likely to be law abiding, diligent, contentious and introverted. He or she will have high levels of self-control and enjoy intellectual rather than artistic pursuits. Psychologically there is some opposition between the characteristics necessary for creative work and those for academic achievement. The problem is that almost all students are chosen for higher education on the basis of their academic results, with the expectation or hope that the brightest will be creative in their work, whether in science or the arts. Fortunately, some survive the selection system with creative and academic traits intact.

Although a very high IQ of itself could never predict a creative bent, nor is it even essential for creativity, an IQ at least above average *is* essential for bringing ideas into a form in which they can be identified as worthwhile. Many studies have settled on a figure of about IQ120 as a minimum for creative work. Both Davids had very high IQs, but their contrasting outlooks and the style of their artistry – one alone and one working with others – made a difference to their lives. Although the unassuming hardworking wildlife artist got a first-class degree, the wildly creative architect barely scraped through his degree exams, but made a much better success of his career. Personality and control of emotion can make all the difference to success in life.

A highly creative individual is able to see and cope with extremes of conflict, to hold complex ideas simultaneously, play with them, and work methodically to resolve them to a new form. Creativity calls for a high level of independence to work out a personal understanding of experience, then make and stick to one's own conclusions. The pull between openness and control, the need to keep an open mind to new information while being aware of inner experiences, also demands a high tolerance of anxiety. Studies of artists and writers have shown them to have a lifelong tendency for unusual and creative ways, particularly the strength of character to withstand social disapproval or disinterest so that they can develop unique viewpoints and products.

In this chapter, I have compared the two Davids in their development to show how artistic talent is affected by opportunity and personality, well beyond school lessons, into the open field of mature creativity in a tough world. Both men have plenty of talent and high intelligence, and both have a determination in their work which has become stronger as they have reached maturity. But fate has also played its part in their lives, notably finding them art mentors at school and giving them encouraging fathers.

Had I stopped this research at the end of these two boys' secondary schooling, David, the potential architect, would have fitted the stereotype of the wild 'artistic' talented stereotype, not least as his school results were disappointing in terms of his measured intelligence. The architect acquired his deep love of architecture at home, but it seemed unlikely in his teens that he would have the staying power to work through a long technical training and set up a flourishing practice. The future of the wildlife artist looked more promising. He was a hard and dedicated worker who emerged from university with a first-class degree. Yet both have risen to creative success in adulthood.

The careers of the two Davids show the tortuousness of the road to being a professional artist, and how easy it is to fall by the wayside. Every potential artist needs plenty of material to work with and teachers to help and encourage. An artist must have an open mind to be creative and be emotionally strong enough to stay the course. Add to that, determination and guts to overcome the inevitable setbacks and grab the opportunities. It's not an easy mixture to organise for yourself at any age, but one to which supportive parents and teachers can contribute to great effect.

6

A good samaritan

Everybody comes to me with their problems and I help
them sort them out.

Suzanne Nolan

Some gifts are hard to define and measure with exactness,
yet we believe we recognise them when we see them. Social
giftedness is one, in the sense of not only being able to take
another's perspective but also to care about it. I've tried to
find out whether empathy as a part of social giftedness was
related to high ability in other spheres or whether it was a
matter of individual personality. From the time they were
children, I'd regularly asked each person in detail about
their emotional reactions to other people and situations.
For most of the gifted, compared with the more average
youngster, I found they showed a higher level of empathy
and social awareness, and this remained true across the 35
years of the study.

In one clever experiment in the USA, social gifts were
measured with children between the ages of three and six.
They were asked to choose from a range of toys what
another child would like as a birthday present. It emerged
that the more intelligent the child, the more likely they
were to choose what the other child would like – confirmed
on the receiving end. So, it seemed that the higher a child's
intelligence, the more empathetic they were.

But this is not so for every gifted person. A speedy
brain can also be impatient, especially with plodding,

repetitive talkers. Quite a few gifted people in the study admitted they could swiftly pick up the gist of what someone else was explaining, then only half-listen while attempting to appear attentive. Highly intelligent people are not always good at small talk.

The idea that some people are better at having finer feelings than others has been around for centuries. In earlier times, though, they were considered to be the preserve of the well-born. More recently, Professor Howard Gardner of Harvard University, suggested a separate emotional intelligence in his theory of multiple intelligences. This, he said, is only one of several intelligences, each being distinct, neither overlapping nor merely strengths and weaknesses.

Daniel Goleman, a journalist, took the idea further in his book *Emotional Intelligence*, taking it to wider popular appeal. Goleman wrote that emotional intelligence is 'the capacity for recognising our own feelings and those of others, for motivating ourselves and for managing emotions effectively in others and ourselves.' Although there has been considerable research on the idea of emotional intelligence, there are still problems with its scientific validity.

The main problem is that emotional intelligence overlaps considerably with ideas of personality. And the theory does not recognise the big variations in culture. What may be welcome as empathy in one culture may be offensive in another. Take personal space, for example. This is the space around a person which they regard as psychologically theirs. This can be seen when you are standing in a queue or at a shop counter where you are waiting to be served. If someone from a different culture stands too close, it can seem threatening. In a social situation, if they stand too far away it might seem unfriendly. In all cultures, richer people and those of higher status are normally given more space. For lovers – personal space entirely disappears.

The spectrum of empathy and autism

Perhaps the opposite of empathy is autism in its various forms. I did not come across any cases of diagnosed autism among the study's 210 participants, whether it was undetected or absent. There were, though, some people who had difficulty in making relationships. Most were scientists and all of them male. In the general population, five times as many boys as girls are diagnosed as having some form of autism. Scientists, mathematicians and computer fanatics are said to have autistic characteristics. The autistic person finds social relationships difficult, if not impossible, because he truly cannot get into other people's minds and feelings, he can't see how to behave socially.

In her excellent introduction to the subject, *Autism*, Professor Uta Frith, a world expert, points out how the autistic gifted pupil only learns what he wants to and doesn't fit in socially with the rest of the class. Her gifted example, Edward, read dictionaries for pleasure, and by the age of five had acquired an extraordinary vocabulary. He didn't play with other children, but loved being with adults. Edward developed an intricate system for classifying his collection of birds' eggs, which he'd started at the age of four. He went on to study mathematics brilliantly at a top university. In a crowd, he stands out because of his high-pitched voice and his strange mannerisms.

Dr Hans Asperger, the Austrian paediatrician who gave his name to a milder form of autism, even implied that a dash of autism was part and parcel of being a creative scientist. But Uta Frith feels that we demand too high a level of social skills from children, so that the loner and the mild misfit are diagnosed and treated as 'Aspergers', sometimes without real cause. The condition is almost fashionable. In previous times, no-one would have worried.

It's important not to confuse Asperger syndrome with giftedness. Children with this mild neurological disorder need the right psychological treatment – the gifted need the right education. A very few children may need both. There is no evidence of any regular relationship between them, but any form of neurological disorder can affect the development of gifts. So often, such problems come in clusters, particularly Asperger syndrome (AS), Attention Deficit Hyperactivity Disorder (ADHD), dyslexia and dyspraxia (clumsiness).

Parents in my study, who had labelled their child 'gifted', were far more likely to complain of higher levels of emotional and physical health problems compared with identically gifted children who had not been labelled. They told me of their children's lack of co-ordination, poor sleep patterns, under- or over-reaction, not thinking before acting, aggression, too little or too much concentration, and great difficulties making relationships. Some of it was similar to signs of Asperger syndrome. Parents and teachers were generally in agreement on the symptoms of individual children. Some parents, though, sometimes took emotional problems as the true signs of giftedness, as Rachel Wallace's mother had done (Chapter 1). Yet because of the careful ability-matching of the labelled and the unlabelled gifted, as well as matching on other aspects of their lives, it was clear that the giftedness itself could not be at the root of these complaints.

Suzanne's gift of empathy

One woman in my sample has always had empathy (or 'emotional intelligence') in abundance. At 16, Suzanne Nolan was beautiful with a pale clear complexion, masses of fair hair tumbling round her shoulders, and a gentle but firm demeanour. She radiated happiness and good will, which she distributed generously. She hit the ceiling of the IQ scale, scoring top marks across a wide range of subjects at her comprehensive school.

Her mother, in her strong North of England accent, took a no-nonsense view of it all when Suzanne was a child:

> She's found that she's of a higher intelligence than some girls that she's first been friendly with. She's not letting it affect relationships, even though she quickly realises that certain friendships can't go any further because of this. At school, she was told, 'We all have a gift', so she asked me what hers was. I told her, 'kindness and consideration'. She's very sensible, but she's also too sensitive to other people's feelings. She'll have to learn to control her emotions.

Everyone who came into contact with her – parents, sister, friends and teachers – were aware of Suzanne's wonderful gift of empathy. She knew it herself, but was keen to assure me that she was neither a sloppy push-over, nor a Polly-anna who simpered through her days seeing only good around her. She had her principles and stuck to them. Her personality was made up of a strong mix of warmth and strength, which made her very attractive. At 16, her moral principles were clear:

I'm a believing Christian. Lots of people laugh, and they can laugh if they want. It doesn't change the fact that I'm a Christian, and it doesn't bother me.

I care very much about almost everyone I meet, even people on a bus. It's very strange. I've always thought that was why I could comfort people. Maybe I have a very happy outlook because my life is happy.

I work hard for things I feel strongly about. For example, a lot of my friends smoke, but I won't tolerate that because my Auntie Hilda died of lung cancer and I've seen the suffering she had. I've managed to persuade my choir-master to cut down from 20 to two or three a day. If people start smoking, I just walk away and they know why. I did try it, but I think everybody does that when they're young.

I do get angry at times, but then I try to think why and what I can do about it. Am I just being impatient? Am I being silly? It calms me down. It's always better when you can see things in perspective, because if you're feeling depressed, you tend to take things out of proportion too. When I was younger, all I could see was what was happening to me, and I used to feel sorry for myself – poor little me – but now I can look at how other people feel. If you think of somebody who's worse off than you, you always feel better because your situation's not half as bad. Mostly I like just about everybody. I'm friends with everybody.

Suzanne's empathy influenced her school-work

When I'm learning English, I'm very empathetic, so that when I read a really good novel, I experience it as though

I were there. To understand someone, you've got to see things from their point of view. You have to do that to exist in harmony with people around you. That's why I'm so good at history; I empathise with times past and also with the people from them. And you've got to do it with a restricted amount of information, because you're never going to have as much information as the person who was standing there.

Even as a young teenager, Suzanne took a mature professional approach in using her sensitivity and wish to help others. Her mother told me that as a small girl, Suzanne had even practised empathy on her dolls. But real change had come a few years earlier when she was 12, living in South Africa for a year while her father was working there as an engineer. Suzanne told me what had happened:

I've seen a lot of cruelty to black people, like white policemen beating them up, when there was nothing I could do about it. Abraham, a black man, drove us to school. Once, a white man overtook us and signalled for us to pull over. He came up to the window and was yelling at Abraham in Afrikaans – 'What are you doing, a black person driving these white kids?' I'd learned to speak it, and I said, 'Will you please stop being so nasty; you're making this child cry,' because my little sister was in tears. Then he realised that we weren't being kidnapped or anything. White South Africans tended to take such things out of proportion.

I try to put other people first, but I don't get carried away by it. In fact, I'm a bit like an agony aunt at school, everybody comes to me with their problems and I help them sort them out. If I'm truly patient, I can always get through to other people. I try to understand things from their point of view to be able to comfort them, and often I can identify with people who are in trouble, so much that sometimes it really upsets me. Cruelty, such as vivisection, which moves me to tears sometimes.

Now that I'm 16, I've been very worried about what to do with my life, and I prayed about this for a long time. My whole family went to hear a lady preaching about missionaries, and suddenly I just got a feeling – that's what I should do – I should be a missionary. If I took psychology training, I'd be able to understand how people feel and be able to help people. I knew that was what I had to do. Then a week after, my parents were watching TV, and mum said, 'Oh look, it's South West Africa.' It was about missionaries, and I got the same feeling and I thought, 'Right, this is what God wants me to do. I will.' I don't know when I'll be going out to South West Africa. I'm leaving God to tell me that. I'll probably carry out my psychology studies in England for quite a few years first.

I could imagine Suzanne dressed in washed-out cotton standing on the red dust under an open corrugated iron roof in front of rows of big-eyed little black children. Her teaching, though, would never be neutral because of her moral Christian stance. She would reach out to the Africans, but on her own terms, giving them her beliefs and her way of thinking. Yet real life was closer to hand. As the years passed, even during the mundane demands of her everyday existence, she had continued to use her empathy to help others, but she did not go to South West Africa and remained close to home.

Practical empathy

In her early thirties, I caught up with Suzanne in the ancient north England city of Lancaster. Built on Roman foundations, the great city is made of stone, dominated by its great grey castle. Parts of it are still recognisable in its classic castle silhouette of turrets and keeps that it had gained in the eleventh century. Suzanne was a jolly singleton, living with many cats in her small grey stone terraced house but blazing with colour inside with lots of fun ornaments. She'd made it a warm and welcoming place (though I do have a strong allergy to cats, and left her with eyes and nose streaming).

The first part of her teenage plan was complete. She'd acquired a degree in psychology. But being Suzanne, she'd chosen an applied rather than a theoretical course – as a way of helping others. Slowly, via a variety of jobs, including looking after children and running a bookshop, she took her first steps in the professional world of caring. She became a community support officer for people with learning difficulties. 'I learned a lot about me!' she said.

Unfortunately, while working in a care-home for children with emotional-behavioural problems, her kindness and willingness were taken advantage of – a challenge for the emotionally gifted. Long, long days with little sleep (and little pay) caused her healthy young body to collapse with physical exhaustion. Her angry feelings of failure brought depression. She knew what it was to be in desperate need of help from others:

Why had I allowed myself to be so abused? When I was a child in situations where I had to deal with adult bullies, I found ways of appeasing them which worked. But the old mechanisms of coping weren't appropriate. I got bullied. After the medication and counselling, I decided to specialise in counselling. Now I work in mental health with adults aged 16 to 60 with enduring problems. It's a very practical place. There's a large lounge with craft area, a laundry, a bathroom if they haven't got washing facilities at home, and a computer room where people can access the internet. There's a quiet room . . . peace away from everybody. We do meals through the day, because a lot of people with mental health issues don't look after themselves properly.

Empathy – it's one of my better skills. For the most part, I'd say I'm pretty good at it. But there are challenges. When somebody's having a psychotic episode, it's quite hard to get psychological contact and understand that person.

It's funny, really. What I was doing at school, I'm still doing. The other people at work, if they want to talk about something that's very deep or heartfelt, something that's really traumatising, choose me to come and talk to.

Just like they used to at school. I feel I'm in the right place. My sense of valuing and supporting people is able to work well. I'm not swamped by social services directives.

One of my own favourite ways of getting rid of anger and stress is to play the piano. It's as though it's coming out through my fingers. Or sometimes I go to a high wild moor where the windmills are. It's very sparse, and you can see for miles in many directions. The elements are raw there, the wind and the storms. I feel myself to be with nature. I also have a number of really good close friends who I can talk to. I meet a lot of people who haven't got any friends, and they are very, very lonely. For me and mine it's mutual, we can really rely on each other. I really like my life how it is at the moment. I've been very lucky to have those opportunities to develop those kinds of things. I'm preparing the house now to start a private counselling practice here.

Suzanne matured into a warm and very attractive woman. Many friends were drawn to her and one or two long-term lovers, though she is not yet ready to marry. She has indeed become a sort of missionary. Not in Africa, but in Lancaster. The strict moral views of her teenage-years have faded, but are still grounded on Christian foundations. She's managed to co-ordinate her natural gift for empathy with practical care. She is open to and accepting of those who need her. It is part of her and is her contribution to the world.

Morality and giftedness

Morality is as much a part of Suzanne as her gift of empathy. That is to say, she has principles by which she works, and at the same time a feeling for others with different views. But morality does not exist in a theoretical limbo for her or anyone else. It is entirely practical, the warp and weft of the way people live together, and it shares with giftedness the infuriating difficulty of precise definition. Both always reflect their era, their time and place.

It is so often thought that there is a relationship between morality and giftedness. But opinion is like a coin with its two sides. Either the gifted are seen as having a higher morality – and so are selected for leadership courses (notably in the USA), or else they are seen as morally more fragile – and will turn to delinquency more readily than others. Even boredom in school is claimed to afflict the gifted more than other children and so cause them this immorality. Yet, in my detailed overview for the UK government of world-wide scientific research on the development of the gifted, I could not find the slightest evidence of either greater moral strength or moral weakness among the gifted.

The social context of morality was played out vividly right there in Suzanne's city of Lancaster in 1612. Nine women and two men were imprisoned together in Lancaster Castle awaiting their trials as witches. They were all hideously caught up in the morality of the times and in that place. In those days, there was absolute belief that some people could work magic. But magic was immoral in the eyes of church and state, so the lives of those who practised it had to be destroyed. The accused, kept in wretched conditions in the castle dungeons, were charged with murdering people with witchcraft. Ten of them were found guilty by the legal and moral code of those days, and executed by being hanged together in a row on an extended gallows. One escaped the noose only by dying earlier in the dire conditions of her imprisonment.

Morality is tied to wisdom, a currently fashionable concern in education. Wisdom too demands action, such as giving advice and getting people to take it – all of course for their own good. Wisdom too depends on the society in its time and place. Wise and moral people – such as Nelson Mandela, Mother Teresa, Martin Luther King and Mahatma Gandhi – all fall comfortably into the current Western mould of wise people. Yet other ideas of morality are held just as strongly, such as those promoted by the Ayatollah Khomeini and Osama bin Laden who are/were adored for their wisdom, as indeed were Comrades Lenin and Stalin. Adolf Hitler was (and still is to some) the ultimate voice of morality and wisdom, as is Kim Jong-il of North Korea today. There appears to be no shortage of people ready to lead others in their dogmatic vision of morality, which may be diametrically opposed to other people's versions. And millions of people may follow any one of them with terrible results.

One of the boys in my study, Melvin, had picked up the popular idea that personal morality is associated with an extremely high intelligence. He was undeniably gifted in terms of IQ and superb school achievement. At 14, he was round and beaming with the manner of a bank manager who knows what's best for you. He explained to me with great care:

> I often feel that I have a more mature outlook from most people my age. It sounds a terribly high-minded attitude to take and some people pretend not to understand me, because if they did, then I'd explode all their myths about their petty little values. Sometimes it seems that the only way that everybody agrees is when they all disagree with me.

Melvin's mother, her brow creased with concern, quietly told me what would happen:

> He was always morally two years ahead of any of his peers. Where they were still hitting each other for fun, Melvin had worked out that this was silly. He used to try and reason with them, but they didn't know what he was talking about. So while they were hitting him, he was busily pointing out the reasons why they shouldn't.

It seemed to me, though, that in Melvin's case, it was neither his extraordinary intellect nor his advanced morality which had denied him friends – a sad state so often said to be due to giftedness. Rather, it was his lack of empathy, a genuine acceptance and simple friendliness towards his fellows. Suzanne, with an IQ that hit the top of the scale, had no such problems. She was not arrogant, her heart was genuine and friends were drawn to her. This study has shown that giftedness of itself, neither attracts friends nor keeps them away.

Morals also change over time. For example, until the end of the nineteenth century, the idea of educating girls just like boys was immoral in the eyes of the religious authorities and still is in some countries. Susan Quinn in her book *Marie Curie: A Life*, describes how this amazing woman met gender discrimination many times in her life, even when her achievements were the best in the world. When Marie won the French science prize, she was bypassed by the judges, who sent the confirming letter to her husband, Pierre. 'Congratulations', they wrote, 'on your wife's success.' They must have assumed he would tell her! Later, the first of her two Nobel Prizes hung in the balance for the same reason; it seemed more appropriate to give it only to her husband. Fortunately, her colleagues banded together to plead her case, and the Swedes eventually awarded it to her, the woman who had earned it.

The world was fascinated with this female first, though reporters still cast her in a feminine supporting role. The *New York Herald* (among many similar put-downs from the world's press) reported that Madame Curie 'is a devoted fellow labourer in her husband's researches and has associated her name with his discoveries.' A French journalist who camped outside her home to watch the Curie's elder daughter, Irene, being served her supper, described Marie's poor morality. She had, he said, selfishly neglected her maternal role and her daughter so that she could win the Nobel Prize.

Morality and the IQ score

A major clue to the relationship between morality and intelligence is to use males and females as experimental control groups. Looking at moral behaviour over the millennia, the evidence is unquestionable. Women rarely start wars, torture people or behave in other highly destructive ways; they are traditionally carers. Indeed, if actual moral behaviour, rather than high IQ, was the entry ticket to leadership courses for the gifted, they would be filled almost entirely by girls – which they are not. Only if it were possible to demonstrate wide intellectual differences between the genders – were the law-abiding girls seen to be significantly more intelligent – could we conclude that morality is associated with intellectual gifts. It is more likely, though, that morality is independent of high-level achievement and thus probably of intelligence too.

In the survey of research by Herrnstein and Murray in their book *The Bell Curve*, the authors were in no doubt as to the relationship between intelligence and virtue, reiterating Francis Galton's 1869 claim that: 'high intelligence also provides some protection against lapsing into criminality.' Arthur Jensen, notably in his famous 1969 paper in the *Harvard Educational Review*, associated crime with low IQ, noting that in the published statistics, on average American blacks have lower IQs than American whites, and that is why, he concluded, they were more inclined to crime. However, he later modified this, writing, 'since as far as we know, the full range of human talents is represented in all major races of man and in all socioeconomic levels, it is unjust to allow the mere fact of an individual's racial or social background to affect the treatment accorded to him.'

Ideas of morality, being part of their time and place, emerge in tests of morality – as well as sneakily in IQ tests. Correct answers to the morality questions gain the testee IQ points. The important thing is to reply in line with current belief. Actual behaviour, though, is not part of the test and could be quite different. Here are a couple of examples from an IQ test written in the first quarter of twentieth-century America, though constantly modified:

From the Stanford-Binet Intelligence Test
'What's the thing to do if another boy/girl hits you without meaning to do it?' The correct response, for which the highest score is given, must involve the Christian ideal of forgiveness. There is no eye-for-an-eye or tooth-for-a-tooth morality here, or the honour-vengeance practised in many parts of the world.

'What would you do when another child takes your toy?' Instead of grabbing it back or fighting over it, a pretty normal reaction in small children, the mark of intelligence is measured by how 'cool' they are. For a high grade, they should rein in any anger, inhibit any reflex to lash out, and say politely that he or she would tell the teacher. How prissy. What a poor lesson for real life. What higher authority would you run to in the cut-throat market place when someone snitches the deal from under your nose?

Many top-ranking Nazis were extremely intelligent and highly cultured, notably Joseph Goebbels, Hitler's propaganda minister. Hermann Goering was an outstanding art collector who simply stole what he wanted. Many of them could easily have risen to the dizzy heights of Mensa, though the Führer himself might not have made it. The IQs of other cruel despots are not known, but it can be guessed that if they were running a country and countering clever plots to topple them, they were probably highly intelligent. Whatever you may feel about their morality, Fidel Castro is extremely intelligent, as is/was Osama bin Laden. Suicide bombers are no less intelligent than those who band together to talk about ways of making peace, and both sides of the coin believe wholeheartedly in the morality of what they are doing.

Psychologists and educators sometimes ask ourselves why we are trying to help gifted and talented children, and in what way we are encouraging them. We may believe that we are contributing to the satisfaction of the individuals and the improvement of the world, but that is also what the ideologists of Fascism and Communism thought. And so did workers in the Eugenics movement in America and Europe, when they weeded out future generations of children by sterilising little girls – never boys – who they thought were likely to be intellectually of poor quality and so a drain on society.

The gifted, I suggest, have no greater claims to morality than anyone else, but what they do have is the capacity to intellectually understand moral conundrums in life and to perceive arguments for what they are, set in their social contexts. Suzanne practises a very high degree of Western morality, caring for others without obliging them to believe as she does. Whether other gifted people choose to use their intellectual gifts to understand and see different points of view is another matter. Some do and some don't.

7

The gift of integrity

It's usually a question of being determined and focused and getting it done.

Gary Booth

As a man who made every one of his gifts work for him, Gary Booth appeared to glide smoothly through the multiple social, physical and emotional barriers that fate threw in his path. Any one of them could have tripped him up. His rise in the world of high finance was extraordinary. Not that he did it without effort; he worked extremely hard and for long hours when this was called for. Somehow, he had resolutely harnessed and focused his youthful energy on a long-term outcome which would be beneficial to himself and those he loved. Not that he had any specific goal – as the achievement manuals always recommend – nor had he any kindly mentor or counsellor who would gently pull him aside for a heart to heart. There was just the fuzzy idea in his head that things somewhere else were better than what he was experiencing as a boy, and whatever it was, he wanted to be part of it.

Time and time again, Gary was presented with opportunities for social-class advancement. He recognised these for their potential, but found them distasteful and never took them up. He was a fine example of all that Rudyard Kipling, the poet, had urged in his wonderful poem, *If*, most notably the advice to 'meet with Triumph and Disaster/ And treat those two imposters just the same'. Gary consciously kept his balance. Whatever he did was weighed and measured for its intrinsic value. Snobbery and syco-phancy had no place in his personal life. He is what he is: take him or leave him. He is a Northern man, in the way that Mrs Elizabeth Gaskell, the campaigning nineteenth-century writer, described in her book *Mary Barton: A Tale of Manchester Life*, direct, honest and self-motivated. His outstanding, but unmeasured and unrecognised, extra gift which he had in spades was integrity.

When Gary was about 14, I set off to find him at his home in Widnes, a small industrial town about an hour's drive south from the port of Liverpool along the River Mersey. I manoeuvred my shiny red MG sports car through miles of drab, low-quality housing. Of about 20 of the local shops, only one was open, though heavily defended with metal grilles. The boards covering the windows of the others were daubed with graffiti. Somberly dressed people slouched by. The area was surrounded by chemical indus-tries. Fat chimneys with twinkling lights on their rims and black spiky towers were silhouetted against the pink even-ing sky, topped by the everlasting flames of burning fumes. Even as the cold salt sea air came over the land, it picked up pollution, a cloud so heavy that the whole area smelled of chemicals. It seemed to me to be a very unhealthy place.

Gary lived there with his widowed mother and younger brother, Alec, in a sweet and neat house where she still lives. His mother glowed with love for her two sons. Gary was tall, well-built and handsome. He hit the ceiling of the IQ scale and his school results were always first-class. This was in spite of being virtually blind in one eye. He was at the local all-comers school, in a mixed-ability class of his own age. It was not a comprehensive school which might have given him support into further education, but an attenuated version which only took pupils to the age of 16. The youngsters could go on to another educational insti-tution from there, but most of them simply stopped being educated formally at the end of school.

Although nothing special was ever offered to this highly gifted boy, his teachers had genuine concern for him, as indeed they did for all their charges. They gave him the positive feedback and encouragement he needed, something

youngsters at much more expensive schools may not have
known. One perceptive teacher introduced him to the area
that was to become his life, economics. Gary told me:

> I was 15. Never heard of economics. And I said, 'What's
> that, Bill?' He sat me down and said, 'This is economics,
> and I think you'll be really good at it.' That's the only thing
> he ever said. We had that one conversation. He was a good
> teacher, a person I remember fondly. My form teacher, she
> never actually taught me for anything, but she had a
> similar mind-set. She was also a good teacher who would
> genuinely be concerned about development of her pupils. I
> bumped into her when I was working in a pub, three years
> later. She immediately knew who I was and what I'd been
> doing. Her pupils were important to her. Nobody actually
> took me fully under their wing, but there were a number
> of teachers who were good influences at important stages.
> And I had a genuine desire to learn.

Both Gary's parents had left school at 14. His situation
highlighted some of the problems of gifted working-class
youth fighting for a place in the professional world. But for
him, somehow, it all worked to his advantage. He would
probably have found it difficult to cope with the middle-
class ethos of a selective grammar school, or could have
been crushed by the snobbery in some private schools. At
his school, he could find his own way with gentle teachers
and mates who spoke with his accent, and with strong
emotional support from home.

To me, Gary's most obvious obstacle to entry to the
professions was that he was not as fluent in his speech as
a middle-class child would be, and what he did say was in a
thick nasal Widnes accent. He had little practice of conversation in smooth well-rounded sentences to beguile the
ear of a prospective tutor or employer. I, who lived less than
two hours' drive away, found him a little difficult to
understand. He was neither accustomed to talking to the
full extent of his vocabulary nor was he reading seriously.
I could see no books in his home, and the only newspaper I spotted was a well-thumbed tabloid. But as a young

teenager, I could see his fine spirit, and was already
fighting hard to overcome his disadvantages.

The one paradoxical advantage he had in not being
from an ardently educational family, was that he was
blissfully free of the hang-ups of being labelled 'gifted'.
Nobody had made him feel exceptional. As well as the top
school grades, he was a keen and powerful rugby player,
becoming captain of the school team. He was at one with
his world. When someone is in such harmony, good things
come from it. Gary had a fine brain, the capacity for hard
work and, importantly, the unquestioning devotion of his
mother. As a gifted pupil, he was a rarity in his school,
telling me when he was 14:

> I give other people in the class help, and they prefer
> getting it off me, instead of them running to a teacher. I
> get on alright with me mates, and just leave the ones I
> don't like. I don't care what they think, but I don't think
> I'm any different from them. If my work's good, I feel
> proud, and if it's bad, it's me own fault. I can't blame it on
> anyone else. They don't tell me I'm a bright lad, but I
> know that if I've got an exam question to answer, if the
> teachers give me just a hint, I'd be able to give the answer
> straight off.
>
> You don't feel confident if you come from a poor
> background, like going for a high-up job when there's
> someone else there from a higher family. You'd always
> feel he'd got the upper hand. That's what I'm working so
> hard at school for – to show 'em. I've joined the rugby
> team, and I play of an evening three times a week.

Gary's father had been a highly intelligent man, well
qualified in the Navy as a nuclear submarine engineer. He
died of a heart attack while supervising shipbuilding at
Barrow in Furness. The Navy widows' pension was not
generous and the family income plunged. Gary was 13.

His only route to improvement was Widnes Sixth Form
College. To move up from there, he would have to wrench
himself away from all that he loved. 'I was never going to
work there in the north. I wanted to go down to London

to show that I could. Who knows where I'd end up?' Facing his first big social temptation, his deep sense of integrity kicked in:

> The tutors at Widnes College wanted me to apply for Oxford and Cambridge and I chose not to. The journey down was too far from home. I chose Leeds University as a compromise, because I could move away from home but not be too far away from mum. I needed to be able to get home within a couple of hours. That was important to me. And there was my brother, Alec. For the three years I was going to be at university, he was going to go from 14 through 17, so I felt I needed to be nearby. Dad had never been around much, and when he passed away, well, he was just away and not coming back. I'd been very aware that I was the man in the family from a young age.
>
> Mum made great sacrifices for us. We never wanted for anything: sports kits and things like that. She took cleaning jobs and went out to work in the evenings just to make sure we had enough money. You know, she learned to drive so she could take us to rugby training. She wouldn't take anything for herself. Once we'd left school, she became a day-care assistant at a primary school to be able to pay her way and still make sure that we didn't do without. She is still there as a 'dinner-lady', 26 years later at the age of 68. Alec still needed rugby boots, rugby kit and all this sort of stuff. I have great admiration for what mum has done.
>
> She'd never have given me any ideas above my status; she'd have got rid of them very quickly. The people I grew up with wouldn't have tolerated it either, especially the guys I used to play rugby league with. She still thinks that Alec does the real job and I ponce around pushing paper – which is not unreasonable. I owe her a lot.

The social divide

Not everyone among the gifted in my study had Gary's honesty and good sense. Those from state schools who made it to the dreaming spires of Oxbridge were often deeply shocked to find that their faces – and accents – did not fit. Both Oxford and Cambridge Universities still take about half their undergraduates from the tiny 7 per cent of private schools, and only about 10 per cent of undergraduates there could be called working-class, so the social dominance is of the privately educated. I found in my study, that the cultural gap was still strong, though easier for boys studying science, and worst for girls studying the arts.

These powerful social effects were to devastate the life of Alison Cranfield. She was an outstandingly brilliant girl whose school, without much consideration as to whether it was the right place for her, had pushed her to Oxbridge for the pride of her school. This meant a big leap across the social–cultural divide and it proved too wide for her. She had slipped, fallen badly and suffered deep long-term emotional damage. Even to think of it, many years after the debacle, brought tears to her eyes.

Alison was a tall, slender, sensitive and highly gifted girl from Liverpool. She had a modest manner, hands clasped in front of her with slightly stooped shoulders. Rather a delicate bird-like figure. She lived not far from Gary Booth and had much the same River Mersey twang that is familiar to the world through the Beatles. Even at ten years old, she struck me as shy and just a little too polite. She lived with her single mother on social benefit in a modest home.

She won a place at a high-level academic girls' grammar school where she had superb teaching. She was an assiduous worker and gave her teachers good reason for their pride in her examination results. But that's where their help and understanding stopped. They aimed her for Oxford University, but without enough personal preparation to see her through the great changes of pace and style she would face. When she got there, the university had failed to give her any help whatsoever. She'd never had an intellectual model to follow nor had a mentor to give her courage. Not one person in her family had ever gone past the minimum school-leaving age. She only had her belief in God. Her face clouded as she told me sadly what had happened to her in her first year at Oxford:

I felt looked down on because of where I came from. They would tease me and imitate my accent, then laugh loudly and say they couldn't understand me. They seemed to enjoy upsetting me. But that wasn't the whole reason I left. I failed my first-year exams because the course wasn't right for me. No-one at school had ever discussed how it might be; it was just, 'OK, off you go.' My background knowledge wasn't sufficient, because I only knew what I'd been taught in school, those few books I'd read for my exams. I had so much catching up to do. I was taking French, though I've never been to France, yet other students had second homes over there.

When I left Oxford, I felt I'd let down my school and the neighbours and the church. The college agreed that it was best for me to leave. It was galling when they suggested I should have done a different course or gone to a different university. Why didn't they tell me before?

After I got back, for the first six weeks, I'd go to sleep at night and pray for the bomb to drop. I didn't have the courage to commit suicide; I wanted someone to do it for me. I stayed in the house all the time because the neighbours would ask me about Oxford. But I was just ending up self-pitying, so I started going to places where people hadn't known me before. I took up new interests, started going to a drama group once a week and made new friends there. And I went to a different church.

I felt very much that what I'd done was wrong – to step out of my caste – to think that I could be like one of them. I hated the students, higher education, and everything that I associated with Oxford. If I have my own children, I wouldn't encourage them to go on to higher education. I'd rather they were on the loose for a few years and sorted things out before committing themselves to something like that.

Alison's road continued to be rocky. Still living with her mother, she took a job as a clerk, eventually resigned from it and enrolled for a degree in education at a small local college. But there she met another type of teaching. This gifted girl found the lectures pitched at too low a level for her: 'the slow pace drove me berserk.' At times she was so boiling with frustration she fled the lecture theatre for the cloakroom to splash cold water on her face. She doubtless offended her lecturers by telling them 'that the concepts they were trying to teach were so simple to grasp that the lesson could be completed in a fraction of the time.' Also, as she was two years older and seriously brighter and better educated than most of the other students she felt removed from them and did not socialise much. The simmering pot of frustration of being highly gifted in a world that was too slow finally boiled over, and she left in her second year – the second academic course she had quit.

Personality matters

Alison wasn't alone in how her school had treated her. Many of the gifted found their high-pressure schools were very limited in their communication with the outside world. They'd call them 'an ivory tower' or 'a prison camp' or 'a train which ran on rails and couldn't change direction'. Success in school, as many discovered, did not necessarily predict success outside it. A positive personality and strong motivation are essential; something she was short of, but which Gary had in plenty.

The figures from my study speak for themselves. Just under half the gifted youngsters said they did not receive the career help from school they needed. About a third said they received no personal, one-to-one career counselling whatsoever. Such poor vocational guidance (not unique to Britain) is very short-sighted in terms of national needs – and a scandalous waste of human resources from any point of view.

Alison's sad stumbling tale was a far cry from Gary's determined and well-judged thrust to higher education. His pro-active personality alerted him to make of life what he could, while hers was hesitant and insecure. He even called himself a 'self-starter', which stood him in good stead at Leeds University. He understood his situation very well, and how wise he was:

Had I gone at 18 down to Oxford or Cambridge, it may have been one jump too far, even though my Leeds degree could never be in the same bracket. I had an absolute ball at Leeds; it was fabulous.

Economics was one of the big, popular subjects, so the lecture rooms were packed. If you don't turn up, if you're hung-over or you can't be bothered, nobody'd come chasing for you. That was fine for me. But for people that came through a more directed school system, it was horrific. They'd been trained to pass exams, and do their homework at special times. Suddenly without parameters it was easy for them to go off the rails and they couldn't function. The freedom was dangerous. And it's the wrong time to begin. [This is exactly what had happened to Jocelyn Lavin in Chapter 8, going from her supportive school to big London University.]

I had a system of working hard the last term of each of the three years. In the other two terms, I had a great social life and played a lot of rugby. I graduated top of the year in Leeds and won the Economics Prize – there was a pretty big distance between me and the next person. After a scholarship to Vanderbilt University, Nashville, USA, I attended the business school there for a year, and travelled around. Then I worked for a major firm of accountants in the City of London for nearly four years. It was the best, very much blue chip, blue blood, good clients, good people. Then I joined a major investment bank. Just four years there and I was head-hunted for an American bank.

Mergers and acquisitions

The City, also known as the Square Mile, is the business centre of London and a global finance hub. It has its own flag, coat of arms, police force and corporation. Founded by the Romans in 50 AD, it is the original city from which the great modern metropolis has grown. The City of London was where the pantomime hero Dick Whittington and his cat returned to when they heard the bells of Bow Church ringing out to tell him he would become Lord Mayor, which indeed he became in 1397. St Paul's cathedral is there, as well as a contemporary forest of glassy skyscrapers. People scurry between them, largely concerned with matters of money. The City is home to the London Stock Exchange, the insurers Lloyd's of London and the Bank of England, not to mention the Tower of London on the bank of the muddy Thames. No church bells rang to draw young Gary Booth to the city. But he stepped into that ancient powerful world of money with barely a backward glance.

By the time he was 34, Gary had established himself. Early every morning he mounted his scooter and negotiated it swiftly into the City. A quick trip to the gym for a work-out, shower, back at the office to read his waiting *Financial Times*, all by eight o'clock. At home he would leave his beautiful wife, recently head of European research at a big accountancy firm, and two children. They lived in two old houses joined together, overlooking green space in an elegant area of London. In front there were two 4×4 vehicles. The family visit their other house in Spain from time to time, sometimes joined by his mother. While we talked in 2001 his two greyhounds lounged beside us. Gary looked much as he did as a boy. He has a turn of the head, rather like Gordon Brown, the Prime Minister, who also has one virtually blind eye. I asked Gary whether it had been a handicap to him. He replied in his casual can-do just-get-on-with-it way that it had not:

I was born with this bad eye. I don't know any different. When I played rugby and people came from that side, they cracked me because I couldn't see it coming. But I've got peripheral vision. It's never stopped me doing anything like being able to ride a bike or drive a car. I don't see it as an issue. I'm careful about my other eye, but provided I'm sensible, I don't have trouble. I never read in a bad light or strain it. There's a slight whiteness over the middle of the eye, where the skin has grown over the lens. I could have a cosmetic contact lens if I wanted to, to make sure it's black. Some people ask about it, some don't.

Yet Gary's transition from Widnes, via Leeds and Vanderbilt Universities to the City had not been entirely smooth. He was not one to bend his knee to anyone else's expectations of him, nor attempt to be like anyone other than himself. Again and again he'd been faced with a way of life he'd not encountered before and had to draw on his inner self – his integrity – to get to where he wanted to be:

Sometimes it was tough. I got slapped pretty hard by a couple of blue-blood banks early on. One individual was a typical product of the snobby private education system, trying to demonstrate his superiority. He asked me, 'What does XYZ mean in Latin?' And this was supposed to be an interview for a job in a bank! I wasn't going to get it in a million years. It wasn't an interview; it was basically half an hour of attempted humiliation. I wasn't prepared to give him that satisfaction. In fact, it gave *me* great satisfaction to get up and walk out.

I called my head-hunter and said, 'Never do that to me again. If I reach a glass ceiling, I reach a glass ceiling.' But it hasn't happened. Certainly, with the influence of American culture those pathetic attitudes are less and less; it's much more meritocratic.

I'd got through every hoop so far and suddenly, there were these institutions that weren't going to let me jump into them. For every job, there were 40, 50 applicants at that level. It was my first real rejection, where people said, 'No, we're not going to give you a job in our organisation,' which I hadn't come across before. My drive started to kick in.

I suppose that walking out didn't help! So I asked around, listened and learned. I needed to seem keener, less easy-going, to sell myself more. But I wasn't going to pretend to be more like them. No. Absolutely not. The institution where the guy gave me a hard time, they are drone-like. They take in a certain type of person. I wouldn't have fitted. They want the fluffy-haired, rosy-cheeked English, the product of a certain way of life, you know, shotgun over one arm, fishing rod over the other. But it's getting tougher and tougher for them. The corporate clients have changed. There's even been something of a reversal: now it's people like me who are starting to hire them, and actually we want something different and better.

Most of the people coming out of Eton and Harrow into investment and merchant banking are pretty decent. By and large, I'm brighter than them, but I'm not a threat. I'm not trying to take social status off them, so I was an easy guy to get on with. We all go to the pub, and there will be the guys who order Bollinger and I'm the one that orders the pint of bitter. And they know it and they laugh. Or I'm the guy that'll look at the rugby league results in the back of the sports paper.

The Oxbridge route has a network I can't tap into. Their peers from their universities get to prominent roles in whatever they've done, be it the law, the corporate world, accountancy, banking, the medical profession. We're not bred out of Leeds for that.

We'd talked for a couple of hours before Gary managed to tell me how really ambitious he was. He explained how it had all begun so long ago at school. It was just a spark that had lit his fire, unplanned but specific. It burst like the flames from the fumes leaving the chimneys of Widnes, his home town. I don't suppose his teachers ever knew what they had done for him. I hope they will read this book and find out:

I'm pretty driven. Yeah, I'm driven. I want to be working with bright people; I want to be working for the best organisations. I want to be successful. I've always wanted to be the best I can. I wouldn't say I felt it from being very small. I'd say it sort of crept up on me. It became more and more important the closer I got to actually doing my O-levels, when I realised that this was a real opportunity. The fact that I got maths a year early I think was the catalyst. I was accelerated just for that one subject. About 20 of us took it early. I knew then that I could actually get out and do well.

My life is a sacrifice of long hours. My alarm goes off at a quarter to six, and I'll be back at about 9.00pm. When I was a junior, if I left work before midnight, that was an early night. I've done so many 24-hour days. The longest I did was a Monday afternoon to Friday morning; I didn't leave the building. You don't really sleep until you go. I may have a cat nap, and send my secretary out to buy me a shirt. You always work through the night if you're doing a deal. The announcements go out first thing the next morning. Imagine the scenario – everything cranking up getting ready to make an announcement seven o'clock on Monday morning that you're going to make a bid. So you work all through the weekend and Sunday night. Then you've got analyst briefings, press briefings, whatever you need to do.

The night before the deal, you're still going to be in all night, because that's what your client's paying you for. And you've got your team. You may be able to leave at three in the morning and ask the team to put the document to bed, or put the announcement to bed. Then they'll be doing the last-minute admin, so you can get a couple of hours sleep, and come in for seven. With just a little sleep, I'm ready to field questions. That's what a merger and acquisitions banker does. That's our job. I'm quite happy with who I am and what I'm doing.

You'd be amazed how you can train yourself to keep going. My wife knows when I'm in deal mode. My adrenalin's going, I'm very alert, my mind is exercised. I sleep badly when a deal is on, but I feel as if I'm sleeping pretty soundly. My mind is still going, so when I wake up, I know what I'm going to be doing that day. I feel very alert. When the deal finishes and the rush finishes, that's when it's tough. After one major deal, everybody went for drinks and I was asleep in the pub at five in the afternoon. They put a little sign round me, 'Do not disturb.'

My wife's a saint, she puts up with it. But I don't bring work home. I put the telephone down when I leave the office because I can't change anything. I don't have a desire to tell her about my day, and I don't have to offload on her about the problems, I just leave them. For many years, I've not taken all my holiday time, so it's stored up. We had three weeks for our honeymoon, though, which was nice.

I try to keep things in perspective. If people are getting cross in the office or tempers are getting frayed and everybody's shouting and screaming – whatever else they do, you know, in the city investment banks . . . I just say to myself, I'm standing in a rugby pitch at 11 o'clock in the morning in Yorkshire or somewhere in the freezing cold. That keeps me out of it.

In 2009, Gary left the City to become a partner in his own firm in the heart of the West End of London. He weathered the 1990s financial crisis, he said, 'with his crash helmet on'. And the family has moved to an expensive semi-rural home in the Home Counties, south of the city. He thinks of his once home territory, but somehow it stays where it is, a long way away physically and culturally:

I'd like to go back up north, to give something back. I'd like my children to be brought up with northern values. But I'm not prepared to take a gamble with their education. They'll go to private schools, but not boarding schools.

My job's to run the office, run the team who deal with customers. It's their money. Very high risk. Clients do trust me. There's something in me that they invariably warm to. They see me as an advisor. I know I can have a rapport with them. But I have to get the business first – not if.

Siblings

On the face of it, Gary Booth was a one-off, a unique member of his family of decent, hard-working English folk. He presents a challenge to any psychologist. Why did Gary soar when no-one else in his family had changed their expected life-paths? His younger brother, with every opportunity that Gary had, works in a local warehouse. Gary told me:

He moves things, forklift trucks, all this sort of stuff. Never left. Just lives across the bridge from mum, married his first girlfriend, then two boys and two girls. He'd like to have more money, but. . . . We haven't got a great deal in common, apart from mum and rugby. We share how we help mum: I do the paperwork and he does the DIY. We'll talk about rugby and things like that, as brothers will. He doesn't know what I do, though I know what he does. I think he's happy.

When we were little I thought he had a higher IQ than me. My mum looks at the two of us, and says he was always the one that was more stubborn, strong-minded, doing his own thing. I don't know whether it was the timing of dad's death, but after that he became the one that was more easily led and I became the more strong-minded. That meant he was just bumming around in class because it wasn't cool to work. He never took advantage of my example. To him, rugby was his life, he'd set his stall on turning professional and he got ever so close. Fundamentally, he was too nice a guy to succeed. It never happened. He doesn't play now.

There are real differences between siblings in a family. Parents not only behave differently with each one, but the children themselves interpret differently the way they are treated. A child's position in the family can have a considerable effect on development, and Gary was in the best position, a first-born.

First-borns and only children strive harder to please their parents and teachers because they identify more strongly with them. In general, they achieve more highly than their brothers and sisters throughout life, including having higher IQ scores. Even their leisure-time activities often have an educational aspect. First-born and only children are more likely to be more concerned with the effect they have on adults and are more responsible, the second-born is easier going and has more friends, the third-born is often more difficult to live with, and the fourth-born is often babied and so learns to be more dependent.

The concept of hereditability is often misunderstood. It does not apply to an individual, but is a statistical likelihood of a thing happening over large numbers of people. Its calculation is an estimate for a particular group at a particular time. One cannot say that for a new-born baby, 80 per cent of its future characteristics are absolutely fixed, with only 20 per cent to be adjusted by the environment. The proportions could be different for each one.

It was clear from my research that there was a spectrum – the more intelligent the child, the better able they were to make use of what was available to them. Gary was able to get a lot more from his school experiences than the less intelligent pupils and his younger brother. His fine brain was able to take in and use information more efficiently than theirs. This means that the environment is relatively more influential for potentially gifted people – in other words, the effects of the environment are stronger for the gifted.

A great mind, though, does not always make for a great bank balance. The proportion of high-IQ people in the population can easily be calculated, and only some of them could be called financially successful, while on the other hand, many people with lower IQs are extremely successful. Personality and motivation make a big difference. Overall, incomes tend to be higher for the gifted and well-educated, but that is not true for serious wealth. I don't remember ever seeing a Rolls-Royce in a university car park.

Dr Jay Zagorsky and his team at Ohio State University have interviewed 7,403 Americans time after time since 1979, and found that each extra IQ point was worth between $202 and $616 a year. But having a high IQ, they found, offered no protection against falling into heavy debt or other kinds of financial distress. In fact, if a child is aiming to be a self-made millionaire, then a highly developed IQ, which could lead to much time being spent at a university, where thought-processes are too often trained to criticise rather than construct, can be a positive handicap. Gary, though, managed to avoid that handicap.

Why Gary made it

The clues to why Gary's life rocketed way beyond his family's are all there in what he did and what he told me across the decades. Emotionally, he was upheld by the immense security and acceptance given without strings by his mother. She would love and accept him whether he spent his life on social welfare, or as in fact becoming more successful than she could ever have imagined. Sigmund Freud described Gary's situation perfectly, 'If a man is the apple of his mother's eye, there is nothing he cannot do.' He was also physically strong, in spite of his poor sight in one eye; and his down-to-earth northern personality served him perfectly.

When his father died suddenly – a man even bearing the same name – this was doubtless a vital shock stimulus. Even though he saw little of his dad, young Gary looked up to him and managed to cope well at the sensitive age of 13 with his death. Yet it shook him into early manhood and a feeling of responsibility for his family, so much so that he would not allow himself to be more than two hours' journey away from home in case he was needed. No Oxbridge privileges could tempt him away. He cared for his mother and his younger brother to the best of his youthful ability. At all times, he would do his utmost in his dad's place, and one day, he vowed, he would go to London to take up the opportunities his father never had.

Essentially, it was his extremely high IQ which enabled Gary to live his dramatic life. In spite of his personal valour and integrity, he could not have taken that extraordinary advantage of the same opportunities which others around him also had. Motivation is not enough to do what he did.

Gary has been on an upward spiral, probably most of his life. When he was challenged at school or on the rugby pitch, he always did his best and his best was usually successful. The positive feedback from success over challenges and the praise from the important people in his life spurred him to even more confidence, more effort – and more success. At no time did he attempt to climb beyond what he felt able to succeed at, notably by not applying to

Oxbridge. That way he avoided becoming frustrated with feelings of incompetence. He also avoided lower-level progress through only coping. Gary did not merely get by; he took charge of his life.

For Gary, the man of integrity, his drive has always been tempered by consideration of the consequences and of others. He has neither stepped over the line of knowing who he is, nor what he is morally prepared to do to promote his career, however difficult his position. Gary's success has been far beyond what would have satisfied most other people from where he started. He has quite a lot in common with Dick Whittington, another man of integrity. And in fact, his road from Widnes to the City was also paved with gold.

8

Musical chairs

I can safely say it has all been a success story.
Anna Markland

That was my peak, and it's all been downhill since then.
Jocelyn Lavin

One fine autumn day in 1974, two wide-eyed, excited little girls set foot for the first time on the threshold of Chetham's School of Music in Manchester. Eleven years old and flushed with their scholarships, both had been discovered and promoted by their perceptive teachers. There was no question about their intellectual gifts or their musical talents: they had passed their auditions with flying colours. The path they had set their little feet on was to be a life of hard work towards the goal of musical fame.

A friendly teacher led them around the school, once a medieval college for priests for the local church. They walked through the pillared grey stone cloister around a grass-filled quadrangle on one side, faced with a windowed wall on the other. On they went through the winding, arched-roof corridors of what is now the city cathedral. Much of the building remains largely untouched since it was built on the windy Lancashire plain in the tiny hamlet of Manchester. It has remained an island of dedicated spiritual endeavour, though now surrounded by commerce and swirling traffic in the heart of the vibrant cosmopolitan city.

In 1421, the first novice priests must have shivered in the same chill inside that bleak grey stone building, and huddled deeper into their brown woollen robes. The bright boys selected for training for the priesthood were never allowed into the Warming House, the only heated room in the collegiate monastery. Two hundred years later, it served as the centre of operations for the Parliamentarians against the Royalists in the English civil war. In 1653, Humphrey Chetham, a successful businessman, took it over to set up his orphanage school for 'forty poor boys'. The fine library, he wrote in his will, was to be 'open to schollars and others well affected . . . as a publick Librarie' and it has been so ever since. Importantly, he left the boys a handsome legacy for their education. Miraculously, almost everything has survived heavy German bombing and the deterioration of centuries. Some of its fifteenth-century furnishings are still there. The library at Chetham's School is the oldest public library in the English-speaking world.

Another two hundred years passed before a couple of its regular readers rocked the axis of the world. In the early 1840s, when Manchester, as the crucible of the world's first industrial revolution, dominated international trade, Karl Marx and Friedrich Engels found Chetham's library a pleasant, quiet place to plan. Putting their earnest bearded heads together across a polished table in their regular quiet bay under a big gothic window, they compiled the Ten Steps to Communism and began to put pen to paper on the Communist Manifesto.

Wind forward yet another hundred or so years to 1969, when the school took on its music specialty – and admitted girls. Now it is the biggest music school in Britain, with a population of 290 highly selected talented students aged between eight and 18. Ninety per cent are funded by the government, with generous scholarships for foreign students. The school received a multi-million pound grant in 2007 to expand its territory and provision. Its standing is world-class. Chetham's School for the 'well affected' is no ordinary place of education.

The girls dutifully hung their coats on the pegs in the cloakroom and followed the teacher on to their big stone classroom, its gothic windows looking out onto the city. They glanced around. Anna flashed her brilliant smile at Jocelyn, and Jocelyn beamed. Instant pals. The 'girls' and I caught up on a BBC radio programme in September 2008. They are still admiring each other more than 35 years later:

> Jocelyn: When I heard Anna rattling off the *Fantasie Impromptu* by Chopin at the age of 11, I knew I could never do that. Then she hurt her right hand; couldn't use it at all for a year. But rather than give up, she learned every single thing in the piano repertoire for the left hand. I didn't realise there were so many things for the left hand. She put in so much effort. I'm sure I would have given up.
>
> Anna: Jocelyn was amazing at maths, just extraordinary. She was top in everything. In my second year, I had a rough ride from several of the girls. But Jocelyn was a rock to me. She was incredibly supportive and really generous with her friendship and her time. And I will always remember that and treasure it.

Both girls left Chetham's School in a blaze of glory. Anna had reaped armfuls of rewards. She rose to be head girl of the school, winner of the most prestigious all-instrument, national competition in Britain, the *BBC Young Musician of the Year*, in front of millions of television viewers, soon followed by a scholarship to Oxford University and a dizzily successful and satisfying professional and personal life. Jocelyn had the most magnificent school-leaving results the school had ever known, or was expecting to ever have again. But her professional and personal life to come turned out to be one of distress and stumbling personal progress; a very different story from Anna's.

Both Anna and Jocelyn have always been open and willing to be talk to me. Jocelyn has a Lancashire accent, though Anna has lost her Liverpool lilt completely, first as a boarder at Chetham's and later at Oxford University.

Had I stopped my investigation when the girls left school, what a different story I would have offered to research in the development of gifts and talents. I could have said with confidence that because these two little girls had been given the right opportunities and moral support, their talents had flowered brilliantly. The evidence was clear in their superb accomplishments. But as they walked through the medieval arch of the school into the city, it was the moment of change. And as the decades rolled on, both girls' lives were to go on changing dramatically.

The girls' childhoods

Anna had never lived in luxury. Her scholarship to Chetham's was a giant step-up for a girl from the toughest part of the port of Liverpool – not the normal nursery of a future concert pianist. All four of her Irish grandparents had crossed the cold grey waters of the Irish Sea to seek a better life in England. Her father described his family to me as 'factory hands', but – and this is where detailed questioning pays – her great-grandparents on her mother's side had both been concert performers, her grandmother having 'got her music degree, her cap and gown, at 14 from Trinity College Dublin'. She'd taught music and played the organ at her church. Her ancestor's talent, though, seemed to have entirely skipped the generation of Anna's parents. Then there was that uncle who drove a motor-bike in a fairground Wall-of-Death, though sometimes he ran a fairground stall, and at others bent his back digging ditches. Whatever genes have come through to Anna, they have cast her talent in fire.

Her parents still live in a tiny house in a large, featureless, pre-war council estate outside Liverpool, built to rehouse the poor from the slums. It must have looked efficient on the town planner's drawing board, without any thought that its inhabitants needed to buy food or might ever own cars. Anna joked that carrying the weekly shop a mile home 'developed really good arms'. From where I'd parked to visit her one bitter December evening, I faced an icy crunch across a hundred unlit yards of spiky, frozen grass to reach their front door. I knocked and her mother smiled a warm welcome, taking me to a cosy room with a 'rather decrepit brown upright' piano (as Anna called it). Anna told me at the time:

When I was ten years old, my violin teacher arranged for an audition for Chetham's School of Music: great fun for about two and a half hours. They told me how I *should* be playing the violin, as opposed to how I *was* playing the violin – and then they took me in to study the piano!

I had to go as a boarder because it was so far, but it was incredibly difficult to leave home. My dad used to keep me and my sister going. He'd be the one who very often would get us ready for school because mum was a nurse working nights. We were means-tested and my parents had to pay school fees because it was only a part scholarship. It nearly broke them financially, Joan. My mum and dad had no money. No money at all. The school worked out a way of paying like £30 a month, and they were backdating the bills. The governors or the bursar wrote to my parents, and said 'Any chance of £35?,' and they had to say, 'Sorry, we just can't afford it.'

When Jocelyn and I started at Chetham's, they were still finding their feet as a music school. Practice facilities were really very basic. Some of the pianos were quite dreadful. They just didn't have the money in those days to be able to buy decent instruments. When I won the *Young Musician of the Year* competition it really put them on the map, sort of justified their existence.

I thought there was too much emphasis on music there, music, music, music all the time, when people should have been going pot-holing, or playing sports. A lot of talented young musicians lose out on that. They also suffer from an adverse amount of competition, especially string players. They get so anxious, going round in kid gloves all day to protect their fingers. Maybe I shouldn't have been playing hockey, but I never came to any harm. I'm careful and look after my hands.

I was truly lucky to go there. The all-round musical training, not just on the piano, but academically and orally was exceptional. I was really fired up by doing four-part dictation at the age of 14, and I was in a class two years older than me doing post A-level oral work at the age of 14. I used to challenge myself just to see how quickly I could do it. It was fab; I really, really enjoyed it.

Jocelyn's background was less dramatic. She started a social step up from Anna's family in her neat semi-detached house in a pleasant area of Salford, next to Manchester. Her parents were always encouraging and gave her every opportunity they could. Her problem was that she excelled at everything. Still in primary school, she read so prodigiously she devoured everything in the public junior library and had to be accepted for the adult library. She was passionate about learning and everything about school.

Anna and Jocelyn became part of my study soon after they started at Chetham's. When I tested them, it would be hard to imagine two more closely matched, sharp and talented children. But there was a difference in their parents' attitudes towards their daughters' gifts. While Jocelyn's parents had joined the National Association for Gifted Children (NAGC), Anna's parents had not. Of the two, only Jocelyn had been given the label of gifted and taken to special classes for the gifted. Her parents appeared to be more ambitious for her than Anna's.

Jocelyn's brilliant results

All the 12 children in my sample who'd been at Chetham's School told me enthusiastically how wonderful it had been, how inspiring and greatly caring. This was true for Jocelyn. Her school-leaving results at A-level were the highest in my study of 210 young people, some of whom were too gifted to be measured. She knew it:

School was a fantastic place, a great atmosphere to be in because it was a school for musically gifted children who were good at things, though not necessarily academically. I was an oboist. There were four others in my year, and I was the worst of them. That's not to say I was bad, but I was interested in all sorts of other things, and the others only wanted to be professionals. They devoted all their spare time to practising to become the best oboists they could possibly be. I didn't like competing with that. I didn't know what I did want to do, though, apart from go into space.

At school they did try to stretch me: several teachers gave me extra stuff saying, 'Oh look, I think you'll be interested in this.' A fantastic music teacher was forever giving me articles, suggesting I look at various things. The maths teacher and the chemistry teacher were great. But in hindsight, maybe they didn't try and stretch me enough, because I don't remember it ever feeling difficult. I love exams; I've always loved exams. If I'd been judged on coursework I wouldn't have got the grades I got. I like leaving it to the last minute.

I'd done my maths O-level two years early and I wanted to do astronomy. They made it happen. For A-levels I did maths, pure maths, applied paths, physics, chemistry and general studies. But I didn't work for any of it at all. That's been the cause of most of my problems since, because I never have learned how to work. I certainly didn't work for my A-levels. It wasn't difficult, it didn't feel like work, it wasn't any effort. Yes, that was my peak.

I found it hard to get a clear answer as to why Jocelyn did not take A-level music along with her other six subjects. Surely that would have been easy for her then.

Music practice took a lot of time and I didn't do enough of it. But I knew by that stage that I wasn't going to be a professional and you can't actually do music practice properly without working very hard. About a third of the timetable was for practice and instrumental lessons. The subjects I did filled all the time I had. I always thought that if I ever needed it I could do it later on at night school or something.

The lack really hit me years later when I enrolled on a teacher-training course. My main subject was primary maths, but I wanted my secondary subject to be music. They wouldn't let me. I told them I knew enough. After all, I'd studied music until I was 18. But there was a strict rule at the college that you had to have an A-level in the subject that you were teaching.

Once again, I found it very difficult to find out from Jocelyn why she had not taken her A-level music at the time she took up teacher-training, her second opportunity. It would have got her onto the course she wanted, and even at that stage it would not have been difficult for her. It seemed as though there had long been a great big brake in her mind about taking that essential music qualification. It could have been due to one of the problems of giftedness, shared by others in this study – a fear of not being seen to be successful. What if she did not gain an A-grade in the subject she had worked at for so many years? What if she had only scored a B or less in music – the love of her life?

Anna, the Young Musician of the Year

The British Broadcasting Corporation set up the televised *Young Musician of the Year* competition in 1978, covering the whole country. Since then, thousands of young people have competed. The route to the top starts with regional heats, then is refined in direct competition with other winners in the same instrument category. The glory at the final competition in each instrument category is to perform in the grand finale in evening dress on television with a full symphony orchestra. It is a very popular series, attracting millions of viewers. Just one young person becomes the overall winner across all categories, of whom many have gone on to fame and fortune.

Anna's extraordinary interpretation of Rachmaninoff's second piano concerto won her the title of the *BBC Young Musician of the Year* in 1982. Coincidentally, she'd played it some years before under the high roof of deep timbers and arched braces of the school hall, with Jocelyn supporting her on her oboe in the orchestra. Looking back, it was at that point that Anna and Jocelyn's stories began to fork. For Anna, it was the start of her musical career and for Jocelyn the start of her life, not in music, but in science.

Anna also has an extraordinary (one can say gifted) facility of being able to harness energy from whatever source:

One of the defining moments in my preparation for the
Young Musician competition was that it coincided with
the break-up of my first big relationship. Devastation was
my main driving force. I threw myself into work, into
practice, though never more than three or four hours a
day, because I wanted to do other things with my life. I
wanted to go to university, I wanted to do history A-level,
I didn't want to stop being head girl, and I didn't want to
stop doing sport. It was important to me to be a well-
balanced, rounded individual. Some teachers told me I
wasn't practising enough. But I replied that *Young
Musician* is not the be-all and end-all. I've got a life to
lead as well.

She leapt smoothly over the hurdles of the competition.
First the Liverpool round, North West regional winner,
then her recording sent to the judges and she'd made it
through the national semi-finals. The red carpet began to
be rolled out. She placed her foot firmly on it:

When I got to the final I knew I was going to win it
because I was playing well, I had a strong programme, a
repertoire I really liked, and I remember thinking I'm in
danger of winning this. Not the school, though. It was a
huge surprise to them. It put me in a very difficult
situation there because I was taking my Oxford entrance
exam at the same time. I didn't give a monkey's about
this silly competition thing. I really wanted to go to
Oxford and study music. You see, I enjoyed the whole
broad spectrum of music. It wasn't just about performing
for me, it was delving deeper into how it's all put
together.
    I was flooded with invitations to perform, so the need
for constant practice reared its ugly head. They let me
use the school as my base until I went to university. But
it was a disaster because all my friends had left and I
reckon the teachers were sick of the sight of me after my
media exposure. I started living the dual life that's
always afflicted me. I was sometimes representing my

country and not my school in really high-powered concerts. Then I'd come back to school and I felt them saying, 'Oh no, she's back again.' I never courted this fame that maybe other people would have wanted. It was just . . . that's what I did. Being told at the age of 19 to go to bed at half past ten – how ludicrous is that. I found my time there very, very hard.

I lived the life of a hermit for two years after the competition. It was because there was so much practice to do. I had no real social life at all. I just practised. I was under pressure all the time, part of which I think I put on myself. I did 70, 80 concerts a year after the competition. How can anybody sustain that level of pressure and not go under?

I'd had to take another year out because of all those concerts and went back home. Problem was that my mum was working nights as a nurse at that time and I had to practise during the day when she had to sleep, so I had nowhere to live after that extra year staying at the school. My wonderful piano teacher, Heather, took me in for a year. Having done ten years at boarding school I was quite naive about living in the big wide world. So that year with her was a sort of transition between school and university. I did another 70 concerts that year; just slipped them in, you know. So it was two years after leaving school that I went to Oxford.

University for Anna and Jocelyn

Anna at 20 was nearly three years older than Jocelyn had been when starting university. Her Anna-style reaction on meeting student life and her relief from the treadmill of unrelenting practice and at least two concerts a week was, 'Wey-hey, this is just amazing!' Her 'easier' schedule meant cutting practice back to two or three hours a day (though she'd wanted five or six) on top of a normal student life of lectures and assignments. Then there were hours of delicious time to be spent with the new man in her life, a romance that has lasted happily ever after:

Philip was literally the first person I met at university. I walked through the gate at Worcester College, and there he was, and he recognised me because of the television. He said, 'Oh, hello, I'm the Organ Scholar: show you where your room is.' And that was that. Six weeks later we were going out together and we've been married for more than 20 years, which is extraordinary.

Basically I'm a very lazy person, and anyway, there's more to life than doing academic work and music. I can concentrate quite easily, but when I've finished maybe four or five hours of solid concentrated practice I'm completely exhausted. At university I usually performed for financial reasons, because some of the concerts were very well paid. But I'd do some that are appallingly badly paid because it's just a good thing to do musically. But that is the life of a musician.

Jocelyn at 17 hit a very different university scene. She was the youngest in her class and until she reached 18 she was forbidden by law to enter the student bar where her class-mates laughed and made new friends. Although it was just for a few weeks, it was enough to interfere with the development of her first social contacts. Unlike Anna, she was not a disciplined student at university. She told me how it was for her:

It was so exciting in London. There were lectures and tutorials, and they gave out these problem sheets. In the first week I'd reckoned to whiz through them while I had my tea, which is what I'd usually done. But they were too difficult. For the first time ever I should have started working properly, looking stuff up and trying to find out the answers. It wasn't the best time for me to learn how to work, all alone in London. My reaction at the time was, 'I'll worry about it later.'

It was a shock. At school, information seemed to go in very, very easily. I'd only had to revise a bit before exams to remember odd facts, and I always used to be able to pull it off at the last minute. I'm absolutely positive that I hadn't ever learned how to work properly. When I was at school I'd thought I was working, but I wasn't, not properly: it was too easy.

There were all these other things to do at university, the Music Society and the choir and the orchestra. In my first year, I played in the orchestra, in the second I was orchestra manager, and in the third – President of the Music Society.

I think of myself as working-class and obviously all the rest of them did because of my accent. In London they tended to treat me like a pet poodle, and it could get a bit irritating. When I came into a room there was always someone who would get to me, like saying, 'Oh look, the working-classes have arrived!' Or they'd call me 'the token prole'.

William Shakespeare had experienced exactly what Jocelyn was to share four centuries later. He too had a strong regional accent from the county of Warwickshire. It threads through his plays, most distinctly in his rhymes. So long ago, reaching London in Elizabethan England, he too met metropolitan condescension when he spoke. For him, a lover of the spoken word, the barbs would have been particularly stinging. Again and again in his plays he points out plainly how accent defined and afflicted social status. For example, in *As you Like It*, Orlando is lost in the Forest of Arden where he comes across Rosalind, an aristocratic young woman pretending to be lowborn. He immediately detects the vital clue in her voice, saying, 'Your accent is something finer than you could purchase in so removed a dwelling.' Another character, Kent, in *King Lear*, talks about 'my dialect, which you discommend so much'.

This British obsession with accent and social class was the focus of George Bernard Shaw's play, *Pygmalion*, later turned into the musical, *My Fair Lady*, by Lerner and Loewe. It has a character, Henry Higgins, who is a professor of phonetics. He bets his friend, Colonel Pickering, that he can successfully pass off a working flower-girl, Eliza Doolittle, as a refined society lady, essentially by teaching her how to speak with an upper-class accent, as well as improving her social behaviour. He succeeded, showing that social class is based on such superficial things.

Jocelyn, in addition, was beset by her yearning for music and told me when she was in her third year at university:

> I didn't go to the lectures after the first couple of weeks in my second year because of the musical I was directing – *Oh What a Lovely War*. It just snowballed. I wrote the score, organised the costumes, and did just about everything else. I spent all day in the theatre from about eight in the morning till midnight, and then extra hours on the phone. It's the thing I've enjoyed doing most ever, and it was a smash. But it was staged the day before my first exam and, as a result, I did very badly.

Jocelyn failed her final examinations and left university without a degree:

> My parents were devastated. I felt terrible guilt, and dwelt on how old schoolfriends would react. Everyone I knew had expected great things of me, and I'd let them all down.
>
> I was so sure I'd made the right choice in studying maths and astronomy. I can't understand how everyone isn't interested in astronomy, it's the most fascinating subject there is. It's everything, absolutely everything. And it's . . . it's just beyond words, I mean just to look and see the stars and know how far away they are and anything could happen there and you think did it happen so long ago that we weren't even around at the time.

Anna's life challenge

Just one of the invitations Anna received for winning the award was to the Women of the Year Luncheon at the swish Savoy hotel in London. I bumped into her there in the mirrored and gilded River Room by the Thames. She looked pale, tired and somewhat uncomfortable in that glamorous perfumed gathering of more than 200 successful women. We spent some time together afterwards and caught up. What she told me was shocking:

After I'd won the BBC competition, the first thing I bought was a pair of decent glasses because I'd only ever had National Health ones. We couldn't afford smart ones. Above all, I was determined that my parents weren't going to have to finance me through university as well as school. So you see, even at Oxford when the concert invitations were pouring in, I did about 25 gigs a year outside term time. It was crazy.

And destructive. Even at school, Anna had sometimes been aware that her arms were tired after long practice. She'd brushed it aside. There was to be no rest for her. But there was a price to be paid and it was a terrible one. Her arms, particularly her left arm, began to betray her again while she was an undergraduate at Oxford University. The piano practice could never stop because the concerts not only brought her satisfaction but much-needed cash in her newfound independence from her parents' generosity and sacrifice. Again and again Anna drew up strong courage, pushed aside the pains from her nerves and muscles and fulfilled her commitments.

She reminded me of The Little Mermaid in Hans Christian Andersen's story, who'd fallen in love with the prince on the ship that sailed by. With enormous courage, she'd swished her tail and swum through the murky depths to the Sea Witch, who gave her legs. The price was losing her beautiful voice, and with every step she suffered terrible pain. The little mermaid danced with her prince, lost him, died and turned into sea foam. Anna, though, was made of sturdier stuff.

Anna had been flying high, her daily life was superb and her future mapped for world success. The pain got worse. After Oxford and two years' postgraduate study at the Royal College of Music it became unbearable, and her left arm became useless. The medical therapy she was prescribed was to rest, completely. Her doctor told her it was repetitive strain injury and she was not to use her arm at all. Anna gave up playing the piano:

> With being left-handed, and that was the arm that had packed up, I had to really learn to do everything with my right hand. I learned to write, I learned to do absolutely everything with the other hand. And it's no surprise that I developed shingles in that . . . 'Oh my hands, what are we going to do?' My husband did all the driving, brushed my hair, brushed my teeth, put on the kettle, all the things I couldn't do, even cutting up my food.
>
> I was a very good girl and did what I was told, but nine months in I thought this is just not getting any better. So I went to see this bloke and he had a look at it. He took some x-rays of my neck and said, 'Yeah, I know what the problem is; I'll fix it for you.' At the first appointment he sort of moved it a bit and said, 'You'll feel a little click.' And then he pressed . . . and 14 years of tension just went whew and exploded. My neck went like those little wobbly dog things you see in the back of cars. It was extraordinary. And that's where the problem was. It was postural. A combination of chiropractics and Alexander Technique sorted me out, and has sorted me out ever since. Occasionally if I'm doing too much playing, I get a bit sore and tired, but I've got a pet physiotherapist at the bottom of the road, and she sort of goes crunch, pops it back in, and it's all fine again.

So that long, long nine months in which Anna the ardent pianist had suffered terribly at being forbidden to play – had been quite unnecessary. It was alternative medicine to the rescue. Nine months for a musician is a long time without practice. But being Anna, she took positive lessons from this experience:

> You do need to take some rest; you need to rest the tendons and what's around them. But maybe I needed a year off psychologically; mentally I needed time out. Because if you think what I'd been doing before then, I

mean it was just crazy, you know. All the playing and then the university thing, and I was at the Music Academy as well. I was performing all the way through my time at the Academy, and singing as well, you see. And in my second year as a postgraduate at the Academy, I already said, 'Look, I really think I need to stop playing, can I become a first study singer?' They said, 'Yeah, OK, right.' There was no, 'How are you Anna, and how are you dealing with the fact that you can't play the piano?', just, 'Yeah. OK. Next.' It was extraordinary. But I've come out the other end, you know. And I think everybody in life experiences difficulties.

I got very, very depressed. At one point I said to Phil, 'Right, I'm going to become a midwife now. I've enrolled at Wycombe General Hospital.' And he was fantastic because rather than saying, 'Oh, don't be so ridiculous you can't do that', he said 'OK.' We went to the pub and had a long chat about it. He said, 'Well, let's work out what your skills are, what you're good at, and perhaps being a midwife isn't the right thing. We might find something else for you to do.' So he was there, he didn't say the blindingly obvious thing, which is, 'Of course you can't give up.' But he took the pressure off. So I'm incredibly lucky; he's a man in a million for putting up with me. His great motto in life is, 'Don't worry about anything you can't do anything about.' We just had to go through it. And you know, we got through. Just go on, do the job, and hope for the best. But I do get more nervous at piano concerts now.

Years later she told me cheerfully that there is no cloud without a silver lining. Like every other pupil at Chetham's School she had learned singing. In fact, she and Jocelyn were together in the chorus in their final-year concert singing Georg Frideric Handel's magnificent *The King Shall Rejoice*. But at Oxford University she'd already begun to put serious energy into training her voice. So although she'd lost the use of her arm and her devotion to the piano, deep in her psyche she had already provided musical insurance to change the emphasis in her performing.

She joined a new university singing group called *I Fagiolini* (Italian for 'little beans'). *The Times* newspaper reviewer called it 'the most inventive Renaissance vocal ensemble at work today'. Their biggest hit, *The Full Monteverdi*, presents Monteverdi's *Fourth Book of Madrigals* through the lens of relationships meltdown. Many singing lovers meet in joy and part in sorrow, moving among the audience seated at tables. My feelings as a member of the audience were first of astonishment, and then a strange mixture of heartbreak and fun. *I Fagiolini* is now the mainstay of Anna's career. Yet she has also returned slowly and carefully to piano playing. In her mid-forties, she 'only', she says, plays about 20 piano concerts a year, and is in a constant whirl of music presentations all over the world. Looking back, she said:

I think that as I get older I feel even more expectation on me. After all these years it still comes from my *Young Musician* prize because the British are great at the pride-comes-before-a-fall sort of thing, though I also put that on myself a little bit. There's so many things that can go wrong. Three weeks ago, I did Beethoven II down in Maidenhead. And four days before the show I woke up and thought, I can't play this, I can't play. I am a strong person, but I can't do it alone.

Jocelyn's life as an adult

By the age of 40, Jocelyn had spent many years as a teacher of children with problems. But it had not satisfied her deep longing for stability. Music and science still fought battles for ascendency in her life. First one would rise to the top of her mind and then the other. A formal music qualification has been a long time coming, but perhaps it is on its way in spite of her poor work habits and easy distraction:

I've eventually decided to do something about it, now that I'm over 40, by doing an MA in music at the Open University. I've found that although I absolutely love learning the stuff, reading about stuff, looking stuff up, finding stuff out. When I have to actually write an essay I absolutely hate doing it. The other day I was supposed to be writing an essay but instead I replied to an e-mail asking me a one-line question. I wrote a 7,000-word reply without even thinking. A critical essay of 1,500 words is much, much more difficult. Too many other things distract me. I find any number of excuses to put it off.

I don't read intellectual books for pleasure. I like things that are easy to read, escapism, sci-fi and that sort of thing. I read much too fast; I skim. When I read a book again it's very enlightening because I find all sorts of things I'd missed the first time. But I can learn like that. I can't work with music on, though, because I just end up listening to it.

Then there's all things cat-related, and I'm fanatic about baseball. I've been to Atlanta because of my interest in baseball. I have singing lessons and do solo singing, and I've got a band and we perform, but not as often as I'd like. I'm fanatical about recycling, and give people a hard time. I do lots of charity and environmental type things – Amnesty, Greenpeace and Friends of the Earth, Worldwide Fund for Nature, RSPCA and NSPCC. I always feel guilty that I'm not doing more. I give them all the money I can.

I'm never bored. I want to do all these things, all at the same time, now, immediately. I can't do anything like read a book or watch something I want to watch, or play music because that would be doing something I shouldn't be doing. But for some reason it doesn't seem to be quite the same if I'm faffing around on-line and that seems to sort of take a day. Just getting led in different directions.

It's a blessing being able to do so many things at once. It's difficult enough to get everything done as it is that I want to do; if I couldn't do lots of them at the same time I don't know how I'd do it: impossible. I'm not really a creative person. I try to compose, but not very often. It's a time thing. Only two songs that I've finished, properly finished, and recorded and performed. I was inspired at the time. I've never actually been able to sit down and write a song. I always go on to something else.

I asked Jocelyn about the picture of a nice-looking young man stuck to the fridge door. She told me about her bad luck with relationships. She seemed to have a problem of control, perhaps a kind of naivety that she had been plagued with all her life:

That was Andy, who was a very good friend for about six months. It was very intense, but he's no longer speaking to me. The picture's a reminder of a nice time. I'm very good at getting people not to speak to me. It's an art, you know, Joan. I've done it six times actually. At first we find we can talk to each other very easily about all sorts of things. Then it gets that I want to talk to them all the time, because I don't really talk to many people, and so when I find one I can really talk to, I want to talk to them more and more and more. They tend to get alarmed.

What makes it worse is that with each successive one, there's the history of the ones before. Each time they've all said, 'Oh well, that's not going to happen, because you know I know, and I wouldn't do that to you.' Then they do in the end because they can't find a way out, I suppose. Six in the last ten years, two in the last two years. I can see it happening but I always, always hope that this is going to be the time. I'm getting paranoid about it. I've developed an obsessive nature.

I bought seven calendars this year. If I start playing a CD, for example, I can't play another one until I've listened to the whole of the first one. So that takes time because you can't actually listen to two CDs at once. And if I decide I need to try something out on the piano, I need to play the whole piece, you know, not a little bit of it. Spelling mistakes, apostrophes and things like that just leap out at me. Teachers are the worst. I try not to do it because I know it irritates people, but . . . I can't stop myself.

In the last year or so my depression's gradually come back. I have massive mood swings the whole time. I mean, half an hour before you arrived, Joan, I was in floods of tears, over just nothing at all. It just takes nothing to set me off. Suddenly anything can be the worst thing in the world. I'm on medication, a tricyclic anti-depressant. It's better than it was before. It's just got gradually worse and worse and worse; several things a day were making me burst into floods of tears.

Singing helps. The choir is fantastic; my lifesaver. It's really the only time that I see people socially. People in the choir like sitting near me, because I'm confident and 99 per cent of the time get everything right because I'm really good at sight-reading. I dread the summer holidays because there's no choir. I do a pub quiz once a week in the summer. But I don't see any of those people ever apart from then. Most of the people who know me best are my on-line friends; better than anyone I know in real life. I've met most of them. All the people I really like, apart from on-line people, are all part of a couple and they've all got families. If a friend asks me to do something, or if a friend needs me, I'm there for them.

The group I feel most a part of is an on-line chatroom. I share a lot of interests with a lot of those people, geeky type things, though most of them are much younger than me. I'm always conscious that I'm over 40 and most of them are about 21. We meet up occasionally. Even though there's lots and lots of common interests, the age thing is always at the back of my mind.

My brother and sister are not at all like me. My sister tried to do well at school but my brother was never taken with it. I don't much care to see my mother much. There's three things that I always said from when I was little I wanted to do. I wanted to be an astronaut and a librarian and to sing.

Anna's support system

In the decades I've known her, Anna has always radiated exuberance for life and sheer happiness. Her husband is a management consultant who also travels a lot, which brings them some tricky organisational times being there for their two musical and educationally advanced little girls. Her family, she says, takes priority in all she does, and their happiness is there for all to see. Many of her neighbours have got the keys to their home in case of emergency. Her singing group, *I Fagiolini*, is admired all over the world. There is barely a country in which she has not performed. So often she talks with love and gratitude about her support network of family and teachers.

The psychologist, Professor Albert Bandura, at Stanford University, has pointed out how a sense of personal control is a vital feature of success. When Anna lost the use of her arm, she was in despair and yet managed a balance between control and flexibility to change her musical path. Although Jocelyn had plenty of flexibility, she lacked and has continued to lack the essential balance of self-control. Bandura also said that a mother with high expectations can contribute to her daughter's attitudes towards commitment and control. She can help her to learn from bad times so that she doesn't get ground down, but instead uses them as positive growth experiences. Anna's mother, and her father too, gave her that, but Jocelyn's parents were less involved in her emotional life. Anna always appreciates what she has been given:

> Part of my positive outlook on life is because I had such a good early background. My support network has been very, very important to me from being quite little, and I've had it all the way through in my life. I find it all so interesting now with having the girls myself; it's treading that fine line between encouragement, which I think my parents did superbly well, and putting pressure on them. I've encountered children who've put immense pressure on themselves and I don't want them to do that.
>
> Mum and dad kept my feet on the ground right from the word go, like Phil does today. They're always very proud of me, but there was never any 'Gosh, isn't she completely wonderful,' and all that sort of stuff. And I can't be doing with that anyway. Musicians, well we're just normal people but we just happen to do a different job. Hm . . . well, maybe we're a bit strange. But I've got enough normal people around me to keep my feet on the ground. My own family is prepared to take my crazy lifestyle as it is. They are hugely supportive just by their

very acceptance of what I do. I can't thank the three of them enough.

I've always been available for my daughters. When they were little, I would never practise during the day. I would always wait. My time was their time. It's only really in the last year or so that I've said, 'Look girls, we're on holiday but I've got to do some practice. If you're really good I'll get a couple of hours done, then we'll go off and do something nice.' So I think they have a fairly healthy attitude to music. They practise every day, and I normally try and do that with them as well, so they're not just thrown into, 'Go and do your practice.' One plays the cello and I'm teaching her the piano, and the other one plays the violin.

Is practice all it takes?

There is evidence from the decades of laboratory work on expertise by Professor K. Anders Ericsson at Florida State University that the difference between an average and an élite musician is entirely down to practice – almost nothing else. He found that among conservatory musicians the longer the hours of practice they put in, the higher their achievement. It is true for many fields – when people are put in laboratory conditions, those who practise harder produce better results. Ericsson reckons that 10,000 hours is the minimum for excellence. That means about three hours a day, or 20 hours a week over about 20 years.

In theory, then, if you put in enough time you too could be a Mozart. But I do not accept that expertise is the same as talent. In fact, musically talented children progress much more quickly during the time they spend practising, compared with more average children. The problem with the 10,000 hours idea is that millions of people put in that kind of time in their work or interests and, although they may reach a level of expertise, they may never reach beyond what might be called competence. A ballet dancer who has put in all that time can know what to do for every step and turn, but if she does not have sufficient talent she will not even make it to the corps de ballet, and certainly not perform solo parts. The actor can know his lines to perfection, the social context of his part, and even the history of theatre, but if he can't act, the audience will see it. In the end, as Jocelyn discovered, it was not her hours of practice that were inadequate, it was her talent.

What's more, not all practice is the same. Professor John Geake, the Australian psycho-neurologist, found that in their practice, musical prodigies didn't just recognise a sequence of sounds, one note after the other. What they heard and felt was integrated intellectually and emotionally with what they'd already heard and what they were about to hear. They could keep in mind either big chunks of the music or the whole piece at the same time. The real key to excellence, Geake says, lies in that ongoing comparative overview which the gifted and talented do all the time, whatever they do.

Above all else, what a true musician puts into their practice is guided by talent. When the musically talented practise, it is of a high and subjectively different quality. They do not waste time on technical errors, but can overlook them in their concern to improve interpretation. Normal young children play the same thing over and over until each note is correct, but the performance stays mechanical and dull – to anyone but an adoring parent.

This is what makes the essential difference between musicians who are merely very good and those who reach musical excellence. Jocelyn had realised this deep down at school. No matter how much practice she could do on her oboe, she knew she didn't have enough talent and love of the instrument to compete with the other oboists around her. No such thought occurred to Anna. She practised for thousands and thousands of hours, not only because she is highly talented, but because she is in love with her music. The lucky ones like Anna start with a friendly teacher who makes them feel at home with their music, then move on to more rigorous, skilled teachers who take them further:

I use as many differing emotions as I can get hold of in my playing. I gained from the experience of the BBC competition and all its ramifications with other people –

even their jealousy. It's useful being a pianist. Whenever I'm feeling fed up, I just go and hit hell out of that piano for two hours.

But during a concert I don't feel moved because I'm concentrating on communicating; it comes afterwards. The emotions are somehow inbuilt in a piece. Take the Liszt sonata I'm doing at the moment. I've thought out a particular theme for it and whilst I'm practising I'm thinking – yes, he's meeting her; he's taking her out to dinner for the first time. But then when I'm playing it for real, I'll play the whole thing through from beginning to end, trying to play it the way I think Liszt would have wanted me to.

Anna knew her value

I'm very lucky to have an audience to play to, with, let's face it, national recognition. I've found something that I'm good at; it's marvellous, and I'm just incredibly happy. From the mercenary point of view, it is nice to be able to go out and buy what you want; I get professional fees now. When I was young I used to think, 'God, wouldn't it be lovely to take the musical world by storm – I'm going to be a performer.' And now I am.

I'm a very tactile person – certainly when I'm memorising music. I can't memorise away from the keyboard, I've got to physically feel and hear what I'm doing, whereas some people can sit on a train from Edinburgh to London and have a piece learned and go away and play it. It's all visual memory; they actually see the music then – actually see the page as they're playing it. I always hear it and feel it.

There's a difference between music as a subject and music as a practical thing, and the two don't always meet. There were quite a few people at school who were excellent performers but death on the academic side. The two must be combined, because if you don't know how music is actually put together and how it ticks, then what chance can you have of communicating something to an audience? You've got to actually know what it's all about.

People talk about talent all the time, but you have to feed the talent with effort. People come up to me after a concert and ask me what I do during the day. They imagine you just turn up and think, 'Oh, I'll do a piano concert today.' They imagine you can put on a superb performance without practising. John Lill once said when people asked him 'How did you find the piano?' . . . 'Well, walked on stage and there it was.'

I do believe very strongly that I've been put here to do what I do. I would be denying myself and denying what I believe in if I didn't do it. As a Catholic I have a God-given gift to play the piano and to sing and to teach, and if I don't do that I'm not fulfilling what I should be doing. There have been times, though, when I've thought I can't do this anymore, I just can't do it. The profession is overcrowded, and you have to find a level at which you're happy in performing. And I think I've found it.

I do about three or four concertos a year, ten, 15 recitals a year, and I do some accompanying. There's a possibility of doing some more chamber music next year. And there's *I Fagiolini*, my extended family. Performing on your own is such a lonely thing. You turn up on the afternoon of a concert, rattle your way through a concerto. And then there's the girls. And that's why the house and the garden looks such a wreck, because I haven't got time.

No two days are ever the same. I'm a musical chameleon. I couldn't imagine playing the piano for the rest of my life. I'm so lucky. Oh God. It's crazy. Really crazy. But it's good. It's great. I can safely say it has all been a success story. Oh, Phil's made us some lunch.

Jocelyn the celebrity

In a strange twist of fate, Jocelyn has found an unexpected celebrity status in the media because she was part of my study. She is always open-minded, honest and ready to take part, although over and over again she has to examine her life and tell her disappointments to different audiences. She knows the score:

Ever since I was in your first book, newspapers, magazines, radio programmers ring up. I summarise it by saying, 'Oh, it's the failed genius thing again.' So I've sort of perpetuated it myself. I don't go through life thinking I'm a failure. It's only when I'm reminded how things used to be, that's when it starts to come into my head that really it's all just . . . terrible. And the failed genius side of it has just become shorthand for the whole thing.

I'd really be better off without the label of gifted because every time I've been interviewed about it, it's never been a positive experience. I have to reflect in public on my failures. It's always looking back, and it's obvious to anyone that was my peak, and it's all been downhill since. And every time I've done it, it's been upsetting. Well, it's not your fault [big grin]. Well, actually it is completely your fault! . . . I always blame you every time!

Jocelyn was like Laura, the sister who ate the delicious poisonous fruits in Christina Rossetti's poem, *Goblin Market*. She was lost amidst temptation. Laura and her sister Lizzie were goaded by the evil goblins, 'Come buy our orchard fruits/ Come buy, come buy.' When she tried to stop herself wanting it all, Laura, like Jocelyn, 'gnashed her teeth for balked desire, and wept/ As if her heart would break' for the 'fruits like honey to the throat/ But poison in the blood.' Luckily for Laura in the poem, she had her devoted sister Lizzie to rescue her. Jocelyn had no one. Even in her mid-forties, the evil goblins will not let her be at peace. They twist and pinch, pulling her concentration hither and thither to bewilder and exhaust her, getting her down, until another day, another week, another year has gone by with little to show for it. Jocelyn is beginning to doubt that her musical dreams are ever going to be realised.

In 2008 Jocelyn, Anna and I were together on a BBC radio programme on how gifted children grow up. I was invited as the only researcher who had ever done such a long and in-depth study on the subject, Anna was the success, and Jocelyn was yet again invited as what she calls a 'failed gifted child'. She was still hopeful and trying not to get sour, but her life is very hard, and understandably she was disillusioned:

> Society doesn't want intelligent people. Over a year ago, I decided to quit teaching so that I can do other things with my musical skills: build them up. I assumed – in hindsight *totally* stupidly – that because I can do lots of things and I have good qualifications, like my six A-levels, all Grade A, and a degree, I would be able to get a job. All I wanted was a basic admin job to pay the bills so I could develop my music side. I sold my car and told myself that I could live on a lot less: I have cut out just about everything. But I hadn't taken into account having to still pay a mortgage. You get £59 a week if you're unemployed, and even that's under enquiry because I'd quit my job, so there's all sorts of investigations going on. They might even take that away.
>
> I was entirely unemployed for six months; not a single interview after really trying. Most of the jobs I applied for, like typing, filing, using a computer, didn't even reply. Then something came up at a music college, which I would have loved, but I didn't get it. They re-advertised the same job, six months later, and I didn't even get an interview. Still I've managed to get a temporary job for a charity for the deaf, which thinks I'm fabulous, but they don't pay me enough to cover my living costs.
>
> I can only assume they think I'm over-qualified, though no-one's actually said that to my face. Month after month, it really grinds you down. I'm so, so broke. I've not had any lunch for the last three weeks. It's that bad. I've only kept my house because of fabulous family and friends lending me money: large amounts in some cases. One friend's paying for my internet access, and she bought me a pair of shoes when mine had holes in them. It's an interesting challenge trying to keep everything afloat with absolutely no money at all.
>
> Teaching was a fabulous job. The schools that I worked at were great places, the people I worked with were great, and most of the kids were fabulous. But the time that it was taking was just increasing. And because

I do lots of other things, I didn't want to give up any of those, specially the musical things. It was getting too much of a strain. It didn't occur to me for a second that I wouldn't be able to get a job. I want to say, I'm clever . . . good at things . . . but . . . But that's the situation. I can't get a job and I don't want to get sour.

The last time I came down to London for an interview for something, they paid for the train and they paid for the hotel overnight, but it didn't occur to them to say, 'Oh well, here's some money for food.' So I had nothing to eat for the whole of that day, and the night before. I was absolutely starving. I can't go back to teaching or even supply teaching because what school is going to want someone who quit? And in any case, I'd just be back to where I was before. I'd have a bit more money, but the reason for quitting was that money isn't everything. If I don't get something musical it would be like quitting on life. But . . . financially, I'm not entirely sure how much longer I can do it.

What had happened?

For these two women entering their middle years, their attitudes to life were already largely formed in childhood. Even in 1976, when they were 12 years old, Anna had more 'psazz' than any other of the 210 children in my sample. Trying to photograph her at home with her fingers flying up and down her piano was a challenge. I couldn't focus the one-girl vibration of sight and sound.

Jocelyn's character at that time was harder to pinpoint. Her personality was quieter but she was into everything. Although she was at a specialist music school, her mind was investigating all sorts of tempting learning attractions. Music was only one of them. Her teachers were delighted, and what teacher would not be? There weren't many pupils such as Jocelyn at the school, a girl with such a high intelligence she absorbed their lessons like a sponge, and took her learning easily and with pleasure, her powerful gifted mind scooping up everything that took her fancy. She was such a pleasure to teach and a potential star to demonstrate to the world what a splendid all-round education this struggling new music school could provide. The school staff did all they could to encourage her and provide her with the broad opportunities she craved.

Noticeable differences between the girls began as they moved into their teens. Although Anna's passion and determination for music were never to the exclusion of all else, she stayed clearly focused on her goal of the concert platform. Jocelyn had yet to discover her life's mission, though she was perhaps too versatile for her own good. The sharp dividing of their ways came after each one's superb successes at the end of school. Anna's *Young Musician of the Year* prize was a stunner and Jocelyn's painless six A grades at A-level taken at one sitting were extraordinary at that time. Anna was overwhelmed by concert commissions so didn't reach Oxford University until she was 20, probably benefitting from her extra maturity. Jocelyn was accepted at London University at 17 for high-powered science. Each had a life-course in sight and rosy success beckoned them both.

Once at their universities, though, both young women continued with the learning habits they'd developed since they were small. Anna threw herself gladly into her music, both theory and practice. But she also found the man she was to love, marry and have a family with. Jocelyn stayed curious and tempted by all the wonderful and irresistible things she came across at university – ah, those delicious fruits. But the bright new goal of her science degree soon began to take second place in her affections, and then third, its lustre dimmed. In her astronomical terms, one could say that her world was turning so fast she couldn't keep up with what kept disappearing over the horizon.

Whereas Anna and the school had together nurtured her focused hard practice, Jocelyn's teachers at the same school had unwittingly nurtured her lack of focus and poor work habits. Perhaps each girl had drawn advice from her teachers that suited her instincts. Jocelyn's sheer cleverness had proved to be a chimera, which fooled them all. Her mind darted more and more frantically along her familiar learning pathways to little avail. Her handy old standbys, enjoyed by so many gifted youngsters, of last-minute learning, skimming through homework, barely revising for exams and seeming to absorb knowledge from the air, soon lost their value when she was faced with difficult scientific concepts. For some of the gifted in this position, the idea of failure is such anathema that they make themselves learn to learn. But when faced at university with that challenge, Jocelyn did not rise to it. She turned away from the idea of sheer work to enjoy juicier temptations. It was not a shortage of brain power that caused her to fail her final university exams but a shortage of discipline and direction. It cast a terrible blight on her future and she has paid a serious cost ever since.

Everyone in Jocelyn's life did their best for her. She flourished at Chetham's, a gifted and talented girl in a world-class school for the gifted and talented. What she did not get, though, was deeper personal guidance. She needed some close counselling by someone who could help her use her brilliance efficiently and purposefully. One problem with specialist schools is that, at such a high level of achievement, those who may not feel able to reach it can be turned off, like Jocelyn. Perhaps at a more academic school she would have remained outstanding, and been better prepared for a higher level of study with a much happier outcome.

For years, it seemed to me that Jocelyn's struggles and disappointments were due to taking the wrong subject at university and deserting her professional music. After all, the big decisions had been made by her 16-year-old self, a well-recognised age of upheaval. But I no longer believe she'd simply chosen badly. Jocelyn had and still has a love and a mind for science as well as a love for music. She could have done anything she wanted. Paradoxically, if she had not been so gifted and open to where her curiosity led her, she wouldn't have landed in that mess. But Jocelyn has never given up hope and is still searching for her own right way.

PART 3

Special challenges to gifted potential

What a blunt fellow is this grown to be? He was quick mettle when he went to school.
William Shakespeare, *Julius Caesar*

Wherefore have these gifts a curtain before 'em?
William Shakespeare, *Twelfth Night*

If there is one group of people who should be good at mental gymnastics and overcoming challenges, it's the gifted. Yet the severe challenges to the development of their great potential come in a bewildering variety of forms which can be hard to spot and overcome. Internal barriers are sometimes set up by the gifted person themselves, lack of progress being explained away through complicated self-justifications. External barriers can come in the way that authority figures see and categorise a child, and so block opportunities.

Some challenges are unique to the gifted and talented, and these can cause havoc in their lives. The people in this part were chosen to show how the gifted cope with the challenges only they face. Margaret and Jack, for example, reacted quite differently to being labelled a gifted child, with all the pressure and expectation that the label entailed. Margaret was harmed by it, while Jack ignored it. Gifted Gail's challenge was in her own mind, due to her self-effacing ideas of herself because of the gap between the intellectual world of her social class and what she later experienced.

Philip's first horrendous challenge was in the mind of another whose 'expert' opinion could so easily have shut off all his opportunities. Family influences on the lives of pals and classmates, Ady and Harold, caused them to take wildly separate routes. Lydia and Francine were both gifted well-off girls with the finest opportunities. But even those did not protect them from gender challenges, which have altered their feelings of self-worth and so the way they have lived.

Underachievement comes from challenges not over-come. It is a particularly difficult problem to identify in the gifted. Those who slip below their potential might be unnoticed because they are still above-average in school class. This is a special problem among the disadvantaged gifted, whose teachers sometimes do not expect them to do well. For some in my study, though, they had all they needed and still did not use it to their greatest advantage.

Just a few had no particular ambition, simply ignored their gifts and lived the lives of the community around them. A once-highly achieving schoolboy, now in early middle-age, still lives with his mother. He is proud never to have missed watching his small local football team play, goes down the pub almost every night and is content with his clerking job. Did he underachieve because he did not live up to his outstanding intellectual promise, or is his achievement in his contentment?

Several had poor ideas about what they felt was appropriate for someone of their low social class. One boy, Derek, had been advanced a year at school and achieved a handful of A-grade A-levels. The school pleaded with him to go to university, but he was adamant. He told me specifically why he had refused to go, even though at that time attendance was free. It was, he said, 'not for the likes of me.' He did, though, demonstrate one unique aspect of being unquestionably gifted. He shone with it.

He was working as a labourer but his boss could see that he had more to him than the ability to wield a spade in the frozen ground. Speaking directly man to man – which was rather more effective than teacher to pupil – he per-suaded Derek to take a part-time course; in time he went on to obtain a first-class degree. Along the way, Derek had also learned that his gifts were valuable and worth recognising, and that his ideas on social status were long out of date. He rose to be a high-level administrator in his line of work.

Personal outlook can overcome real challenges to progress and fulfillment. The great American psychologist William James must have been a pessimist. He recommended lowering your expectations so that you wouldn't be disappointed and quotes Thomas Carlyle: 'Make thy claim of wages a zero, then hast thou the world under thy feet.' But pessimism, we know, undermines performance. The optimist is the winner.

9

The label of 'gifted'

I suppose because everything else in my life wasn't particularly good, it was nice to have the attention for the music.

Margaret Sweeting

The one big reward that little Margaret Sweeting could offer her parents was her talent. There seemed to be plenty of it. After years of yearning for a child, they had adopted her as a baby of ten months. How fortunate and happy they were then. They loved their pretty, sweet and obliging little girl, someone any parents would delight in. At five years old, seated on a cushion at the piano, she would flex her tiny fingers and display her musicality.

No expense was spared in providing piano lessons for their daughter. Day in and day out, she practised her scales and her exercise pieces. She was a precious only child, with a talent which they told me was the envy of other parents at her primary school. The heavy tuition and practice paid off when she was seven years old and accepted for Chetham's School of Music in Manchester (see Chapter 8). Her musical life looked very promising indeed. In her sweet accepting way, Margaret took up her role with pleasure. When she was eight years old, her parents told her she was adopted. In her considerate way, she accepted it without any fuss, and it seemed perfectly all right – at the time.

The first threat to the family's smooth life, when it came, was not from the lack of consanguinity with her parents (that was the second threat), but from her role as a gifted musician. After four years in that highly selective music school, it became clear to her teachers, as well as to Margaret, that her aspiring classmates had far more talent than her. All those years of dedicated practice had got her through the auditions; even those experienced judges seem to have been misled by her polished performances. Chetham's had taken a chance giving her a place; but not all chances pay off. Her talent was looking a little threadbare.

Frantically, she practised harder and harder but simply could not reach the extremely high level expected of her in the school. In spite of her continuing heavy work-load, Margaret's performance had slowly begun to slip, to languish somewhere along the bottom ranks. The shiny label of gifted child which she'd worn with pride most of her young life was becoming tarnished. Something had to be done if it was to stay bright. Practice without the talent was clearly not enough.

Using face-saving reasoning, her parents explained to Margaret that the intensive music education for which they had sent her there so joyfully and proudly, was no longer suitable. She needed, they said, a broader education. Accordingly, they removed her at the age of 11 from a situation where she was seen to be less talented than others, and placed her in a small girls' boarding school where she could shine. Margaret didn't complain: she never complained. Instantly, she had been removed from the pressure of that powerful competitive league. She unpacked in her dorm, found her way around the school and discovered the piano. Being a dutiful daughter, once again she did her best to fulfil her obligations to her parents in her familiar role as an outstanding musician.

More than 30 years later, at well past 40, she could see all too well how what happened afterwards, the extraordinarily tortuous path of her life, had been moulded so early on by being labelled gifted. She saw the expectations it had engendered, how she could not live up to it, and how her parents had tweaked her life so that she could still wear it and honour them. Were they being kind to her, letting her believe she really was a highly talented musician, or were they manipulative? She seemed rueful and spoke softly:

That was a big part of my problems, being labelled a musically gifted child. There was just a handful of us at boarding school who stood out as being musically gifted, and we were the stars of the school. Part of me enjoyed the limelight. Part of me enjoyed winning classes and competitions and being singled out. I suppose because everything else in my life wasn't particularly good, it was nice to have the attention for the music.

Margaret left the boarding school at 16. No further mention was ever made by her parents of the broader education she'd been sent there to acquire and the exams she was to have passed. The fragile tower of cards on which her life had been constructed began to shift in the draught from the opening door. She had totally accepted her label. It was what she had been told all her life. But now, the core of her being, who she believed herself to be, was due to be blown apart.

Margaret went into hiding

It was the most beautiful summer's day Scotland had known for many a year when I visited Margaret three decades later. With the town of Dumfries at my back, not far from the birthplace of Scotland's national poet, Robbie Burns, I set off across the Galloway countryside. During the last ice age, glacial material had dumped and shaped little hills called drumlins along the way. Not yet dried out by the rare hot sun, these bright green mounds bordered the narrow road as I drove towards her isolated farmhouse. I knew she lived in that low, white building with a partner, but not much more.

Margaret had been off my radar for about 20 years. I could not find any recent school or work records to chase up. I could not find her parents. It had looked like the end of our relationship. But one contact led to another, until eventually I had an e-mail address and then her friendly voice on the phone. On that sparkling day, she told me what had happened and where she'd been:

At 16, I was desperately unhappy at the boarding school and life at home was very, very difficult; my mother was clinically paranoid and my father was at his wit's end. So they sent me to live with my piano teacher, who got me to the Royal Academy of Music in London to study piano. I worked very, very hard. I was one of the top pianists in the second year. But . . . oh dear . . . in my third year, I had a nervous breakdown. I don't know how I managed to pass my final exams. I'd been suppressing a lot of emotional pain.

I felt my life was falling to bits and I wanted a religion that would tell me what to believe and how to live. I've always been moved by religious music, and the spiritual, liturgical and mystical meaning within Catholicism was very attractive to me. So through college contacts I converted to Roman Catholicism. The change, the learning and the religious life I was leading were all intense, and so was college and all my emotional baggage from home. Everything came crashing on top of me. I went to pieces. Physically, I couldn't sustain the piano practice. So many tears. I started to take an overdose, but couldn't see it through and panicked. On the very, very edge. Did I really want to wipe myself off planet earth or not? I was terribly depressed.

Quite alone in the metropolis of London with no help at all from the college, Margaret did not think of seeking psychological help but turned instead to her new welcoming church, which offered her the services of a chaplain with some church training in counselling. Of course, he was a dedicated Catholic worker, and by the nature of his calling was obliged to practise chastity to seek spiritually higher realms and find salvation. It would have been difficult to find anyone less suitable to counsel this lost, clinically depressed young woman.

Never in Margaret's life had she known a warm family environment with parents who accepted and loved her just for being Margaret. It had always been love with strings, a life of obedience, of years of discipline and dedication on the piano stool. She had always been a quiet girl with no intimate friends, but of a sweet nature. Who could have known how well her life so far would prepare her for the next stage in her life. She had light brown hair, clear grey eyes, was of medium height and could be described as mousy.

The chaplain took her in hand, and together through their sessions they worked towards a solution to her problems. They arrived at what she saw as the 'joint' decision that she had a calling. With that, the best place for Margaret was a convent, where she was to dedicate her life to becoming a nun in the service of God and her church. This conclusion, though, brought her the extra stress of deciding which order to join. But again the chaplain managed to sort that one out. She was best suited, he thought, to a closed order. This emotionally fragile girl took his advice and opted to stay apart from the rest of the world. It was perhaps surprising that the Carmelites accepted her in the mental state she was in. They believed that her calling was genuine, and that were she to live a regular life with them, with their support she could become one of them and stable.

The monastery was a pleasant yellow-brick nineteenth-century building. Its four acres in the city centre were surrounded by a seven-metre high wall, keeping out the busy urban life around and providing an oasis for prayer. Margaret felt welcome and liked what she saw, believing gratefully that the chaplain had been sent by God to direct her to this place of peace. For the first time in her life she was in a community where she felt loved for herself and not just her talent. Her parents, who were not churchgoers of any kind, were horrified, and (not without reason) felt rejected. They would never be allowed into the convent itself and visits to their daughter were strictly limited.

Carmelites, men and women, trace their origins to hermits living on Mount Carmel, now in Haifa in Israel, in the late thirteenth century. The order has stayed hermit-like and austere; each Carmelite is alone with God and prayer within the monastery, rarely, if ever, leaving it. Their lives of solitude and silence within the community are devoted to their three vows of chastity, poverty and obedience. They pray for closeness to Jesus; his companionship is valued above all else, and for all the suffering in the world. Only he, they believe, has the answer. Becoming a Carmelite is far from easy. For Margaret, whose days had been filled with working to develop glorious sound at her fingertips, to be in a world of absolute silence was a terrible and deep shock. Fortunately, she was able to draw on her long-practised skills of discipline and obedience.

For her first year she was a Postulant guided by her personal Vocation Director in prayerfulness and service. In her second, she was given a simple nun's habit as a Novice, praying and learning to be a member of the community. She would rise in the dark at 5.30 to spend most of her days in silence and solitude. But she had plenty of domestic duties, also carried out in silence, and she ate in silence while a holy text was read aloud by a sister. Chapel was seven times a day. The stage of Simple Profession followed, in which she took a three-year vow to remain in prayer and the silent study of holy works.

The next stage would have been life commitment, wearing the traditional nun's medieval black or brown robe with a white wimple under the head covering, devoting her life totally to Jesus, belonging to him completely for life after her marriage to him in a white wedding dress. As part of the ceremony, the nun bride lies face down, her head towards his statue with her arms spread wide in a cruciform shape. Margaret was sincere; even though she tried her best, slowly it trickled through to her understanding that this cloistered contemplative life was not for her. Drawing up her courage, she asked the Mother Prioress to let her go back into the world:

I was given permission to leave the convent three months before my vows expired. The nuns were very kind and supportive because they realised I didn't have the calling to stay for the rest of my life. It had been a complete break from the music which had dominated my every day up to then. There was no piano – the best thing that could have ever happened for me musically. Nothing, nothing. We did a bit of singing, I used to write some of the chants for big feast days, and community entertainment when some of the novices would sing to the rest of us. It gave me space, and because I'd always been good at music, it was always the obvious thing for me to do.

Margaret had seemed to be happy at the convent. She was loved and well integrated in the community, and felt that it was a healing place for her. But she was not, in fact, being healed at all. It proved to be just a long break. Her accumulated emotional problems had neither been helped nor removed by silence and prayer. They quickly bubbled up again. But not knowing what to do, she went straight back to the same Catholic chaplain. This time, after the gap of five contemplative years and the maturity it had brought her, she recognised with startled dismay his counselling ineptitude, and that he now had her going round in emotional circles. There had to be another way.

Margaret's world of women

Margaret moved from the enclosed community to another type of intimate association:

I knew I was lesbian before I went into the convent. I'd had a couple of girlfriends before. But at that point it was totally irrelevant, because I was going to be under a vow of chastity for the rest of my life. I've never been part of the gay scene. Most of my friends are heterosexual.
Having been at a girls' boarding school, I wasn't used to boys and it still takes me ages to get to know men. Angela and I met when I was playing the organ for a service at a liberal Catholic chapel. We were friends for three years and then moved into a relationship. I've been effectively married for over five years. It's the best I've ever felt in my life. I've come through some tough times.

Now, I'm an ecumenical hotchpotch. I play the organ at an Anglican church and attended the Church of Scotland for a while, but nowhere on a regular basis. My beliefs are too borderline heretical for me to feel comfortable. But despite that, I'm doing a theology degree with a very evangelical course. I've told my parents about it, but my mother just blanks. She takes it as a slap in her face, that they've given me all the support to go to music college, to be good at music – and I'm doing something different from what I'd been programmed to do. I know there's a lot of people out there who are much better musically than I am, but that doesn't negate the fact that I am still good at it. I'm very rusty, because I just don't have the time to practise and I'm not a regular performer. My main work now is teaching the piano. I have about 50 private pupils on my waiting list.

Angela and I have no social life whatsoever. I'd love to set up a retreat house one day, to be able to offer space to people to move in a spiritual direction. I'm nowhere near as emotionally fragile as I was. But it probably wouldn't take a huge nudge to tip me off-balance. I still have a problem handling anger. All my life I've learned to suppress it, to pretend that I was just this nice sweet person. I sometimes let it out by playing the piano, pounding away. I feel successful at a personal level. I've got a good relationship, good work that I enjoy, I'm doing well in my studies, I know I'm popular as a teacher. I'm contented with my life.

Margaret made her break

Margaret and her parents never made up her five-year rejection. They refuse to answer their phone to her or anyone else. This was just one reason why I couldn't find them or her, and I did wonder why they have a phone at all. But deep down, the biggest split between them was not her years in the convent, nor her mother's mental illness, nor her lesbian relationship – it was her teenage action in tracing her natural mother. It was a rejection too far for her paranoid mother. Their rift deepened into an unbridgeable chasm. Even so, Margaret remains immensely loyal to her mother, who she feels has done her best over the years and brought her up:

They gave me an ultimatum that if I had anything more to do with my natural mother, they would have nothing more to do with me. It was too late by then; I wouldn't be blackmailed.

I was brought up by a mother who was a very strict disciplinarian. She's paranoid, and that's what led her to start opening my letters, which I couldn't take. There's a history to this. Her own mother had to be kept locked away because she was mentally ill. I was a daddy's girl and I miss him a lot. He knows that and he misses me too. My mother's a recluse and dad looks after her full time, and he also suffers from depression. My mother would never let him meet me. No, no. He's got no life whatsoever. But he's an adult man and he could ring me on his mobile if he wanted to. It's always switched off, but I leave him messages. He's glad to see me settled. After all, he's never lost me to another man!

My natural mother is my friend now. She was scared to meet me at first because she'd gone on to have two other children, who hadn't known about me. I suddenly turned up as an older sister. I like them all. Funny thing is that she is also musical. I don't call her my mother, but she's opened her arms to me. I get invited to her family dos, but don't go to them out of loyalty to my parents, even though they wouldn't know.

As I walked away up the farm path, in the late evening of the long northern summer day, I turned to see Margaret, her beloved dog in her arms, smiling rather wistfully after me. I was leaving her in her isolated farm and returning to the big world outside. By the side of the road, I came across a farmer who'd been watching us hug goodbye. He asked me suspiciously, with a slight sneer, what I'd been doing there. I read his face to imply that he thought I must be one of their kind. It must have been difficult for the lovers.

Margaret rejected her label of gifted child

The most extreme and sure way to slip off a label imposed by others is to utterly reject all that it stands for. That's just what Margaret did. She had been firmly placed by her parents in the role of musically gifted child. The label had identified her, but she knew that she had to provide her parents with constant confirmation of her giftedness. The trouble was that by the age of 11 she could no longer keep up the image. For all her childhood, her parents had loaded the burden of fulfilling their dreams on to her slight shoulders. An obedient soul, she always devoted her best energy to their wishes centred on that role. Her final destination could have been the concert platform – a life of glorious music, excitement, applause, gossip, praise, companions, an agent, a world of noisy communication. In fact, hers was a life of hard practice with modest rewards.

Margaret obviously had talent. She'd been accepted at two prestigious music institutions, Chetham's School and the Royal Academy of Music, through audition. But her talent was not in the top bracket. She was heavily tutored and had practised unremittingly to reach those places. But however hard she worked, it wasn't enough to take her to national excellence as a pianist. In spite of those 10,000 hours of practice which are said to make latent ability into expertise, it was clear in Margaret's case it did not lead her to a life as a famous pianist.

Performance competition is most extreme for pianists, and it is getting harder. Thirty-five million Chinese children have taken up classical piano on the back of the phenomenal success of Lang Lang, and the likelihood is that Chinese pianists will feature more frequently on the world stage. Margaret, because of the label she'd been given, and like many another labelled as gifted – was destined to fail her parents' hopes.

Margaret needed what she did not get, consideration by her parents and her school teachers to find out what this little girl herself might have wanted in life, and what else she might be capable of. During her time at Chetham's, she had been interested in nursing, she told me, particularly nursery nursing, but no-one cared to hear her, and any thoughts in a non-music direction were discouraged. As she said, 'Well, if you're good at music – therefore you do music.'

Because she was practising so much, there was little time for a social life or having fun; though I suspect that fun is not a strong element in Margaret's make-up. She is a serious person. Her tension built until it burst like a boil, spilling its venom in her mind. The devastating depression and her rejection of the label came towards the end of her course at the Royal Academy of Music. She had completed her obligations to her parents to the limit of her capabilities. It was as though her inner self cried out – enough! She couldn't take any more, blocked it all out and entered a world of silence. No music and not even easy communication with her fellow nuns.

It is one of the jobs of a counsellor to help someone find themselves, to help them understand their needs and hopes and find direction in their lives. However, the Catholic chaplain had aided Margaret in a direction which seemed to fit his own needs better than hers. Had she sought advice from professionals who could have dealt with her depression, her life choices might have been very different. Since that dreadful time, Margaret, now in her mid-forties, has painfully manoeuvred herself into a good life. She is at peace with her partner and very successful indeed in her work as a music teacher. It took a long time.

Possible effects of the label

The question I started with in this long research, was why some children were designated as gifted, while others – of identical measured ability – were not. I wanted to know how the label of gifted child had affected the bearer as they grew up. Margaret, in her complicated life, mirrored a lot of what I had found in others. Most importantly, the children who had been volunteered by their parents as gifted were more likely to have more emotional problems. They were likely to have fewer friends and be more 'difficult', meaning that they were often more troubled by problems of a 'nervous' type, such as poor sleep, poor co-ordination, and asthma. These were problems associated with a stereotype of the gifted child. But I discovered that such problems were not the result of the gifts themselves, but of other matters in a child's life, as Margaret's showed so poignantly.

How each individual reacts to their classification as gifted also depends on individual personality and outlook. Not every child I have seen who had been given the label of gifted attempted to fulfil it as slavishly as Margaret did in her childhood. Sometimes, even from an early age, a child is able to reject the gifted role which parents have given them, like Jack Abroms.

For Jack, his label slid like water off a duck's back. His mother had devoted her life to him, her only child. Every photograph in the house was of him, and since he'd been a toddler he'd been allocated two rooms, one as a study and one as a bedroom. By the age of four, he was having four outside-school lessons a week, and when I first met him aged six, it had increased to seven subjects a week – chess, swimming, elocution, French, Hebrew, etc. – at least one a day. The stereotype of the problem gifted child dominated his mother's thinking, even to the extent that she wouldn't have any more children, as this one was so 'demanding'. As she said, 'All my friends, they were very amazed!' She had the common stereotype off pat, complaining constantly about his poor sleep, high energy and insatiable curiosity. He wore her out, she told me, and she expected sympathy. Jack was at a private school:

> I made an appointment to see the junior headmaster, who I couldn't stand at all, to get him to put Jack up a year. When we'd finished, he said, 'I've never had a parent speak to me like you've spoken before!' I said, 'Well, I don't frankly care.' He put Jack up.

To me, though, Jack, seemed not only decidedly incurious, but I had heard more interesting views on life from much less able youngsters. He had taken a very 'laid back' approach to his mother's view of him, seeing it as her opinion rather than his obligation. He had a fine sense of self, so that unlike other youngsters under pressure to perform, he felt the need neither to make excuses for potential failure nor to strive frantically for success. He continued working steadily at his own very high level, with plenty of friends and a good social life. He appreciated his mother's faith in him, and they understood and loved each other well. Taking his mother's attitudes in his stride, he has become a dedicated and very successful medical consultant.

I admired Jack's fortitude. I did not find his mother an easy woman to interview as she talked without drawing breath, going on to describe all her relatives and their children. I'd been aware of myself sitting keenly on the edge of the armchair as we began, then slowly sinking further back into it as I struggled to concentrate, until the sound of her voice became like rain pattering on the window. Yet from his parents of modest education, and I suspected modest intelligence, had come this happy, secure, gifted son. Though he benefitted greatly from his excellent schools, his success in life is not entirely due to his education, but in large part to his mother's faith in him.

From the child's point of view, being labelled gifted is always a challenge. Whether to call a child gifted or to avoid the description is a delicate decision which must be based on respect for the truth and total acceptance of the individual child concerned. Sometimes a label is simply a valuable and short-hand way of describing the state of things, but sometimes it is based more on hope than reality. Working out what a child is capable of is part of the art of parenting and teaching, and in the end the decision of whether or not to label is complex. And a label of giftedness can have different effects. Whereas an already over-worked child, such as Margaret and others, might be driven to low feelings of self, even depression, under the threat of failure, another might benefit from the challenge and love being distinguished as gifted.

The balance that parents and teachers have to achieve in making decisions for children is far from easy, considering the interacting factors. Big parts are played in this complex by the children's personalities, the facilities available, the rest of the family, finance, culture and all the subtleties of daily living. No-one can get it all right, and fortunately most children understand that most parents do their best for their families and are able to forgive them their mistakes.

10

Barriers in the mind

If only I could live to my full potential for just one day.
Gail Pattison

I've had to build up a sort of shield for myself over the
years.

Philip Bessant

One bright autumn afternoon in the mid-1980s, while Gail
Pattison was an education student in the English Lake
District, we walked together in the college grounds, kicking
through thick russet leaves in the earthy crisp air beneath
the sage green hills. It was a shimmering Lakeland day,
and Gail was a striking pre-Raphaelite figure. She was tall
and slender, her pale earnest face framed by wild red hair.
Within minutes of our meeting, she began to talk and continued with little pause for several hours. The essence of
her message was that nobody around her could understand
the depth of her gifted thinking, and how uncomfortable
she felt among her fellow students with their lesser brain-
power. Her barrage of words struck me as the combination
of a hook to hold my attention and a defence against hurt.
Gail had picked up on the stereotype of gifted and saw her
life as inevitably hard because of her gifted mind:

It's difficult for people like me with a very high
intelligence, because we think we know so much and are
influenced by bigger things. I say a lot of things that

other people would never say, and do things that other
people wouldn't do. I live how other people wouldn't live.
I've got a lot of thoughts that other people can't possibly
begin to understand because they've probably never
thought that hard before. It's unfortunate, but they just
don't know what I'm going on about. Last week, I thought
about truth – nothing's real because what you see one
day may be seen the next day as totally different. So
reality is always real, but it changes and it's a different
reality. When I say things like that, they say, 'Yes . . . I
think I'll go and have a cup of coffee.'

When I'd first met her at the age of 11, Gail was in her first
year as a pupil at a high-level girls' grammar school with an
excellent academic reputation. The entrance examination
had been taken along with the rest of Gail's class, so getting
a place there had been a complete surprise to her plumber
father and housewife mother. They lived in the heart of a big
council estate where life was relatively straightforward. If
you were a boy, you would most likely follow your father's
trade or a similar one. Girls left school for temporary work
until they married, had babies and became housewives and
mothers, sometimes with part-time jobs, but not careers.

   Because she was so outstanding in her giftedness, especially maths, Gail's primary school teachers had strongly
advised her mother to join the National Association for
Gifted Children. However, in line with her parents' general
lack of effort for their gifted daughter, it proved too difficult
for them to take her to the Saturday morning classes. Her
primary school-class had been grouped by ability, but in the
egalitarian 1970s, this was played down – the children were
not supposed to be aware of any differences between them.
But little Gail was too perceptive for the system:

   The kids on the top table tended to look neater than the
   kids on the bottom table. I didn't have any notion at all
   that I was particularly bright. I knew that I got a lot of
   gold stars for my written work, but I assumed that if you
   did good work you got one, and the rest of my table got
   them too.

There was no link between the school work and my parents. I would never have come home and mum'd say, 'Ah! Gold stars.' She was never proud of what I'd done. The most she'd say was, 'You'll be all right, love, you've got a good brain.'

My parents never took any interest in what I did or my dreams and hopes. None whatsoever. They weren't like that. It was shopping in the city, then home to watch the telly. Till my teens, every weekend we went to see the grandparents. That's what we did. They were rock solid and they were there for us. They gave us a hug when we were sad and shouted at us when we were naughty. Mum washed the clothes and dad went to work and brought home the bacon. They told you what you could and couldn't do. That's what mums and dads did.

She'd been expected to go on to the school up the road to join her sister. But getting that place at the grammar school made her feel she'd won a golden ticket. But to where? The shock at the social-class jump she found there began a lifetime of emotional problems and decades of navel gazing about who she was:

I was just as much of an oddity to most of the teachers as they were to me. Most of them were very, very middle-class, and I was scared stiff of middle-classness. My name was always at the top for exam results. I got to expect it to be there. But it wasn't me: it was my whole identity that scared me. I hardly had any friends.

As at most selective schools, vocational guidance was largely limited to deciding on which university. Gail was not the only youngster in my study to feel let down, telling me:

They didn't know anything about me. They didn't hear what I was saying.

During her teen years, she'd developed a passion for horses, helping out at a local stables every weekend. Neither of her parents ever went to see her ride or took the slightest interest. Not until her thirties did she blurt out her resentment to her mother, who replied calmly, 'We just didn't do that kind of thing. But we were always here for you. You had a secure loving home.' Gail understood this in her head, but not in her heart:

> I wanted to work with horses, so I left school at 16. There didn't seem much point in staying on, and nobody objected. My dad did some plumbing work in Saudi, so he got extra money and put some in a bank for me. I moved into a cottage with a friend and worked full time for a riding school for no money. The payoff was being trained to be a riding instructress. Suddenly, my workload tripled when two of my colleagues were off ill, and I'd already been doing twice what I should have been. They were sat in the tack room, having coffee and counting the money. So I walked in and said, 'You can find yourself another skivvy. I'm going. Bye-bye.' I cycled home, got me a copy of the *Horse and Hound* and looked through the jobs at the back, went to the phone box and started phoning.

Social class bites

That's when Gail really had her eyes opened to British social-class divisions. No more gentle banter and feelings of resentment with her school teachers who wanted the best for her, or with small-time, local riding teachers trailing little girls around the stable-yard on plodding ponies. No more visits to granny on Sundays and shopping trips with mum. She took a train to the soft south, then a taxi to her first job. It took her up a long drive to a fine mansion:

> It was a summer job, working for titled people. I was thrown headlong into this other world with shooting and swimming. Rather fun looking after children and helping them with their riding lessons, but almost no pay. What did they think I lived on?

By the end of the summer, Gail was financially no better off, but she had learned a lot about how to live the good life.

She had adapted, albeit in a serving capacity, and was able to cope with the mores of that tribe. They'd said they liked her, though not enough to either pay her properly or ask her to stay on.

With that experience under her belt, she found an even higher social rank in her next job. This time, the drive to the grand house was even longer and the people snootier. Her position was like that of so many half-educated young women for generations – as nanny to the children. Her social learning curve shot up even more steeply. She was trusted, after all, to teach these aristocratic children how to behave. Unfortunately, the behaviour shown to Gail was not kind or courteous, not a drop of *noblesse oblige*:

> They were the most upper-class people possible – playing polo with Prince Charles, and all the rest of that stuff. They worked me absolutely into the ground. They just expect that kind of service from their servants. I was virtually dead.
>
> I was so bad that even mum and dad said you've got to leave it. Come and take some A-levels at the tech college. I gave in and did them in one year instead of two. Then I chose a little teacher training college because it looked easy, and it was free. I suppose I did look down on other students. I couldn't understand why they didn't ask questions. I got a good degree, even though I didn't do any work.

Gail, a 'Career Gifted'

I call Gail a 'Career Gifted' because her life was centred around promoting the image of herself as ferociously clever. I coined that term to describe people like her whose self-image is absolutely tied up with their giftedness. Even in conversation with strangers, before long Career Gifteds will let others know in one way or another how difficult it is for them as intellectually superior people to cope with the normal world. As children, their parents were often supportive of that presentation. Career Gifteds are likely to insist that were it not for . . . *insert excuse* . . . they could show their true and brilliant colours. Behind the facade lies the fear of being exposed as normal and unexceptional – not gifted at all. Such fear has inhibiting spin-offs to making one's way in the world, especially to creative expression of every kind which needs courage to carry out.

Since she was about five, Gail's teachers had spotted her outstanding intelligence and designated her a gifted child. Like some others in my study, she'd taken up the stereotype of the-gifted-child-who-finds-it-difficult-to-live-in-a-mediocre-world with enthusiasm. Her confidence in the justification of the label was, however, weak. So, to protect any threat of damage to her status, she'd learned over the years to avoid any real test of her abilities. Like others who adopt that defensive way of thinking, her prime manoeuvre was to demonstrate disdain for the educational system. She began to do badly in school exams because, she said, it was beneath her to work for them. Logically, taking this further, her next big self-harming defence was at 16 to leave school altogether, the place where she was expected to continue to show her mettle. Gail took up the care of intellectually undemanding horses. Mucking them out kept her well away from challenge. They provided a perfect shield to prevent damage to her fragile self-image as a gifted child, even though she had to endure long, hard hours for extremely little reward.

Gail took her equally ill-paid work among the upper-classes in her stride, but there was no jumping up that social gap. She either remained as their lowly servant, a step down too far, or took some action to better herself. Back she came to her own folks, re-geared her fine brain to study again and scraped together enough qualifications to take a teacher training course at a small and not too demanding college. She was already a student there when she flipped back into her long-practised Career Gifted mode, dropping into my ear – oh, so casually:

When this college said I could have a place, I didn't bother about it very much. I occasionally remembered I was taking the exams, got them and came here.

Three major barriers had impeded Gail's intellectual progress. Each was encouraged by adults, and underpinned by her own insecure personality. The first was from her parents, who had taken little interest in Gail as a complicated developing human being. She loved them, but felt somewhat rejected because they hadn't shown much interest in what interested her. The second was being labelled a gifted child. This set up high-level expectations of academic success and general cleverness, which frightened her because in her heart she didn't believe she merited it. The easiest way was to avoid putting the label to the test, which clearly worked because no high-level achievements were gained.

The third barrier was her deep-rooted working-class outlook, limiting what she saw as acceptable for one of her social standing. But even the fragile ambition she'd managed to develop was insidiously squashed by one of the few college tutors she respected. Perhaps he was justifying his own modest success in life in advising her to lower her sights, telling her with what seemed like the wordly sophistication of an older wiser man which she found irresistible:

> You can only really expect to move so far from where you start; you can only get a certain distance, so don't expect to reach the moon from where you are. Be happy with that and content with that. Join the local Liberal Party, do *The Guardian* crossword.

The dynamics of these three barriers took their toll. Although she was more than capable of going to university, the potential challenge of sparring with her intellectual equals posed too much of a threat to her carefully built defence system. It was different at the small college. As part of her daily performance there as a brilliant philosopher, she produced what she described as 'deep unanswerable questions' with which she taunted her teachers, though not her fellow-students, who she rather disregarded. I found that trying to follow her non-stop, undisciplined flow of words was like chasing a zigzagging rabbit throwing me, the pursuer, off the scent.

Gail graduated from college with a good but not the best degree, because, as she stressed in her Career Gifted mode:

> I didn't do any work for it. I could have got a first-class degree, but I didn't realise how easy it was until I'd done the exams.

Her deep defences made it difficult for Gail to make progress in a career and earn a living. For more than a year after qualifying, she attempted to find a teaching job, but somehow never made it past the first interview. There were always 'reasons', such as not knowing how to interview, not being able to drive, or that it was obviously an inside appointment.

Memory plays strange tricks, which is why autobiography sometimes has to be taken with a pinch of salt. So many times in this very long study, I could see that the backwards look was not always accurate. Gail, in her forties, had completely forgotten – or repressed – dominant forces in her childhood, which I had carefully audio-recorded and documented at the time. She told me earnestly:

> I didn't have a clue that I was gifted, and that cluelessness has probably been largely the reason for the cross I bear. I failed to notice the plot, largely on account of the naivety of my parents.

Her three years at the teacher training college, followed by her year's intense search for a teaching position, were treated with the same defence of denial:

> I never wanted to teach. I don't like what they expect of you nowadays.

Harmony

Once again, in the summer of 2005, I drove across the hills and valleys of the Lake District to see Gail in her beautiful town. She was waiting for me on a bench in the small garden outside her pretty house, watching people walk by.

The sunlight glinted on the flint in its grey stone walls. She welcomed me into her home filled with colour and life. The family – Gail, her husband and their adored son and daughter – lived in harmony and comfort. Her daughter is like her, she told me, 'different' – and a potential genius. They had become firmly middle-class. 'For my daughter, it's something she takes as the norm. We both feel that we are bridging the gap for our kids, and they'll be able to move up a bit further.' The children give her, she said, 'freedom' to think and be herself.

Straight out of college, she'd married a man from a similar background. 'We're a similar age, with similar minds. I'd marry him again tomorrow. We're building a bridge away from that fear of fitting someone else's image of you.' They survived the hard years while he set up his building business, Gail supporting them both financially with short-term unskilled jobs, as well as doing the housework in the evenings.

Since she'd left school, Gail had suffered from clinical depression. When she was at college, she'd told me:

> I can't help myself crying if I'm depressed. It's a natural reaction. But I can't stop it. I can cry and cry and really get myself into a state, and then I stop and sort it out; then the depression will just go. I'm never going to be happy until I've got what I want, which is a very small farmhouse with a farmer. That's all I want, with a four-poster bed to make love in. I want to make my four-poster bed and carve it and make my patchwork quilt, and build the house too, stone by stone.

As Gail neared 40, the sudden death of her mother triggered panic attacks. Gail went to a psychiatrist:

> I felt like a sponge that hadn't been squeezed out properly. He gave me Prozac. It enabled me to stand back from myself, to see things clearly – truths that I was afraid of and couldn't really acknowledge. I don't need to be afraid of them now.

She still has her philosophical approach to life, and has come a very long way in understanding herself:

> Most things were and still are a mystery to me. I'm very naive, oblivious to a lot of things. I live a bit in my own world. I was ashamed of being vain. I was afraid of failure and of being hurt. I had a wall round me. But I've found that if you can accept everyone else truly and honestly, you can accept yourself. It's dawning on me that if I really do want to achieve the best, well, I can. It's something I've always been told, but that penny never really completely dropped until now. If you just start climbing a mountain one foot after the other, you'll eventually get to the top. It's about getting over that feeling that you can't do it.
>
> I'm just really happy. I've moved from being less aware than the average person, to being more aware. We've both become different people. My husband is doing very well. I practise my fiddle every day, and any child that comes to the house, I hand it to them and say, 'Here, play this,' and they all have a go. I show them how I pull my finger up the string as they bow it and it makes different notes. The house is very, very me. People come in and say – 'Wow, what a house!' And our children know that. The house has got personality that they breathe in.
>
> I love dancing; I pick my children up and dance them round the room. The world's just a big exciting kind of place and you can do absolutely anything you want. I've got absolutely 100 per cent security – financial and love – and I'm not taken for granted. We have fun and we laugh a lot together. We can resolve problems because we've both learned to listen to each other. We're just best mates. I no longer expect him to be my dream husband.
>
> You remember what I said about wanting a four-poster, well, it struck me the other day that that's what everyone wants isn't it. That's what I wanted – and that's what we've got.

Gail owns her own business making sweet English puddings for the many little hotels, tourist shops and walkers in the Lake District. She has rented a room to cook in and set up a website. Her mouth-watering range includes date and sticky toffee, chocolate and damson, chocolate and cherry, and cranberry and orange. She delights in discovering still more creative gifts in herself that neither she nor anyone else could have imagined.

If I'd stopped seeing Gail at the point of her leaving primary school, she would have been a great success story, a gifted child who had been given great new opportunities. Had I stopped when she was 16 and had just left the grammar school, she could have been described as a gifted underachiever, and stayed that way right through until she was about 40. It has taken Gail three decades to get rid of her distorting childhood mental barriers. My long-term research has shown once more how the ups and downs of fate can affect the development of natural gifts and talents. For Gail, the label of 'gifted' given to her as a child had been, she said, 'the bane of my life'. In her maturity, she delights in her family, her greatest success. Her final release came through her children who, she said, didn't know about the label – and loved her for herself.

Mental barriers from other people

Whereas Gail's barriers to her gifted fulfilment were in her own mind, the more dangerous barrier to Philip Bessant's was in the mind of an authority – his doctor. Like other gifted children with physical disability, or learning disabilities such as dyslexia, he was at serious risk of being denied a suitable education. His narrow escape from his doctor's diagnosis of physical – and mental – incapacity was entirely due to the extraordinary courage and determination of his mother. In fact, several mothers told me similar stories of being ridiculed by the family doctor over their concerns for their children.

Philip had severe spastic problems of muscle control when I first met him at nine years old. We met again when he was a student of 19 and had grown very tall and gangly, with a pale, delicate little-boy face. His movements were clumsy and he had a constant tremor. It took him a long time to make us coffee in his icy university room. He was studying chemistry, a subject needing some fine motor control holding test-tubes over the Bunsen burners. I had to concentrate hard to tune in to what he said because he had difficulty controlling his mouth. He told me that he talked too fast for people to follow, though I suspected they became impatient waiting for the end of his slow, laborious sentences. He also had problems with social relationships, but it was difficult to distinguish how much was due to his personality and how much to his disability.

His mother, still angry after so many years, told me what had happened:

Our doctor had seen Philip going upstairs at about the age of three, first one foot then together, like a younger child. Without any concern, he just turned to me and said, 'You know you've got an ESN (educationally subnormal) child there.' I said, 'He may be anything but he's not ESN,' because there were all sorts of things he could do. Once, when he was under two, he and his grandma weren't speaking because he said a certain car was a Minor and she said it was a Mini! He's probably ten years ahead now of what he would have been if I hadn't seen to it all.

They really didn't know what to make of Philip when they assessed him at the Children's Hospital. Co-ordination-wise he was way down, clumsy, but he'd got great concentration, and was intellectually gifted. I found a remedial teacher, without qualifications, who did a lot for him. I taught him how to write. His worst difficulty was with reading, because he couldn't co-ordinate his eyes along the line, so he was reading encyclopaedias with short lines for the information, but he couldn't manage stories. The school was very kind, but they couldn't understand it.

We chose a private, more disciplined, traditional sort of education, because we felt that with his problems, he would flounder in a free-expression kind of school. He needed to know where he was. At first, the less-able boys teased him, but when he was put with boys of similar ability, he seemed to cope pretty well. His writing was appalling, so the teachers didn't upset him. Most of them used to just tick it, and say, 'Yes, that was fine.' The English master gave him real confidence when he said, 'I don't care how you write; I love your ideas.' Philip did so well with him.

He's helped himself enormously, because he's got determination and discipline. Of course, he can't be sporty, but he doesn't seem to mind that at all. He can hold his own in company, but when the time comes for him to look at jobs, I worry that he's not had enough practice in dealing with people.

Had his brave mother not overridden the doctor's professional advice, little gifted Philip would probably have been sent to a school for slow learners – at least until maybe the teachers found him out. Few children from special schools of any sort achieve, like him, a PhD in instrumentation and analytical science. He was particularly fortunate to receive an excellent science education. This is a valuable way of encouraging intellectual investigation, and working out problems and solutions, in spite of physical limitations. Science suited him perfectly, providing a way for him to be challenged in a creative way, and he has excelled in his specialist field.

When I flew up to see him at home in Scotland, in his mid-forties, he seemed delighted at our reunion. He is working at an extremely high level, researching new automatic catalysis and better computer chips to deal with it. He lives alone in a house he has paid for himself. His once strangled speech has smoothed out somewhat so that he is much easier to listen to. It is rare now, he told me, for anyone to mention his problem. He is tall, good looking, warm and hospitable and we talked for hours. He seemed to have gained a good understanding of himself:

I've had to build up a sort of shield for myself over the years. It's made me very much more of an individual. I'm slightly withdrawn. I don't enjoy parties, or pubs or restaurants much. Makes me different. A handful of boys at school teased me until I was about 15 or 16, but they were the sort of boys who'd always have found somebody else to pick on. I've always been too big to bully – I was 6 foot 5 by the time I left school, and had already realised that I was gay.

At my age, I'm an old maid. I did the whole gay scene thing and I found it tremendously superficial. It's all about looks and personality, and nobody wants to know you once you've had your thirtieth birthday. It's basically for picking up. I'm not pretending to be any different to everybody who is out there looking for the 20 year old. There just aren't enough young ones to go round. My sexuality doesn't actually make very much difference. My own space is essential to my happiness and I'm content with my own company. It's the way I am.

A gifted person can have learning difficulties

A gifted individual can have disabilities which interfere with the development of their bodies and minds. Unfortunately, very many with problems like Philip's have to spend so much time coping with their immediate physical troubles that their intellectual development can be neglected. Often, too, those who are specially trained to help people like him see the physical problem as the first priority and care for any gifts trails behind.

Philip, with his combination of gifted intellect and physical problems, is called doubly or multiply exceptional. His problems show in muscle control, but others have sensory problems like blindness, or chronic illnesses such as epilepsy or asthma. Gifted people can also have learning problems, such as dyslexia, which last for life. Many have a combination of such problems, any of which can cause the gifted to underachieve.

For a small child, so much depends on adult decisions, the effects of which can last a lifetime. Philip's doctor, the respected medical authority, diagnosed the toddler's unusual way of climbing the stairs as a symptom of an untreatable condition – with a poor mental prognosis – and

suggested putting him in a 'home'. But his mother perceived her little son's stair-climbing method in a completely
different light – not as a mental disability, but as a sign of
his giftedness in beating his physical disability – using his
brain to great advantage.

Philip's disability had made it difficult for him to learn
through normal babyhood physical exploration, but his
mother recognised his great memory, his curiosity and his
keenness to learn. Even as a small boy, she said, he'd had a
dry sense of humour and an outstandingly mature insight
into his condition. Her unquestioning faith in him and the
opportunities she provided for him are not always there,
alas, for other children with similar conditions. Every day,
as a grown man, Philip appreciated what she had done for
him. He well knew:

No matter how unlucky I am – I am very lucky compared
to lots and lots of other people.

Professor Diane Montgomery, of Middlesex University,
London, has worked for years with gifted disabled people
and provides practical details in her book, *Able, Gifted and
Talented Underachievers*. Underachievement, she says,
means that gifted potential is not fully realised, which can
be true at any time in life. Underachievement comes from
many causes. The gifted, for example, may refuse to work
hard enough to achieve well because they feel the job is
beneath them, or that it is too boring to bother with.
Philip's life has shown that underachievement is not
inevitable when there are physical problems, though the
fulfillment of his gifts was more difficult and took longer.
But what a gifted disabled child might receive by way of
encouragement and opportunity is to some extent a matter
of chance.

There is a difference, though, between underachievers
and non-producers. Underachievers often submit to the
obstacle of low self-esteem and emotional distress. One way
or another, they feel useless, and often feel ashamed that
other people can see it. Non-producers, on the other hand,
are confident. They positively choose not to conform, but

can achieve perfectly well in any direction when they decide to make the effort.

It is important to reiterate that gifts do not develop all by themselves. They need help, as Philip was fortunate to receive. In his maturity, he provides a fine example of a man with multiple exceptionality, who with the right support has made a highly successful life. Philip and his mother can teach the world to be perceptive about the intellectual as well as the physical side of an exceptional child's life, to never to give up hope for the best outcome and to think positively.

11

A gifted gambler

I like gambling and I'm good at it.

Ady Toms

I never wanted to know my teachers, I just wanted the instruction.

Mark Harrison

One grey winter's day in 1993 in the old industrial city of Nottingham, Adrian Toms saw an advertisement for Thailand. It exploded with colour and promise of adventure. There would be hot sun, hot sex, flowing booze and unending fun. He looked at his life as a milkman, with its severe discipline and distorted hours of work. Every morning he fought warm sleep to rise in the dismal gloom of the early hours, running hard around the icy suburbs to put his bottles of milk on doorsteps, falling exhausted into bed by eight o'clock, which cut out almost all his social life. The money was good, but his relationship with his long-term girlfriend was fading. He was 30 years old, big, handsome, healthy and highly intelligent. He sold up his milk-round and headed for hedonism.

I'd measured Adrian's intelligence as within the top 2 per cent of the population when he was eight. He could have excelled at just about anything he fancied. As a young boy, he was sweetly sensitive to language and wrote poetry for himself. Also being strongly built and good at sport, that too could have been his life. But a deep restlessness beset him and so many other things lured him, one more powerfully than everything else – gambling.

Stirrings for the betting life began when he was small and by the time he reached high school he felt it had always been part of him. Nothing on the school curriculum could compare with its special buzz. He is a big, cheery, handsome man who jokes about his academic ignorance and inability to study. Not for him the dry life of books and paper. For Adrian, it's the thrill of the game.

Home life

According to his father, Adrian had been emotionally disturbed by the culmination of not less than three generations of unhappiness, demonstrated by his gambling. On the surface it was plausible; disturbance in families does happen across generations. The British royal family is a well-documented example of disturbed parents producing disturbed children who pass this on to their own offspring. But this off-loading blame on to dead great-grandparents did not ring true. The everyday lies and anger, and the tempestuous marriage which eventually broke up, had severely crippled little Adrian's feelings of security, as well as the development of his high-level intellectual and creative potential.

Even when Adrian was only ten, his mother had told me how she blamed her several attempted suicides entirely on him, her only son. Without any change in her voice or any apparent concern, she added, 'I detested him when he was little.'

Adrian's father was a pale, sad-faced man, who believed that because his son had an extremely high IQ it should automatically have brought his boy a personal magnanimity and maturity beyond anything that would have been expected of a normal youngster – or adult for that matter. Adrian was in a no-win situation. On the basis of his outstanding intellect, his father had set him up in a situation of conflicting expectations – damned if you do and damned if you don't.

By the age of eight, Adrian was expected to fulfil the role of a mature and kindly priest who would close his eyes to normal moral principles and provide his parents with absolution if not an actual blessing for their chaotic relationship. At the same time, he was expected to be highly achieving at school. Adrian failed at both, being neither a child-priest nor a fine scholar. Not only had Adrian rejected his parents' life-style, his father complained, but worse, he had spoken up against it.

When Adrian was a young teenager, I sat alone with his father in the front room of his pleasant red-brick home in a leafy suburb. He looked at me through pale mournful eyes while he spoke of his deep disappointment in his son. Patiently, in his sorrowful droning voice, he explained what he'd hoped for:

I'd rather expected Adrian's intelligence to help him understand his mother and her problems, and he did try until he went bitter and he still can't forgive. To an outsider, the life my wife led was pretty unforgivable; I have the most enormous amount of tolerance, which bordered on stupidity. The basic cause was that there were so many men in her life, mainly because, poor girl, she was too damn good-looking. Adrian couldn't take it. It was he who eventually said to her, 'You can't stay here and have that fellow; it's got to be dad or him.' 'Well, you can't tell me what to do,' she said, and off she went. He's been desperately unhappy since then. I know that fathers and sons don't often get to talk to each other very deeply, but I have managed to talk to him a couple of times.

He used to have so much imagination as a child; I gloried in his humour and his wit. When he was very young he'd read and written a lot, but in his first weeks at the secondary school, a most dreadful English teacher made him look a fool in front of the class. She ripped up the poem that he'd worked so hard over, saying that it wasn't on the subject she'd asked for. He never wrote another thing; stopped absolutely, even reading for pleasure. I was appalled because his imagination still shone through.

Adrian's father's body language told me how very sorry he felt for himself. He was a man of average height, dressed all in grey. As he spoke, he slumped forward, hands clasped together on his lap, the top of his head of thinning grey hair often directed towards me looking hard at his shoes, sometimes glancing up to meet my eyes. He was a victim, he told me, and no-one else could ever understand his point of view, which made it all the harder for him to bear. It wasn't because of any fault in his own character that he'd had to tolerate other men in his marital bed having sex with his wife on a fairly regular basis. It was due to his true and noble love for her, he explained, because 'she was a woman of extraordinary beauty.'

Adrian, in his mid-forties, can look back with some objectivity:

> I can see three themes in my life. The need for an impossible level of perfection, the unquenchable need to feel loved – I once referred to myself as an emotional vampire – and the desire to be emotionally unfaithful to a girlfriend before she has the chance to be unfaithful to me. I find it hard to fully trust most individuals and I *never* trust groups or institutions. In fact, I delight in behaving deviantly towards any large organisation.
>
> Maybe it's all been part of some Oedipus-style saga. My dad felt threatened by me when I was still very young and my mum has confessed that she had an unhealthy attraction towards me as a boy. She used to give me soft porn magazines as Christmas presents, for example. Indeed, immediately after I lost my virginity at 14 she lost interest in me completely and soon after moved to the other end of the country. My mother left and returned on several occasions when I was a child.

Adrian was in a constant state of mental pain. His potential to gain high marks at school seemed irrelevant. Every day when he returned home he faced his morose father and blatantly sexy mother. By 17 he knew well that life at home was relentlessly eating away at his feelings of self-worth. There had to be some other way to live. He could not give his parents the respect they felt was their due, and had told me bitterly:

> I suppose I stored it inside, which is what gave me all the trouble and guilt later on. I used to get very intense bouts of anger. It ended up once in my taking a few tablets, tranquillisers and booze, or I'd zoom off on my motorbike as fast as it could go. I used to get a terrible feeling of desperation. I always thought of myself as very mature at school and yet I acted very immaturely, but I have eventually developed through the trauma, learned through experience.

Not surprisingly, Adrian's school achievements were way below his gifted potential. He knew that he had ability; his teachers knew it too and did what they could. He felt that he was watching at a distance as his educational chances slipped through his fingers. He dearly wanted to have a father like everyone else's, and told me:

> My dad cherished the way that I dealt with English; he loved the stories I wrote. I still love writing, though, and I do some when I can get round to it. In junior school we were told to write a book, to take a week, and I filled about three books in a day. But it wasn't what the teacher wanted, so to make sure that everybody else was more diligent, she read it out then ripped it up in front of everybody, with some of my funny poems too, which everybody else had appreciated. She ripped them up to general amusement. If I'd say anything that the teacher didn't know about, I'd be seen as a real Smart Alec, and she wouldn't ask me again.
>
> It was better later on. The teachers at my comprehensive school were very supportive and encouraging. It was much more than I deserved. They tried everything, even ringing me up at home. I really let them down and I still feel guilty. I was amazed to pass my A-levels, because I hadn't turned up for months, so I decided to take them again to improve my marks. I went to ask the headmaster, but he treated it as a joke. I didn't blame him. It knocked me back, though, so that's how I

ended up on the dole [welfare] for the best part of a year when I was 18. It was terrible and I reckoned that anything was going to be better than that.

An attempt to follow the straight and narrow

I enrolled at the polytechnic and left after a year by mutual consent. I'd picked the wrong course: history of art, design and film, and I couldn't draw a stick-man or name ten painters or one designer – I'd never even heard of Turner then. The only thing I knew was ten films that John Wayne had starred in, and what Captain Kirk did in *Star Trek*. I met my fiancée there, so it did do something for me, but not education-wise.

That was it. Adrian made no more attempts at formal education. He had to earn some money. There was rent to be paid for his four-roomed terraced house and a living to be earned to keep him and his fiancée, who'd also dropped out of higher education. He went for a highly structured, physically demanding job which didn't allow much time for thought or feeling. He brought milk, juice and eggs – sweet nourishment – to hundreds of still sleepy families. Milk, the food of innocent babes that he'd enjoyed in a time before his rejections.

I was very, very lucky to get this job as a milkman. I'd go into the Job Centre and they'd say, 'You've had no experience,' and also I was competing with cheap 16 year olds. Fortunately, I knew someone who recommended me – and it's not temporary. I've enjoyed the job a lot. It's a physical release. I can run everywhere, and the faster I go, the faster I'm done. I've got the afternoons free to myself, though I'm zonked out by eight at night – I'm up at half-three in the morning. I must have a good memory, because this is only my sixth week and I can remember most of the people in over 400 houses.

It's a pretty weird situation: I'm driving a milk-float round and worrying about what time I'm going to get finished today. How can that be so structured and so definite on this planet, and yet on all the other millions of planets, you've got a simple little amoeba floating around in space? It's such an imbalance. I get so wound up with all the thoughts and theories. It's very much easier to get back to today, driving the milk-float around, and trying to get finished by 10am. So I concentrate on that.

For the first time, Adrian put his many gifts and talents into action. In four years he rose swiftly from employee through self-employed franchisee to independent operator. The more milk he delivered, the more he earned. His personal challenge was to deliver the greatest number of bottles between midnight and 8.00am. His yearning for risk, his love of physical activity and his obsessive nature combined to set him off every day. He called himself a 'manic milko' with this efficiency plan:

Everything had to be streamlined to save time, so I studied the best method of loading the float every morning, sometimes even drawing a blueprint. No time to pick up broken bottles. Not much of a problem until you take a corner too quickly and shed 100 full bottles. No time to stop though.

I carried a small oil can to use on any sticky gates that might hinder my progress.

No kind of mechanical malfunction would matter, including loss of brakes, unless it prevented the vehicle moving in both directions. I had to run at the highest possible speed over the shortest distance between doorsteps; flowerbeds, bushes and fences beware. I'd ignore any traffic regulations that would cause me to slow down. A policeman was once astonished to watch me drive through three red lights in a row.

Everything had to be memorised, so no time was wasted opening a book or writing.

Twenty years passed

In spite of my great efforts, not least phoning every Adrian Toms in the land (not unlike the prince searching for

Cinderella) and explaining patiently to each startled man what I was after, I lost track of 'my' Adrian for the next 20 years. His father, in a rare act of paternal concern, had made him join Gamblers Anonymous, and anonymous it was. His telephone number was not anywhere I could find it, even if I'd known roughly where he was living. All normal routes were closed, but now there was the internet, so I tried Friends Reunited. Two months later, in August 2005, he replied – from Thailand. Still cheerful and open, we spoke for hours on the phone and have since regularly exchanged many a long e-mail. He wrote, 'I was going to come back to the UK to seek psychological help so you are saving me a fortune!' Not easy without eye contact and body language, but he sent me many photos and it seemed to work. He has a quirky, lively mind, a fine use of words, and is a delight to correspond with. I was glad to know more about this gifted man who now called himself Ady.

Strangely, at about the same time and in the same way as I'd rediscovered Adrian, I found his equally gifted class-mate, Mark Harrison, who I'd also lost for 20 years. Each was glad to be put in touch with the other again. Adrian considered Mark to be one of the most naturally clever people he'd ever met, writing: 'Mark was very level-headed for a teenager. In an odd way, maybe that worked against him because he was seldom given credit by the teachers for having such a good brain.'

I'd measured these two friends as having identical gifted intelligence, but each had used his in a diametrically opposite way. Where Ady had rebelled, Mark had striven to conform. Unlike Ady, Mark's home life was highly directed but to him it seemed crushing. When he was 21 and at university, I'd written this about him:

> The nasty crop of acne which Mark was enduring cannot have helped him in his unkind world. He said he did have a friend once. His intense reserve was off-putting to anyone who would have liked to get to know him, and he lacked some basic social graces – such as offering me coffee during the three hours of the freezing morning we were together in his university room. Like Mark, his

father was a scientist and a man of firm views, especially about the roles of males and females. His mother was a housewife, who, I noticed, always waited for her husband to speak first.

Any teacher would have recognised high-scoring Mark as gifted and would have recommended him for special gifted classes, had there been any available. Instead, he'd been shot into the easier and cheaper route of acceleration. He was grade-skipped by two years, thus missing all the preparation and building up of learning skills and the understanding that those two lost years would have given him. There was no regard for the development of his social skills. He was simply thrown in at the deep end without any counselling or special educational help. The one sure thing he knew, though, was to study hard and to memorise his learning. Disregarding his fellows and keeping his nose to the grindstone he managed to overcome the gap in his school learning caused by his acceleration. He gained a first-class honours degree as a teenager, and by 22 he had been granted his PhD. An outstanding feat.

But no matter how hard he worked, no matter what academic accolades he laid tenderly at his father's feet, Mark told me he felt that nothing was deemed good enough. Sadly, each of his scholarly successes seemed to turn to dust in his hands. He had to aim higher and higher in his search for what he felt would bring him his father's pride. But he was running out of academic qualifications to aim for and was seriously worried that he wouldn't be able to keep up the hard pace he'd known all his life.

As he left formal education at 22, Mark was well built and in the prime of his young manhood. But he was withdrawn, caught in a mild state of depression and anxiety. Long ago, he'd stopped thinking beyond the work he had to do to gain his next qualification. When I asked him how he imagined the future, I drew a blank. He couldn't even muster some youthful optimism about the world. His work methods, even at school, were dogged, immature and without a hint of imagination. He didn't use his gifted brain to challenge ideas. His fear of getting things wrong and his desire to conform and please had pushed him into the work methods of a less able pupil. Although he read assiduously around a subject, he would note the details in his tiny script, summarising it over and over until he understood it. It was information, examination fodder, that he craved. He told me:

> I never wanted to know my teachers, I just wanted the instruction.

During Mark's doctoral studies, he'd slipped further into isolation, sliding closer and closer towards the stereotype of the backroom scientist; poring over microscope slides by day and returning alone to his student room at night. He never took any steps to alleviate his emotional pain. I felt him sinking lower into his abyss:

> I feel alienated; maybe I'm too sensitive. If people like me, I don't understand why, though I don't usually notice other people's reactions, and anyway, nobody's ever told me anything about myself. I give up very easily in social life, probably because I never concentrate on what people say. I just watch them talking. I know I'm selfish and negative, and a bit of a snob as well. I may be 21, but I don't think I've grown up yet.
>
> Getting depressed holds you back. I spend my time on my own really. It's getting worse, and I don't always know that I'm going to come out of it. It's especially bad because I'm not in an environment where I'm forced into contact with people, so I have to go out to find them. If I'm thrown together with somebody, I get on with them alright, like I might go out to the pub, unless of course I'm feeling depressed. It's quite a while since I felt angry. I feel disillusioned, and I've given up wondering why I'm here because it just depresses me.

The fathers and their sons

For both Ady and Mark, it was their extremely high potential which seemed to have set off negative reactions in their fathers. Doubtless unconsciously, both men had ensured that their sons felt themselves to be failures. The two fathers had done this by setting the achievement stakes at such a high level that it was impossible for either boy to reach them. It was as if the fathers were saying – 'Oh, you think you're so clever; let's see if you can jump high enough to get through this hoop' – while holding it high above the young boys' reach.

In the mid-1950s, David McClelland, Harvard Professor of Psychology, showed how children react to such out-of-reach goals set for them by others. Their inevitable failure is felt as a deep personal fault in not trying hard enough. Parents of gifted children may make unjustifiable assumptions from a child's gifts in one area of development such as early reading, to expect high achievement in science. The child is faced with impossible and painful expectations. It's a labour of Sisyphus, the king in Greek mythology who is sentenced to push a boulder up a hill forever, because every time he struggles to get it to the top it rolls down again.

For each of these boys, his father's out-of-reach goal was very different. Adrian's father tried to use his son's gifts to provide emotional absolution for his own and his wife's immoral behaviour. Mark's father wanted his son to bring him more academic credit than any gifted child could manage. Each boy had a different personality and so had reacted differently to the impossible goals they'd been set. Adrian took the biggest gamble of his life by rejecting not only the chaos of his family but also his excellent educational opportunities. Mark, a more subdued character, dared not fight, and instead shut down his thoughts and feelings in obedient scholarship, striving with all his great intelligence and young strength to satisfy his father's unsatisfiable ambitions.

Other fathers in this sample had also felt threatened by their son's gifts. Poignantly, two had walked out on their families just weeks before their sons took their important school-leaving A-level exams. One was even a college lecturer who knew so well how important that time was for his son. At 15 the boy had told me:

I hadn't known he was going to go. He just said, 'It's like this, son, I'm going away.' It wasn't particularly good timing, but he wasn't going to ruin my chances – they were more important. I retreated into my room into my revision, and it probably made me do more work.

The shock had been terrible for the two deserted families. Fortunately, both those boys had strong personalities and survived that deep blow, though now in adulthood they admit it knocked their confidence in relationships. One of the two deserted mothers told me quite explicitly:

One of the chief reasons for him leaving was having a son who's bigger, stronger, cleverer and generally more socially effective than himself.

Such fathers are abusers, and for these boys the abuse was triggered by the child's gifts. Each shining boy in this situation acts as a mirror to his father, but the father cannot cope with the difference between his self-image and his son's. Fathers have different ways of dealing with this. Where one tries to bask in his son's reflection for his own glory, another attempts to devalue his son's image so that his own looks better, while another runs away from the threatening situation.

Adrian and Mark were their fathers' victims, and although each reacted in his own way, for both their emerging sense of self was damaged. In the short and the long term, both fathers had been successful in blunting their gifted sons' lives and happiness.

The dark secret

Ady's father's abuse was spread more widely though than only directed towards his gifted son. The man had also been systematically destroying the life of Ady's only sibling, his non-gifted half-sister. Her step-dad wasn't aiming for her mind, though, but her young body.

How devoted a husband he had seemed, so convincingly playing the angelic martyr to his wife's sexual largesse, until he was suddenly and shockingly exposed as a preda-tor. The revelation came when Ady and his sister were in their forties and their father was 70 and failing in physical and mental health. His wife said she'd discovered by chance that he'd been sexually abusing her daughter since the little girl was three and a half years old. The mother, in her self-centred way, had not been paying much attention. The girl's ordeal had continued until she left home at 15. Now a wife and mother herself, she tries to push the events of her childhood out of her mind and doesn't want to talk about it. Ady was shaken at the discovery:

> I sat and thought about it very deeply, and my mum and I talked a lot. I could see things that had happened 20 or 30 years previously very differently: why certain comments were made, how they were made, certain actions, I understand them more fully now. My dad had a stronger motivation than blinding love for my mum. He wanted to keep her and my sister happy so that they didn't fight, and the awful truth didn't come blurting out during an argument. It explained things in a somewhat grotesque way.
>
> My sister had turned to the wrong people. She'd said something to a friend of the family years ago, and even her natural father had known and done nothing. My mum overheard something from this so-called friend, but didn't believe it. My mum then confronted my sister who told my mum about her sexual abuse by my father in some detail. She remembered the house where the abuse had first taken place when she was so little.
>
> My mum feels hugely guilty that she hadn't been a good wife and all that kind of thing. My dad was keen for my mum to be the villain, so that nobody ever looked too deeply at what *he* did. My mum and I went through a 180 degrees turnaround out of the blue. We'd always been at each other's throats, and now she wasn't such a villain after all. It seems that we were the only people who weren't aware of what he'd been doing. The twist is that if I inherited any serious moral deficiencies, they weren't from my mum as I'd always suspected but instead they

came from my father – not that I've ever been sexually attracted to children in any way. It completely redefined everybody's attitude to everybody else.

My dad ruined my relationship with my sister because looking back she was always very wary of me, especially when she had a daughter. There was always a distance between us, as though I was guilty.

Dad admitted it: he was obviously terrified by his huge guilt. He was deteriorating and my mum was taking care of him, getting him dressed and feeding him and all things like that when she had this huge sudden hatred of him, and that was very difficult for her. There was absolutely no point shouting and screaming or doing anything, because this was a man who was shortly going to die. There was no point getting a whip out and beating him with it, however you felt. He had a stroke and after a few months in hospital, passed away. My mum had to carry on and deal with the cards she'd been dealt. She was there to comfort him and hold his hand and everything. It just seemed the only thing to do.

There's one benefit: I don't feel so guilty at having underachieved at school. Suffice it to say that the role I played as a teenager suited my father. He never said much to me, but one story he was fond of repeating was about the sword of Damocles. He said over and over that it was hanging around, which was slightly odd, even to me as a child. It's easy to see now that my dad thought of himself as Damocles and that the imaginary sword above his head was the punishment awaiting him if he was ever found out. I am almost sure that he never felt a personal moral guilt for being a paedophile. There was some evidence that he had suffered some sexual abuse as a young child himself.

Now in her seventies, Ady's mum lives in harmony with an old friend and her 48-year-old new lover. Ady no longer blames his mother for his troubled childhood. 'My mum, my sister and I were puppets and my dad was pulling all the strings; he was devious beyond belief.'

Doomed to disappoint

As a small boy, gifted Mark soon learned, not only of his
father's extremely high expectations, but the sting of
failure attached to every effort he made to please him and
his mother who went along with all of it. He told me about
it in his forties, when he was a father himself:

> My parents are still not satisfied with what I've achieved.
> I would think they thought that my brother [who has a
> high rank in the army] was more successful. They're
> quite difficult; they never seem to be satisfied, always
> moaning and groaning. I've given up caring actually. I
> don't mind sitting quietly just watching the world go by. I
> don't get bored. From my parents – ah, how can you put
> this – there was never a positive assertion of my being
> good at anything. I was never good enough.
>   I tend to be self-deprecating. I had a terrible self-
> confidence problem, but I'm getting over it now, having
> had children myself and grown up. Throughout my life,
> I've preferred my own company to other people's, because
> I never feel I fit in or belong. I was always worrying about
> what other people were thinking about me. So I always
> found it much easier to just not interact socially. When I
> first got married and we'd go out with friends, I'd come
> back with this terrible sort of self-examination – 'Oh, why
> did I say that?' But now I've ceased to care so much about
> what people think.
>   Part of it was that I was never allowed to fail. But I
> never had good school reports throughout my junior
> school: I used to get hell for that. It got better as I got to
> secondary school, but you know it was always, 'could do
> better, could try harder', and all the rest of it. It was just
> not good enough, as far as my father was concerned. He
> was very strong. I don't know why he wanted what he
> wanted from me. I was always scared of my father, no two
> ways about it. He used to shout. He had a terrible temper.
> All my life he made me feel small. Mother kept out of the
> way. She certainly didn't stick up for us. No. I used to get
> the brunt of it. I don't like blaming my father, because I

still have certain personality traits similar to him with my own children, which makes me feel absolutely terrible.

Ady went for gambling

Ady had attended Gamblers Anonymous (GA) groups for 12 years. In December 1993 he became the youngest person to ever receive a ten-year diamond pin from GA for complete abstinence from gambling – the only institutional prize in his life:

> I would have been attracted to gambling under any circumstances. There were no role models for me to follow into gambling, far from it. Nobody around me had any connection with gambling.

I saw it very differently. Because of the very long and intimate style I'd used in this study, I could see how he was induced into gambling, and how early his addiction to adrenaline had started. One way that Ady's parents had demonstrated their love for him was by placing a small bet for him each year on the Grand National (horse race). It gave him attention that he craved and he found it satisfying and exciting. He was able to associate that early gambling with feeling good, and he wanted more of it. When Ady read this chapter, he changed his mind completely. He said he saw then how the subtle influences of his upbringing had formed him and his outlook. 'It was all true,' he said.

Ady's own first stumble into gambling began when he lost all his pocket-money in an amusement arcade at five or six years old. Soon after, his grandmother suggested they wager 5p on the outcome of the Oxford and Cambridge University boat race. He picked Oxford and won. He told me:

> Each time I encountered gambling as a young child I was energised by it. At age seven I was given a pound to go to the cinema. When I got there, the film had started already, so I went across the road to play in the

amusement parlour. I started putting pennies into an
elaborate machine and was thrilled each time as I waited
to see if I'd won or lost. As there were 240 old pennies in a
pound, it took me quite a while to lose all the money, but
once I'd started, I couldn't stop. I was fixed to the spot,
even though I soon realised that all the money was going
to be lost.

Serious compulsive gambling came at 13 when he discovered that because he was tall he could pass as an 18
year old to get illegally into betting shops (bookies). He lost
money every day for two weeks after his first bet. A pattern
was taking shape:

While I was still 16 and at school, I got a job as a board-
marker in a local bookies. I often lost my wages before I
even earned them! Then I got a better-paid job in another
bookies, this time working up to four afternoons a week. I
loved it. I had money to gamble every week and I was
mixing socially in the betting shop with the fathers of the
kids I was at school with – very exciting. That all ended
after the bookies was taken over and the new owner
dropped my wages without even telling me. I got back at
him in the last week I worked there by organising a sting
with a couple of school mates. I 'after-timed' a football bet
and ended up sending in a pal to collect £600.
     That was a lot of money in 1980, because most of my
teachers were probably only earning £100 a week. I can
remember the look on the games teacher's face the next
week, when he asked all the boys for their valuables for
safe-keeping. All the other lads handed in their conkers,
marbles and watches – and I gave him 200 quid.
     The only useful thing I did with the money was buy
my mum a Barry Manilow LP [not that useful then!]; I
lost all the rest in a fortnight. I was completely hooked on
gambling by then; I would even memorise horse-form and
write it out in my school books during lessons. After I left
the second bookies, I worked at up to five part-time jobs a
week. Anything, so I could get the cash to gamble. My
father could see the way I was going, and after I stole

some of his money to go to the local dog track, he decided
he'd had enough, and in May 1981 he took me to
Gamblers Anonymous.

One of the problems for anyone who escapes into a gambling dream world is that before long the gambler has
handed over responsibility for his mood. Win and he is
happy, lose and he is sad, in spite of anything else that
might be happening in his life. Ady was the same:

I built up my milk business until I separated from my
girlfriend in 1993, then sold out, took what was left of the
proceeds and ran off to Thailand. Since then I've been
ducking and diving and I've gone broke a few times but
I've had a great time, basically trying to live a Hugh
Heffner lifestyle on a Homer Simpson budget. I came
back to the UK last summer to see if I could make any
money on the poker circuit. I didn't have much success,
but undaunted, I headed off to Vegas. I ended up winning
26 tournaments in three months and whilst most wins
were only a few thousand dollars, I did manage to snare
one first prize of $44k at the Imperial Palace. Apart from
that, I gamble on the internet from my base in Thailand.
I used to run a book locally in the bars, until I got busted
by the police.

In a cold, emotionless way, it is possible to marvel at
places like Las Vegas where every nut, bolt and light bulb
in the entire city is focused on one thing, getting the
gambler to lose all his money. If a person has any
potential to be a gambler, then that already slippery slope
has been treated with some super-special grease to
hasten their descent. Each brand of gambler, from those
addicted to slot machines, to horse betters, to casino
junkies, has their own identifiable personalities, but
above all, gambling is an escape from everyday life.

I definitely feel different from everybody else. I can't
bear normality. I'm clever in some ways, but
horrendously stupid in others. I can't stand doing things
I've no interest in, so I go to enormous lengths to avoid
them. That's why just walking on my milk-round was

unacceptable: I had to run hard to make a dull, repetitive job into something dramatic, to see what was possible. When you interviewed me as a milko, I was taking home £120 for a seven-day week; four years later, I was taking home £1,000 for a six-day week.

Ady's addiction to adrenaline

When Ady bought a one-way ticket to a life far from everything he'd known, he settled in Pattaya, Thailand, as he said:

> a twin town for Sodom and Gomorrah, though Pattaya has 'raised the bar' for towns wishing to incur biblical-style destruction. It's a 24/7 full-on action hell hole that makes Las Vegas feel quaint!

In 1998 he had a *mia looung*, first wife (who he married in Germany) and a *mia noi*, 'small' wife. At night they shared the same bed, although both wives had their own apartments to retreat to if they got fed up. This arrangement worked, he says, pretty well for four years. First wife had a daughter who lived with her Thai husband and their little son in their home village. This made Ady a step-grandfather.

Days were spent gambling, going to the gym, reading and writing poetry. Evening entertainment was the company of the 'bar girls', slender-hipped young Thai beauties who sell their favours. Then back to relax at home with his wives. He knows he has obsessive-compulsive tendencies, and paranoia is not far away:

> I'm too fond of being anxious. I hate being controlled, even by my own emotions, so instead of retreating from uncertainty, I seek it out. How can the future frighten me if I deliberately and independently raise the stakes myself? I've been in Thailand for most of the last 12 years and during the first few, I had sex with a large number of women, always unprotected. I put myself in

so much danger of becoming HIV-positive that I stopped having sex with my first wife, so the risk was mine more than hers.

The stakes Ady has set himself are life-threatening. Sigmund Freud, in his theory of psychoanalysis, included a death wish, Thanatos, which he said everyone had. It is a desire to give up the struggle of life and enter the peace of the grave. He argued that all our lives we do things unwittingly to bring about our own deaths. Critics say that this is not proven, but Ady is a prize example of it.

Ady craves the thrill and excitement that comes with risk and that lifts him out of everyday life. Addicts must have more and more of their addiction to get the buzz they are after. What would the actual pay-off be if Ady did get full-blown AIDS – misery and pain – but followed by the peace of death? Staking your life is a symptom of depression. There are very many ways of putting an end to one's life not all of which are obvious, like driving recklessly or guzzling food to dangerous levels of obesity. Unprotected sex in a known danger zone is another.

When it comes at the right time, a one-off event in childhood, such as a dog bite or an unexpected kindness, can affect the rest of a life. It seems that Ady's grandma did that for him. She offered him a tasty bite of the forbidden fruit thereby giving him her 'psychological permission' to gamble. She conspired with him and encouraged him into it. She was a significant figure in his life. But his parents contributed so much more. Both of them were living very risky lives at home every single day. Ady lived in a pervading atmosphere of risk. As a highly intelligent and sensitive boy he picked this up. Risk was a familiar feeling: it was what he'd always known.

The early satisfactions which told Ady he was loved encouraged him to gamble. He soon learned to look forward to the emotional lift that the sweet surge of adrenaline produced. It helped him to counter the chaos at home and to repress the other feelings that he didn't like, such as regularly disappointing both his parents. Though depression did take over for a while in his teenage years, he has a strong spirit which has kept him going well. Ady's way out has been to take life on the wing. Stability and planning ahead for years were not for him. A swift bet and its result took his mind off all else, at least for a little while. But strong forces are still at work:

I don't try to control the demons that make me a compulsive gambler. I know what their powers are and where they live and I try not to visit them at home, on their own turf. They cause havoc if I let them get a grip of me. They are the forces that drive my obsession, make me lose control. Fought singly they can be defeated and in certain controlled situations their power can even be harnessed to produce something positive, like dedicated gym work. They normally try to cohabit with anger, passion, jealousy and lust and it's when mixed together with these emotions that their power is magnified exponentially.

I have a general love of excess. It's as though my volume knob has always been stuck in the max position. If something isn't vibrant or dramatic it doesn't hold my interest. This creates a problem because there is no filter in place that allows moderation, although I can choose to avoid something altogether. The reality is, though, that just like everyone else, . . . I'm trapped. It's just that the trap looks different. Since most of the world makes me feel I'm in slow motion, it's no coincidence that I've ended up in Pattaya.

For the ultimate excitement, Ady has diced with death. He has challenged fate and paid for adoration from the bar-girls, while knowing (and yet not caring to know) what they thought of him:

I got something from having unprotected sex with so many girls. It's for vanity and the feeling of being wanted. If I walked into a disco in Europe/USA, nobody would pay much attention to me. If I walk into a scruffy bar in Pattaya in the afternoon, wearing an outfit direct from *Starsky and Hutch*, when I am the only man amongst 20 girls, well then I would get a very different reaction. If the girls are used to taking care of some slobbering, pot-bellied Westerner for 500 baht and I put down 5000 and say 'come on, let's have a party,' the response would be even better. In Thailand, given that a man is presentable, his stock rises with the opposite sex if (a) he seems to have loads of disposable cash, and (b) he can be easily separated from said cash.

I eventually perfected a style where I could pick up a bar-girl early evening, take her to the sexiest dress shop, then on to the beauty salon and hairdressers. In each place, the people would know what look I was after, and by 10pm, wham bang, there would be another doll rolling off the production line. Needless to say, the girls loved it – an expensive makeover, drinking all night for free and normally getting well paid without having to have sex. Most nights would end up with me getting drunk in a go-go bar, surrounded by the sexiest girls. This would be fine if I was a millionaire with a replacement liver! A night out was costing me 300 quid!

It was also causing BIG problems with my wives: huge fights. One once completely trashed my condo, causing 5k of damage. I was attacked twice when my behaviour made other guys jealous. Once, three English guys beat me up and broke some ribs, and another time somebody paid for two Thai thugs to cosh me unconscious. I'm under no illusions that if I walked down the street wearing a t-shirt that said 'flat broke', I'd be drinking alone all night.

I'm not depressed, I love life. Since I stopped getting drunk I'm happier than I ever have been. We laugh together from the moment we wake up until the moment we go to sleep. There's much less tension this time around because I made it clear I didn't want to complicate things by having any sex – No sex please, I'm British!

I see this as a form of denial of depression which is called manic defence or a smiling depression, when people make a great show of being happy. It could be that Ady is in that state:

The three of us sleep together – sexlessly – every night when we are together. It is a bit like school camp. We're like Enid Blyton's famous five, only we're the Infamous Three. If they sold ginger beer here, we'd be drinking lashings of it. It's mostly good fun and it beats the normal husband–wife tedium. Anyway, how could I send either of them back to a life of prostitution? I'm always the first one out of bed, and each morning I sing a song about them being lazy gits; if I didn't sing the song they would complain. When it's time for lights out, there's a scramble for who gets which pillow and who has to sleep in the middle, the worst position. I then sing 'Goodnight campers, see you in the morning' and afterwards, someone always shouts 'Hi dee hi!' followed by the other two shouting 'Ho dee ho!' If either weren't happy they would find excuses to be absent. It's quite the reverse; I have to boot them out of the room every Saturday so I can lose my temper at the football alone. I need both so they can do different shifts in the kitchen. The problem for the future is that at 41 my first wife isn't yet ready to hang up her thong just yet.

Worlds apart

Ady's life is so unlike the home life of his dear class-mate. Mark has managed in his maturity and away from all that he had known to escape his cage of scholarship. Love finally came to him and he married a woman in his scientific field. They have two children and live in a beautiful part of the country, far from his boyhood home. He doesn't even need his precocious PhD for what he does. His work is creative and his ideas are spreading through his publications. He adores the hills around and mountain-biking with his family – 'You get out onto the top of the hills and you look around at all the beautiful scenery, and you just think there's no way I'd move.'

This idyllic picture has been hard-won. He told me:

I'm very law abiding. At school, I didn't like people who tried to make friends with me – even teachers. I didn't feel it was appropriate for them to try and be friendly to people that they were teaching. And I also didn't like it when pupils tried to befriend teachers. I was always happier being taught by more strict teachers.

I know that my father is looking over my shoulder all the time. I'm not telling my kids off because I personally disapprove, I'm telling my kids off because I think *he* would disapprove. When I can start to stop caring about that, then I'll be getting somewhere.

Before I got married, I always felt it was a fairly desolate, lonely world and I didn't particularly like being in it. But now I've got my comfort blanket which is my family. And I don't think about what's going to happen in the future. I have to say, though, that my parents have been pretty generous financially. So that's helped us out a great deal.

I always feel very uncomfortable around enthusiastic people. Well, I can't understand them, you know. Some people would say I was lazy. But sometimes, when I'm doing something, I'll be absolutely totally 100 per cent focused; nothing will disturb me.

Mark's life shows that in whatever way gifts may develop, even if they are lying fallow they are still there and ready for service throughout life. For these two men, Ady who fills his purse by gambling and Mark the salary man, both have built a form of independent happiness. Each has made his peace with his parents, yet lives far from them. They have each adapted their mental powers and personalities in their own ways to suit their early experiences.

Gambling

Gambling in children is different from other forms of potential addiction because it is more difficult to spot. Britain is the only Western country which allows children of any age to gamble, even though most cannot have developed the emotional skills they need to control it. Gambling is an addiction. It dominates the addict's life.

Like all addictions, the earlier the gambling addiction begins, the harder it is to cope with it. The novice gambler believes he or she can stop when they want to, and often becomes mentally agile at disguising the truth by making up believable stories, like why they are skint. Unlike other forms of addiction, such as alcohol or drugs, gambling has no physical symptoms. But there is a strong possibility of depression and mood swings. Gamblers, again like other addicts, are preoccupied with their addiction, usually have low self-esteem, turn to rituals to lure luck to their side, and yearn for instant gratification.

Gambling suited Ady particularly well because it has the core addictive aspect of uncertainty. That is what makes it so pleasurable to someone like him whose whole life and reward set-up with his parents was based on not knowing. He had to grab love and security where he could. Today's online gambling suits him particularly well. He can play all day and every day, with no wagging finger from authority figures or Gamblers Anonymous telling him to stop.

Ady started as a boy in a small way, introduced to gambling with his family's support, playing the gaming machines and having a flutter on the horses. Gaming machines are interactive and solitary, and research shows them to be highly addictive. Child gamblers have little understanding of the commercial odds stacked against them: the sparkling, colourful slot-machines promise the great pull of easy money. Only painful experience demonstrates the opposite to those who are aware.

I understand that first childhood hook, because at the age of ten I used to blow all my pocket money on slot-machines as soon as it was in my hand. There was no legal barrier in those days to little girls in school uniform throwing their money away in the sleazy arcade in the centre of the city, its cement floor strewn with cigarette-ends. No-one ever approached me. Nor did I ever win anything other than a bit of plastic tat picked up by the mechanical claw. I hoped fervently to increase my money as I shot the little silver balls to the top of the machine and watched as they darted down again bouncing off the barriers, while I willed them vainly into the holes.

Although the silver balls did not drop where I wanted them to in the slot machine, eventually the penny dropped in my brain – nothing would ever come of this. Fortunately the machines were so strictly fixed that there wasn't the slightest encouragement for me to continue. I stopped after about six months. The great psychologist, B. F. Skinner, of Harvard University, called my reaction 'negative reinforcement'. I'd never had the positive reinforcement of winning, so I had to put a stop to the negative loss of all my pocket-money by quitting the scene, my action being reinforced by the jingle of coins in my pocket. I did not end up like Ady, and have always been grateful to my parents who trusted me to discover the futility of 'amusement arcades' for myself.

The easy accessibility of gaming machines to children carries a very real danger, as it did for Ady (thankfully not for me). The lying and stealing which can follow are highly detrimental to fulfilling any other form of potential, however high the promise. School absences, broken relationships and a lifelong search for the bluebird of happiness can become a normal life for young gamblers. Indeed, as Ady's addiction grew, his gambling detracted hugely from his school performance, bringing him debt and the need for more gambling. Now, he dips into the infinite variety of easily available gambling, such as the 2000 sites or so on the internet, against which gambling help associations, such as Gamblers Anonymous and Gamcare or national governments have little strength.

Ady's way of life is always under threat from disease, thugs and fellow gamblers. His goal is to live life in full technicolor. His lifelines are his gifted intelligence, his high-level empathy and his sweet nature; his tribulations are in his emotions. His gambling was not a rebellion against his family's way of life, but an unwitting fitting in with it. Had he rebelled, it could have been by working hard at his lessons and then getting away from home by going to university. It is a major problem, though, for youngsters in emotional turmoil, as he was, to concentrate on what appears at the time to be irrelevant to their lives. What were geography, maths and history to do with his mother's bringing men home? In his own way, just as his classmate Mark aimed to please, so too did Ady. He would show his father how he would make lots of money. Mark went for superb examination results.

Ady could not have done what he did without his high-level brain-power. His international successes using extremely complicated formulae and strategies are not for those of more average mental capacity. He employs skill and experience in what he does. And he is an expert. Looking further at this approach to his profession is very well explained in the dramatic book by Kushner entitled *Jonny Magic and the Card Shark Kids*, which Ady sent me. High stakes require strength, perseverance and courage.

In the end, Ady has used his gifted IQ to his advantage. It got him the money, the girls and the wild life he wanted. His life-path, though, has been truly precipitous and he's had some very nasty experiences. But he still writes beautiful poetry:

a wild embrace with fortune's favour
can turn to stone before a heart beats twice
the fiery rush from a potential saviour
can in half a furlong become watery ice

When at last our eyes stay closed
when even ashes turn to dust
when we reach that sweet repose
we recall our love, not lust

12

Gifted women

I still think it's a terrible thing to think highly of your abilities.

Lydia Robbins

It's so very important to my happiness, to have intellectual challenge.

Francine Exeter

Once, not so long ago, boys were seen to be better at school work than girls, especially in the sciences. Yet now, in countries where there are equal educational opportunities, girls are scoring more highly at school in most subjects. Naturally, though, in parts of the world where expectations and educational opportunities for girls are poor, boys will still do very much better.

In Britain it starts in the nursery, and by the time they reach five, girls are performing better at school while more boys are getting extra help for learning and behavioural difficulties. By 16, the gap has expanded so much that girls are scoring higher than boys at a significant level in every single school subject (except physical education). At 18, they are still, for the moment, behind in taking up physics and mathematics. The university turning point came in 1992, when more women than men became students. Every year women get proportionately more first-class degrees, notably in medicine, law and business.

The widest recorded gap between girls' and boys' achievements at school is among the gifted, shown up particularly in mathematics. The Third International Mathematics and Science Study (TIMS), in 1999, for example, found that boys and girls scored much the same – except for the top 25 per cent – where girls outshone boys. Not so in the United States. Educational comparisons between Britain and the USA are particularly interesting because the two countries have a similar genetic make-up and aim to provide equal educational opportunities. The essential differences lie in expectations, in culture, and because of those differences it is not always wise to apply American results elsewhere. George Bernard Shaw supposedly quipped, 'We are two nations divided by a common language', or was it Oscar Wilde?

In the United States, for example, a 1995 University of Chicago survey found that in mathematics, of the top 10 per cent of teenagers, there were twice as many boys as girls. In the science top 10 per cent, there were five times as many boys. These proportions are significantly very different from what has been happening in other countries, such as Australia and across Europe. Yet failing to look beyond their own shores, the Chicago researchers decided that the differences they found were innate.

American gender expectations also show in the selection of children for gifted programmes. Professor Ellen Winner, of Boston College, in her book *Gifted Children*, has pointed out that boys and girls are selected in equal proportions at kindergarten level. But by junior high school, girls have dropped to less than 30 per cent and the percentage shrinks even lower at high school. Still, the American situation is changing fast, and conclusions will soon have to be rewritten to fit the new facts.

Everyone has a different explanation for this modern Western reversal of gender position. Brain and behaviour scientists have found only negligible differences between the genders. Some say books don't appeal to boys unless they are about sport; others say that since there have been equal educational opportunities, the girls' repressed intellectual superiority is now being revealed. One sour response is that girls are merely drones and boys would surely be the more brilliant if only the level of work was not so low and unchallenging. In fact, surveys show that girls are becoming more confident, and able to believe in their own abilities, while many schoolboys are now muttering that girls are more intelligent than they are.

In spite of these figures, gifted girls are still influenced by social pressures to be feminine from parents, teachers and the media. For so many girls, their great successes at school seem merely to delay the age-old conflict between family and work. And school achievement is not life achievement. In the adult work-place, since men still far exceed women in earning-power everywhere, girls see far fewer female high-powered role models. Women are also less likely to work mainly for financial reward because they often prefer greater emotional satisfaction. Quite a few high-flying girls have whispered to me how difficult it is for them to find a boyfriend, or for that matter a life-partner who can keep up with them.

The tender trap

The lives of two top-of-the-IQ-scale women in this chapter show how being female has affected their outlooks and achievements. Both Lydia Robbins and Francine Exeter had an abundance of everything beneficial in their childhoods. Each was dearly loved, lived in a beautiful home and enjoyed the best education that money could buy. But as the years passed, looking deeply at what they said and did, I could pick out the threads of how very different their demands and expectations were compared with their brothers. The social influences which both girls absorbed through their formative years have had life-long effects.

When we'd first met, Lydia Robbins was aged ten: a slender, pretty, fair-haired little girl, with laughter in her eyes. The daughter of what appeared to be an open liberal family, she had an IQ too high to measure, plenty of personal ambition and took great pleasure in her school learning. How perfect her life looked, and her brilliant future seemed assured.

This is where my in-depth investigation paid off. As a teenager, Lydia's responses to a ticked questionnaire or a phone interview would completely have missed the depth of her despondence. A subtle and unrecognised worm was already burrowing into her sense of self – entirely because she was female. Her brother was entirely free from her obligations. He was entitled to stand or fall on his own merits, which were in fact much fewer than hers.

My car crunched up the long gravel drive to Lydia's fine home, set in several carefully gardened acres. The big house glowed with comfort and contentment. Flowers were in bloom, and as I reached the gleaming front door, I could see through the long windows either side of it, rooms of antique furniture lined with books. It was a cherished dwelling. Yet I found the story of the daughter of that beautiful home distressing.

Lydia was then in her first year as an undergraduate at Cambridge University, and was glad to talk to me about what had happened to her:

My mother died over a year ago, and it changed everything instantly. I was suddenly responsible and in charge of things. I was 16. I spent nine months at home before university and got the frustrated housewife syndrome. Mummy's friends became my friends, and I took over some of her voluntary social work with them, which is alright up to a point. Daddy said I was having a kind of marriage without the good bits, just doing the housework.

Rationally, I know I don't have anything to be depressed about, but I still cry quite a lot. And when I cry, I really cry. I can't turn to my father, because either he'd not understand why, thinking it was all connected with mummy's death. At university, I see my boyfriend. It's wonderful. But though I'm quite happy to be superficially cheered up by him, I feel kind of guilty because it's not really a solution to my problems.

During these holidays, I've only been out twice, and after both times daddy said, 'You left all this washing-up to do, and I had to do this, and we didn't have enough potatoes on Saturday night,' or something. I want to be a student and I've got to be a housewife too. He doesn't ask my brother because he's away at school, and he's different somehow. Day to day, I never seem to have enough time to do the ironing or the meal or whatever.

I suppose I am growing up a bit, though, because I'm feeling more responsible. When I go back to university, I tell my father he's got to feed himself properly, leave him instructions as to how to do his washing and ring him up to check if he's alright.

This last term at Cambridge, I've found concentration incredibly difficult. It's very irritating, because I'm not used to it. I sit in the library for three hours and think I'm working, but I know I'm not. I read the things we're told to read, but I don't get inspired and write impassioned essays, which everybody else seems to be doing. It gets vaguer and vaguer and less and less controlled as I go on, and I find I have to discipline myself more than I used to.

I feel much less intelligent than I was about ten years ago. Even in concerts now, I don't concentrate for two seconds together on the music, because I'm thinking about other things, like what I'm going to say to the person next to me when it finishes. I have too many things in my mind at once. I'm always thinking about what I'm going to do tomorrow and why I didn't do the washing-up tonight.

Lydia's father, who obviously loved his daughter dearly, seemed to me a somewhat old-fashioned man, a little gruff and brought up in a patriarchal system. I felt myself put on my mettle, psychologically taking a step back, when he and I talked briefly. He was polite and crisp. Both Lydia's parents were older than usual at her birth. His expectations for his daughter appeared to have been tragically distorted by his beloved wife's early death. But even so, it seemed to me that her lifelong need to please her parents had started early. From childhood, her conflict between trying to be a good daughter in her parents' eyes yet wanting to enjoy the excitement of her extraordinary mind had brought her guilt. Nearly all children feel some pull between home and the outside world, but Lydia seemed to be trying especially hard to please.

Hearing her tale, I wondered why Lydia's father hadn't employed someone to take care of the domestic drudgery that he was laying on his academically brilliant daughter. His Cinderella had no wicked stepmother to put the blame on. Obviously he felt it acceptable to take her time and mental energy into his service, which should have been going into her learning. He had severely cut her fun and pleasure among companions of her own age. Chuckling, he'd even joked to her about the arid life he'd imposed on her. Sometimes her mother's friends helped, but essentially she took all the responsibility of an unpaid housekeeper's job on her young shoulders. It wasn't a matter of simply being a child of the family: her brother was completely absolved. It appeared to me to be a situation which was emotionally and mentally crippling to Lydia, not least at a time when she should have been discovering her wings and learning to fly high.

Lydia's girls' boarding secondary school, one of the most expensive in the country, had added its weight to increasing her feelings of inadequacy. She winced at their petty and persistent criticism, which she found pointless and destructive:

> They wouldn't let on if they thought you were intelligent, because they thought it was bad for you. It's probably a hangover that I still think it's a terrible thing to think highly of your abilities. In English, I was told it would be a struggle for me to take the exams – and now it's my subject at Cambridge. I used to be marked B, with oceans of red all over my essays. It really discouraged me.
>
> They used to get so uptight about petty things, like your hair's sitting on your shoulder and it's not tied up with a blue ribbon; they think it's the end of the world. It could go on for a fortnight – 'That wicked girl in the second year.' You go to bed at night, and you've got to face

it all the next morning, and you haven't been able to tell anyone or go home and get away.

In her final two school years, she'd moved to a top boys' boarding school which had begun taking in a few girls at aged 16. To begin with, she found it a great relief:

> The boys' school was much more relaxed; no uniform or regulations about bedtimes, which were ridiculous for 18 year olds. I found a teacher who used to rave about my essays; I thrived on his encouragement.

However, the worm was still burrowing. Always an outstandingly good scholar and a keen mathematician, Lydia had chosen to specialise in science. But now in a class of boys, she was shocked at the male physics teacher's laughter when she put her hand up to answer a question, and he turned to a boy for the answer. Rachel Wallace (Chapter 1) had been in a similar situation and had been given the same treatment. Lydia's experience was explicit:

> When I first went to the boys' school, they'd say, 'Good heavens, a girl doing physics – can't possibly be right.' There were four girls in the class and the physics master used to just teach to the boys. If we girls didn't know anything he used to say, 'Oh, don't ask. Don't ask.' Even on my school report, he wrote that I asked too many questions. He didn't want to know the girls. He just talked to the lads.

As at home, Lydia did not complain or fight this bigotry. Being wonderfully broad-based in her giftedness, she simply switched to English. Would a keen and brilliant male mathematician radically change course because of such slights? Was this a female reaction, or her personal way of coping? Being supremely all-round gifted, Lydia still got top marks in everything she attempted and was accepted by Cambridge University for a highly prized place to study English. She made the same discovery as some others in the sample:

I'd expected everyone at Cambridge to be brilliant, and that I'd only just slipped through the net – but I am actually very good.

Alas, Lydia's dedicated housekeeping during her precious undergraduate years inevitably took its toll. She did not get the first-class degree her tutors had anticipated, and felt ashamed because she knew she'd been capable of it. When I asked her, 15 years later, why she hadn't done as well as she could, she replied that it was because she didn't do much work as she was 'having such a good time'. Ah, memory!

In her late thirties, Lydia cares as well as she can for her rather lonely younger brother, and daily misses her adored father:

It's so sad to lose the one person in your life who thinks you're perfect. I spent the last two weeks of his life with him, going to the hospice three times a day, reading the paper aloud to him. We had a really nice time, actually. He died holding my hand. I felt so lucky to have been there. My brother and I didn't know what to do with the beautiful house. We sold it and didn't get very much for the antiques and the books. We didn't feel like bargaining. I didn't want anything more to do with it.

Lydia has lived with her boyfriend from Cambridge, who is now a university professor, for more than 20 years. She would marry him, but he won't marry her. He was astonished – and amused – to hear from me that I'd measured Lydia as having an IQ of 170. She told me:

He wouldn't want a church service for our marriage. But I'm a Christian and I would want a blessing on our relationship. So there's no way round it. Of course, we now have a shared mortgage, so we're pretty strongly tied together!

Lydia goes frantic

From university, Lydia shot immediately into frantic gear, far from any form of academic study, running hard from one commitment to another with barely time to breathe – or to think in any depth. Lydia explained:

> There doesn't seem to be time to have children. I'm too over-committed. I'm all meetings and this kind of thing. When my father was dying, it brought home to me the need to be available to the people that really matter. But I can't be as responsive as I want to be. It's important to me that I do something for people. I get so much out of all that human interaction with all these different groups of people. But I've been doing something like 40 hours a week – absolutely ridiculous.

Lydia was also the director of her own company producing exhibition design, business cards, books, most things print-able, as well as websites:

> I catch up late into the evenings and at weekends. I feel on the brink all the time. It comes partly out of my faith; I think one should give as much back as one can. I come from such a privileged background with a massively good start in life. I had two amazing parents, a good education and all that. If I'm not in a position to volunteer, who is?

She took up politics, ran a socialist journal until it closed, and worked for an important political society until she clashed with a 'very ambitious, massively sexist general secretary'. The worm continued to burrow. Lydia fled the gender battle-field but the man continued in his post. She freelanced from home, working on trade-union newsletters and with an educational publisher for a few years, until she set up her own business.

Her bitter disappointment was losing the vote to be a Labour councillor for her local town. But she did become a governor of a primary school and an executive member of the local Chamber of Trade – 'Fascinating, most of the others are over 60.' She did the Christian mission 'soup-bus' once a week, wrote the church newsletter, sang in the choir and worked for the parish council. She organised the village fair. And so much more – Vice Chair of the Chamber of Trade, Secretary of the town Credit Union, Secretary of her village youth club, Secretary of the village safety forum, representative for the Association of Local Councils on the District Council Safety Forum:

The village youth club is a complete waste of time. We don't have premises; we even have to borrow the dilapidated football. We meet out on the field, or take them in buses to other places. I apply for grants to keep it going. The kids are complete horrors. And their parents are absolutely not into being involved at all, which is why the kids are the way they are. We all spend so much time trying to generate something for them and they're still getting cross with us because we haven't built them a new clubhouse. It's very wearing and thankless. After all the time you've spent with these kids, there's not a speck of gratitude out of any of them. They smoke the whole time, and they're all about 14. We're all thinking, 'Oh God, if only I could give this up.' And that's a terrible way to do anything.

I'm always planning. I'm sort of dragged forward by my diary, living six months ahead. My goal is to complete all those things. So I'm always dissatisfied and frustrated. I can never succeed. I have things on my to-do list which are frightfully important to me, which never get done. On my desk, I even have a grid of things to tick off every day. I have singing lessons . . . another thing I worry about, not doing enough practice. And I've just started trying to play the piano again, but I neglect family phone calls and friends that I never get round to ringing. I try to read something that isn't work or accounts, papers or the crossword before I crash out at night.

I always loved maths when I was little. If I had all the time in the world, I'd study it again because I loved it. I don't use my brain-power well. Juggling all these things in my brain, switching between them is the hardest thing I do. I could have been anything really. I'd like to do a PhD or something like that. All our friends seem to have them.

Who am I?

Pressure, like Lydia's, can become a habit, so familiar and comfortable that she wanted more of it. Many people know that feeling – that adrenaline rush – especially those who take their work on holiday. Who would you be if you weren't so busy? Doesn't bear thinking about, does it? A frantic life can also provide a form of status, demonstrating that because your time and energy are in such demand, you must be important. And if so many people want you, well then, you must also be popular.

Popularity was a constant thorn in Lydia's side. Being accelerated a year in school had also separated her from the age-mates who might have been her friends, and had disrupted the development of her social skills. As a sweet little six year old, she'd had to deal with skipping a year of lessons all by herself, using only her own personality and strength. She had only her own experience to go on:

> When I was very little, I had intellectual self-confidence. Everybody was saying how clever I was. I knew deep down that school was something I was good at. And that's a nice thing to feel. When I went to boarding school at seven, I was always coming top in tests, so they called me 'brainbox', which wasn't exactly praise. It was my parents who decided I was bored and got the school to push me up by a year. I was the youngest in all my classes in all my schools. Other kids didn't like it. But it was beyond my imagination to sabotage my maths results to be popular.
>
> When I was a teenager at the boys' school, I was incredibly unpopular. The boys used to shout at me. It was only verbal bullying but it will stay with me forever. I still feel unpopular. I'm quite self-conscious, easily undermined. They didn't like me because I didn't look

anything special, I wasn't dressed fashionably, and I didn't come from London. I didn't tell my parents because I didn't want to upset them. Those sorts of things just hurt enormously. I wrote lots of really angry poetry. When I switched to doing English a couple of terms late, I was instantly top of the top set. And, well, boys don't like that either.

Once I had a tendency to speak up in social groups, which is deeply unattractive and often wrong. But I don't do that anymore. I've really tried to get rid of it. I much prefer listening to people really. There's this idea that clever people will have enormous foreheads and just want to do equations all day or talk about nuclear physics. They won't want to have a beer.

At her three boarding schools from the age of seven, Lydia's loneliness was only sometimes alleviated by being bullied by both classmates and teachers. Her favoured method of dealing with such bad situations was to remove herself from them, as from science and the mathematics she loved. The bullying boys, though, left their psychological mark. Fortunately, her feelings about her unattractiveness were clearly not shared by her long-term boyfriend at Cambridge and her many loving friends. I found her sharp, quick and cute, slim with short spiky orange hair; a delightful witty companion.

Bullying is associated with being exceptional in some way. It happens to children who do not fit in, when power is uneven. In William Golding's book *Lord of the Flies*, it was the clever fat one with glasses who got bullied by the other boys until they killed him. There are gender differences in styles of bullying: girls are more verbal and boys more physical. Girls are also far more likely to report it (80 per cent of all girls, when asked), while boys keep a stiff upper lip (20 per cent, when asked).

Whether it is physical, verbal or psychological, bullying – so often out of sight – is a very painful experience for the sufferer. Lydia did not seek help in her suffering – whether this was being called names in childhood or shouted at as a teenager – and none was offered to her as nobody seems to have noticed. Yet in schools where the whole staff takes a positive attitude to eradicating bullying, this can have a beneficial effect. When children know that reporting bullying is not just telling tales, it can be stopped. Peer-group pressure can often be high, though, and it takes a lot of courage to speak out. Lydia had taken up the ethos of the upper-class boys' school, keeping a stiff upper lip. She had long since learned to put the interests and feelings of her family and others before her own. Once again, this highly gifted girl had retreated in the face of conflict.

Lydia reaches an even keel

Lydia and her partner relieve their pressured lives by walking in the hills and taking long holidays. They've moved to the English Lake District, to sweet air surrounded by beauty and green mountains, a place they had always wanted to be.

But poignantly, long ago when she was 16, Lydia had mused into my recorder, 'I picture myself marrying an alcoholic or something, and having a really tough life, but satisfied because I've redeemed that person.' She'd remembered that sentence which I'd quoted in an earlier book, and now she could also see some truth in her teenage prediction:

> We both drink too much; that's our other form of
> relaxation. Lots and lots and lots at weekends. And
> some every day. Thursday night down the pub. Nine
> o'clock until closing time. Three pints of beer, maybe
> four pints. And then Friday night. Well of course, on a
> Friday night, you go drinking, you know. You go down
> to the pub for a couple of pints and then back with a
> bottle of wine and whisky or whatever. Saturday night
> obviously you drink, and on Sundays and Saturday
> lunchtimes, you might find yourself passing a pub
> and having a pint. I don't get drunk-drunk. I don't
> ever sort of fall over or throw up or anything like that.
> My partner obviously does. Gets drunker than me.
> Now I'm just as bad as he is. I remember thinking that

was something that would happen. My parents used to drink, not to excess, but I sometimes saw both of them drunk. My father drank a lot and I thought he was wonderful.

Lydia's business had too many disparate parts to build into a recognisable career or a structure of real help to others. By 2009, she'd given it up and was working for a publishing company. She is aiming to make a clean break from her old ways, though those old habits do seem to be creeping back. She e-mailed me from her new home:

I resolved not to volunteer for anything at all for the first two years while I found my feet. I pretty much stuck to that, although I and with a small group of women set up a local Businesswomen's Network. I did join the board of the local volunteer centre but had to give that up because they meet during the day when I took my current full-time job. My volunteering today is limited to: church (I write intercessions every six weeks or so and draw up the rotas quarterly), volunteer centre (I produce a very tiny newsletter for them once a quarter – very little work), local cycle group (I help them keep their website up to date, as the previous person absconded and left them in the lurch) and the Labour Party. There's so little activity up here, but I did stand in last year's council elections – hopelessly – and I may stand in the Euro elections.

I cycle seven miles down country lanes to work every day, I love the books we work on, and I love the people I work with. I get to use all my publishing experience – writing, editing, design, pre-press, production. I don't have to worry about finding work/getting paid/selling myself day in, day out any more. I'm very, very lucky. We've met lots of lovely like-minded folk up here – and we walk, run, cycle whenever we can, inspired by the place we live in.

I really need to get back to a pile of work, but let me know if you need more 'facts' and when you want to ring. Not today, though, please.

Intellectual life can be dry

There were many similarities between the lives of Lydia and Francine Exeter. Both were exceedingly intelligent, each lived in a comfortable home, had the finest education that money could buy, and both were girls. The Exeter family lived in a lavishly converted huge old barn set among the rolling green hills of the Cheshire countryside, with a couple of acres of ground. There were books everywhere, fine art on the walls, and several large dogs lying around.

At seven years old, both girls had become boarders at different expensive girls' prep schools. When she was ten, Francine knew the score. She informed me that her school was, 'totally geared to the entrance exam system'. She was an earnest child, but her animated little pixie-face with its wild mop of curly brown hair often shot me a cheeky grin – as though we shared a secret. She'd taken great pleasure slicing through my intelligence test like a hot knife through butter, to score with unnerving ease a mental age of 19. Her responses to the test's highest level of 'Superior Adult' were perfect. Nothing was too difficult for her, showing that her intelligence was far too high to measure by any test. She was probably the most intelligent of all my testees. What's more, I found myself talking to her as an adult, a sure sign of a gifted child. What an amazing potential.

Her mother pointed out the difficulties of having a highly gifted child, especially as the firstborn. When she took Francine and her little brother round the garden teaching them the names of the flowers, Francine was way ahead. But then, she had two huge advantages, being much more intelligent than her brother as well as older.

There is a problem of having one gifted child in a family if the other members feel less able. Sometimes parents hold the gifted one in awe, listening to their juvenile pronouncements as though they'd emerged from years of experience. Others feel that all their troubles are due to that 'cuckoo in the nest', blaming arguments and everyday problems on their presence. Some feel that tantrums are acceptable in a gifted child, as Rachel Wallace's mother had done (Chapter

1). One American psychologist even suggested that being gifted in a normal classroom is like being a normal child in a class of children with learning difficulties. But in the hundreds of gifted children I have seen in normal classrooms, I have never come across this attitude or reaction from them towards the non-gifted.

Francine's wise mother asked her daughter to hold back her answer so that little brother could get it right sometimes. It seemed to me a good lesson in learning kindness and patience, while at the same time understanding that she was being recognised as bright and more mature.

When she was 19, her life still seemed like an ideal – looks, brains, charm, money and a precious place at Oxford University. But Francine also had something in common with Lydia – that unrecognised worm which had been resolutely eating away at her early childhood confidence. Her mother was obviously distressed, drawing closer and lowering her voice when she told me about it. She appeared to assume that there was no other way of educating her daughter than sending her away:

> Francine hadn't found it easy to make friends since she was six or seven, so it was really hard for her as a boarder. When she was 15, she became so very depressed and lost an awful lot of weight in a couple of years. The doctors were reluctant to diagnose it as anorexia, though it seemed to us to have all the signs. So she came home for two terms, had psychotherapy, and the school sent lessons by post.

> Then she went back into the sixth-form to stick it out right through. She seems to have got over it now, in so far as one ever can. It really was a reactionary school, and with hindsight, a mixed education would have been much better for her.

Unlike Lydia's parents, Francine's knew very well at the time how unhappy she was. They knew the distress it caused their daughter to be sent as a boarder at the tender age of seven and how unsuitable it was for her. But, her mother explained, there was no suitable education for such a gifted child nearby. By 15, Francine's long-buried symptoms of distress were erupting, mentally and physically. She was sent home with the starving disease, anorexia nervosa. She stayed at home with little help to recover. Was it to put iron in her soul that her parents sent her back again and again? Maybe it was because that was the way it had always been done in their well-off middle-class society.

But as with Lydia's brother, Francine's brother was entirely spared pressure. Indeed, for both the girls' brothers, their schools and their lives were very much easier. Soon after she left school, Francine and I talked about her illness, once again sitting in the sun among the scented flowers in the garden. She felt herself responsible for her unhappiness and undeserving of sympathy. Her illness, she explained, could have been due to sibling rivalry because her lively and popular young sister had just joined the school. Probably, Francine said matter-of-factly, she had been selfishly 'seeking attention' by being ill. At no time did she even consider that with her extraordinarily high intellectual capacity and her sweet loving nature she had been wrongly sent away from home and to the wrong kind of schooling:

> I couldn't say I was ill just because I was unhappy at school, because I used to get depressed when I was younger too. After I'd gone back, after the anorexia, I lodged in the town and went as a day girl, but that was awful as well, because the day girls are very much looked down on, and I really felt it. It's a disadvantage not to be able to make small-talk, which was important in terms of how the girls evaluated each other – and it was very boring. Then I went back as a boarder for a further two years.
>
> When I wasn't eating, I still took care of myself, you know, with lots of exercise and things. I didn't have to be force-fed or hospitalised or anything like that – that was the threat, the stick. My parents, especially my father, took a firm line which had a lot to do with me getting better. But it nearly didn't work.
>
> I still have bad feelings about it. The whole thing changed me. I'm more reserved than I was. At school,

there was the extra real problem of lack of communication between the girls and the teachers – a hands-off approach. Now, I know I have to do something to take my mind off it – after a little interlude of self-pity. I rarely turn to other people; in fact, no, never. I really don't. My parents have helped me more than anything else, but also a lot of it was my own determination.

In her mid-forties, Francine has been able to take a longer-distance view of her teenage malaise. Again, this is a benefit of this long-term in-depth study. Her parents were no longer together, and she now felt able to tell me what had really happened, and what she could not tell me when she was younger:

My father was very critical. He'll always knock what I did. He'd sometimes praise, but then he'd follow it by really pulling the rug from under my feet. My mum was not very self-confident. I'm sure her self-deprecating way had an effect on me. Maybe it was the combination. I have to stop myself from being like that with my children, because I don't want the same things to happen to them. And my husband can also be quite critical too.

So many times, the two girls blamed themselves for their unhappiness. Yet, as with Ady and Mark (Chapter 11), both their fathers had been manipulative and domineering. Francine had punished herself by refusing to eat. But directed by her father, she'd had to go back to boarding school to face a sentence of two more years of tedium and loneliness. Unlike Lydia, she had never been directly insulted for being female, but instead was limited to the stilted education offered to upper-class girls, rather than the free-spirited investigatory style that boys at similar schools enjoyed, and on which she would have thrived. At 15, her fine brain buzzing to learn and explore, she told me how it was at her school:

The style of teaching is uninspirational, uninteresting. The teacher talks and you take it down; homework is essays and more writing. They don't look for new ways to interest the class. The teachers themselves are bored, and of course so are the girls. I'd like to be taught in a way that is more relevant to the actual world outside, to involve more personal experiences both on the teacher's side and on mine. I'm trying to fight boredom and frustration, just to get through my exams with good grades. I expect the teachers think I'm very lazy, but I don't actually know what they think because they don't really speak to me.

There's no time to explore subjects outside your syllabus, though we do public speaking and those sorts of activities. I would have liked computing, and more languages, to have explored more areas. The school doesn't focus enough on the individual; doesn't bring out enough of what you've got to offer. But it does get great examination results. I would have been happier if I'd just stayed at home and gone to a day school for the last four years.

The cage door opened and the bird flew out

Once released from school, Francine spent three happy years at one of the best colleges of Oxford University, taking unaccustomed delight in exercising her mind with philosophy, politics and economics. She left with a first-class degree – 'without much work'. Many of the gifted students in this study even told me they felt lazy because they didn't have to work as hard as their fellow-students. To begin with, she'd thought:

I shouldn't really be there, I'm not clever enough. Then suddenly I got a distinction, which made me realise – well maybe I should.

She shot through further qualifications at double speed, became a chartered accountant with a top firm in London, and gained an MA at the Institute of Latin American Studies. Francine began to scent real and irresistible freedom. She hoisted her back-pack, pulled up that deep courage she'd used to return to the torment of school, and set off alone to Latin America. She leapt with joy into a colourful, hot and sensual world where her once-caged curiosity and emotions could find expression – and they certainly did in the form of a Latin man – handsome, dashing Pablo from Ecuador. Her face smiled broadly and her body visibly relaxed as she told me:

He was the guide on my boat in the Galapagos islands. Then again in Quito and in Bolivia. We've been married for 12 years, though it took me about seven to persuade him to live in England. He's a scuba diver and teaches it, but he's originally a biologist. Now he teaches diving in the UK. Not quite as exotic as the Galapagos, but more interesting than he expected – apart from the fact that it's freezing cold. He's exploring marine life.

Pablo doesn't have the same kind of intelligence as me. He's more instinctive. He quickly sees how to fix a situation or resolve a problem on a much more technical level than I can. That's one of the things that attracted me to him, someone who could immediately see a solution to a problem. He's not intellectual, in the reading, theoretical thinking, way. He's not an erudite person at all. But we're both very active. We're not competitive; we complement each other.

My parents were a bit wary at the beginning about me marrying someone from the other side of the world. Now they think he's great. So it's all worked out perfectly well.

Francine has a career

That South American jaunt lasted eight years, during which she mostly kept herself by working as a well-paid 'stringer' for major journals. She has now found her feet intellectually as a civil servant in London:

I work with a lot of very talented people which is immensely stimulating and enjoyable. I'd definitely fallen behind while I was in Latin America, and it was an intellectual challenge to get going again. The quality and the quantity of my work make it impossible to be bored. It sounds an awful thing to say, but most of my colleagues are also highly intelligent. It's so very important to my happiness, to have intellectual challenge.

Now I have a family, I wouldn't necessarily want to be in a senior management position, with a lot more responsibility and lot longer hours. It's bad enough being away from them for three days a week. You have to make compromises somewhere along the line. I work three days a week in London and two days from home at the other end of the country. I expect that to be less stressful when we've moved down South. I could get posted abroad, which we'd both like.

As long as there is somewhere with good diving and the sun is shining, Pablo will be alright. His daughter, who's eighteen, lives with us. She studies and occasionally she helps out. He's always at home, but even so all the family administration is left to me. I brought them back here, he says, so I'm responsible. There are never enough hours in the day.

I know I don't make the most of myself as a female, in terms of dressing. I don't care anymore what people think about my appearance. [She had a dark-suited office neatness and still the same sweet pixie face.] I don't have time to go shopping. I care more about being seen as intelligent and being able to present a reasonable argument for what I'm doing. It hits me when I wait with the other mums at the school gates. They may think I'm being snooty, but I really don't have anything very much to say to them. But it even happens with friends, who say, we can't speak to Francine about that, she knows too much.

I want my children to be exposed to lots of different experiences, to travel, to be adaptable to change and speak different languages. Definitely not to spend their whole education in a single-sex school. I've had most things – lived abroad, happily married, children, fulfilling job. Sounds alright, doesn't it . . . at the moment anyway?

My brother and sister had the same negative family dynamics to contend with as me; a lot of it was dad's doing. He'd say sarcastically to them, 'It's no use asking you, I'll ask Francine.' They're not very suc . . ., well, I wouldn't say they're that confident in their own abilities. They could both have done better professionally than they have.

Francine's mother has a large farm in the South of England where her second daughter lives across the farmyard breeding rare sheep. Francine and her family have joined the homestead.

Gifted boys and gifted girls

The effects of being a boy or a girl are sometimes difficult to put your finger on in an advanced society. In psychological tests, gender differences are shown over and over again to be negligible. Yet both Lydia and Francine were caught in the female stereotype, which interfered with the development of their unquestionable gifted potential. One has only to imagine them being allowed the mental freedom of their brothers to see that it could hugely have improved their confidence and outlooks, and what they might have made of their lives. Both were well into their adulthoods before they found their feet. Neither of them proved to be outstanding as late starters.

Women face strange and baffling handicaps. Rosalind Franklin, for example, was the scientist who deciphered the vital bases for the discovery of DNA in the 1950s. Even then, in the middle of the twentieth century, because she was a woman she'd never been allowed to set foot in the Senior Common Room of University College, London. No male colleague ever invited her in. All her breaks were taken in her laboratory or office, often alone, while the men took their coffee together and discussed their work. Her gender made her a pariah in the business of science. The stealing of her vital research results from her study by Crick and Watson when she was out of the room, was described with glib amusement in *The Double Helix* by one of the thieves, Nobel Prize winner, James Watson. He also threw in some nasty remarks about her sense of dress and femaleness. In 2009, I attended a talk by James Watson when he suddenly admitted, 'Yes, we were too hard on Rosalind Franklin.' Brenda Maddox details how it all happened in her book *Rosalind Franklin*.

If Virginia Woolf, the writer, had been allowed to go to school at all, would her genius have flourished to gain the admiration of the world? Probably not in a girls' school at the end of the nineteenth century where she would have been taught to be a 'lady'. Instead, Virginia, by the age of 11, was being put to work by her father – not as his house-keeper like Lydia – but as his biographer. He respected her writing and research, saying, 'She takes in a great deal and will really be an author in time.' It was a well-connected family, as Virginia later wrote, 'Every one of our male relations was shot into that machine at the age of ten and emerged at sixty a Head Master, an Admiral, a Cabinet Minister, or the Warden of a college.'

In her twenties, she rebelled against her stuffy back-ground, and moved to be with other creative young people in a rich intellectual ambience, styling themselves the 'Bloomsbury Set'. Days were passed in artistic endeavour and evenings in deep discussion of the arts. But she'd had to get her basic education second-hand through her brothers. They would feed her tit-bits of what they had learned at school when they came home in the holidays. She yearned in vain for what her brothers took for granted. Her bitterness at being deprived of the schooling they'd been given so generously lasted through her life and nurtured her feminism described in her book, *A Room of One's Own*.

It is still true that to make full use of their intellectual abilities, gifted girls still seem to need an extra measure of independence of spirit. Both Rosalind Franklin and Virginia Woolf were rich girls like Lydia and Francine. But they were made of the stuff that enabled them to break out of the family mould and expectations and make their own lives. Had Rosalind not died early she would have been awarded a Nobel Prize, and Virginia is internationally regarded as a genius author.

The 1995 findings by Carole Holahan and Robert Sears of the 70-year Terman follow-up of 1,528 so-called 'geniuses' in California has shown that, although the proportion of career women was high for their generation, more than twice as many of them were unmarried compared with equivalent career-level men. This testified, the authors wrote, to a clear 'incompatibility between career and home-making roles'. And for the women who did marry, having children was strongly detrimental to their careers. Women who made it to the top of their professions had an extra determination, noticeable from childhood, able to make plans and stick to them, and to have a self-confident cheerful attitude to life.

Even today, some of the most able women have difficulty in reconciling high achievement with social expectations of the female role. In some countries, female independence of thought is strictly prohibited. For anyone to become great in the world means inevitable conflicts, whether internal to develop creative thought or with colleagues and authorities. There may also be responsibility at world level, and maybe living in the limelight. Most meaningfully for mothers, it often means time away from the family. Although the middle road, running family and work, like Francine, is hard, taking one's career to a higher level has a price which gifted women with children may not wish to pay.

Many gifted girls are now aiming higher than their mothers' traditional female occupations, which can bring them some relationship problems. These may be at home when a girl may feel anger with her mother for low ambitions, or there may be difficulties with boys who are striving to be macho. There is also evidence, though, that highly talented teenagers are more likely than youngsters of average ability to reject gender categories. Mihaly Csíkszentmihályi, a psychologist at Chicago University, referred to these as 'androgynous traits' where the gifted of both genders are more likely to accept each other for who they are than average ability youngsters.

For so many of the gifted girls and boys in this study, they had to fight against all sorts of labels and assumptions, including gender, to assert their individuality.

Lydia's and Francine's gifted lives illustrate the unconscious assumptions which many parents make, notably that girls and boys do not merit equal treatment. Lydia's father knew that he was misusing his gifted daughter to peel his potatoes and knock her confidence; other parents clip their children's wings with apparently the best of intentions. The key is parental self-awareness, knowing what you are doing – and why.

PART 4

Beyond gifts and talents . . .

13

Genius

Talent is like the marksman who hits a target which others cannot reach; genius is like the marksman who hits a target, as far as which others cannot even see.

Arthur Schopenhauer

What can you expect from life if you are gifted? If you have sturdy self-confidence, enough creativity to make plans, the tenacity to stick to them and a spot of luck, the world is your oyster. You will probably live more healthily and longer, and can look forward to ageing with competence, remaining involved with the world. You may be able to contribute to your country's benefit, and may earn a lot of money on the way. Or perhaps you can bring peace where there was once strife.

But you also have the choice of ignoring your gifts and living your life at a modest level, like a few of the people I've met, who showed that their contentment did not depend on fulfilling their gifted potential.

Genius, though, is something different. The term implies some inexplicable mystical quality inducing awe, and is a far rarer accolade than even a Nobel Prize. But ideas of genius change. It cannot exist independently of a culture – one has to be a genius in something.

At different times in history, certain areas of creative work will attract more potential geniuses than at other times, thereby increasing the likelihood of amazing discoveries in those fields. In art, for example, during the late middle-ages, the Italian Renaissance brought astounding artists to the top, such as Leonardo da Vinci and Michelangelo. The Dutch Golden Age in sixteenth-century Holland produced geniuses like Rembrandt and Franz Hals, along with greatly increased trade and science.

The period of the Enlightenment across Europe in the eighteenth century, produced extraordinary talent which changed thinking and cultural life. It was a time when reason was sought as the main source of intellectual life. It produced the French and American revolutions and the ideas of equality for men as well as women. Isaac Newton was the genius of the time. He made it to Cambridge University very early, but had not shown recognisable signs of his genius to come by the time he left there. He, after all, was to be the prime scientist in the world for hundreds of years. Now, even three centuries after his birth, he is still acknowledged by many to be the greatest scientist ever born. His work encompassed, not only science, but also religion and alchemy.

In the twenty-first century, though, independent geniuses seem to be getting rather thin on the ground. Scientific creativity, in particular, is now so often dependent on teamwork with highly specialised and expensive equipment that it is hard to distinguish a single genius. Even by 1676, Isaac Newton had detected the trend away from individual discovery, writing, 'If I have seen a little further it is by standing on the shoulders of Giants.' Teamwork operates against the old romantic idea of the solitary mad professor with wispy white locks who, like Archimedes, can cry 'Eureka' at his moment of insight and change the world. Of themselves, no amount of assiduous study and hours of homework can bring the insight or flights of fancy that a scientist like Einstein, Curie or Faraday used for great discovery. But study and knowledge provide the platform from which to jump and the means of testing the insight; science always means checking and correcting.

The world-changing creative experience, what T. S. Eliot in *Four Quartets* called 'The thrilling wire in the blood', is not given to many. In a way, the most famous geniuses have come to act as our mental filing cabinets by morphing into a concept, such as 'Shakespearean' or 'Freudian'. Yet the more one knows of creative geniuses, the more human, fallible and less mystical they seem to be. With the increase in communication, contemporary brilliance in such world-figures as Bill Gates is often cynically dismissed.

In his book about twentieth-century literary geniuses, *Married to Genius*, Jeffrey Meyers investigated the relationship between their emotions and their writing. Which comes first, the creativity or the emotional outbursts? By the final page, I felt as though I'd been tossed in a pit of passion, tempest, reconciliation, immaturity, selfishness and incipient madness, into which all these creative husbands and wives had dipped. 'Try it yourself, living with a genius, see how it is . . .,' Frieda Lawrence wrote of her husband, D. H. Lawrence. Their passion was so overpowering that they nearly killed each other. Virginia Woolf, though, throughout her years of mental illness and eventual suicide, was supported and nursed by her husband, Leonard, who sacrificed his own brilliant career so that his wife's should prosper.

Genius often needs physical excellence and stamina, along with talent, although perhaps poets are less sturdy. Segovia, the superb Spanish guitarist, once said that if he had not been born with a strong right thumb-nail, he would not have been able to make any progress at all. Sporting geniuses need an inborn physical advantage. Other essentials for genius are the material things, like instruments and paints, and dedicated teaching, plus a fine set of genes and ferocious motivation. Although there is an idea that not only does practice make perfect, but it can even produce a genius, it is not the birthright of every baby to have perfect pitch or the potential of being an Olympic gold medalist.

Times change in standards. Instrument playing, for example, has improved greatly over several centuries, with a heightened intensity of practice for public performance and the proliferating competitions. This is particularly true for children, so that prodigies today can take less time to reach an equivalent level of performance compared with those of earlier centuries. Even the audiences are likely to demand higher standards. As with athletic records to beat, these get tougher and tougher.

Unlike giftedness, genius can't be measured by any test; certainly not an intelligence test. The germs of genius usually start with a joint focus between parents and children. Mozart is typical of a very young musical genius. Not only was little Wolfgang obliged to live under his father's iron discipline and teaching, but he must also have inherited some of his father's genes, although some say it may not have been Mozart who wrote down his earliest compositions, but his father. Nannerl, his sister, also practised hard and performed as brilliantly, but when still young, she was obliged to give up the piano to be a carer for her father – while Wolfgang left home to seek his fortune. It is hard to know whether Nannerl's early childhood brilliance would have proved to be as creative as Wolfgang's, had she been born a boy and received permission to behave as he did.

Geniuses are not any madder than the rest of the population, and those who become so find their creativity diminished or stopped during periods of insanity. Professor Hans Eysenck in his book *Genius*, suggested a relationship between the two. Both schizophrenic and creative people, he wrote, share a facility to widen attention and so take in more information than most. But whereas the schizophrenic can neither select the relevant information nor store it well enough in memory to use it efficiently, the creative person takes the incoming stimuli and makes something new with them. Eysenck described the quality as largely inborn, though statistically, real geniuses have some experiences in common. The most likely genius, he said, would be a 'high-Psychoticism [on his scale], high-IQ, introverted, highly talented and creative Jewish boy who had lost a parent before the age of 10.' But how to promote this?

The childhoods of geniuses

Any relationship between early precocity and geniuses is unsure, as John Radford found in his overview *Child*

Prodigies and Exceptional Early Achievers. He concluded that it is almost impossible to predict true adult giftedness from childhood. The most reliable signs are probably confined to music. A child's main problem is time. A ten year old hasn't lived long enough to put in the minimum hours of practice – ten years and 10,000 hours – to reach even the basic level of recogniseable expertise. You can't do that as a child at the same time as attending school. Only when a parent of a potential genius, usually a father, devotes his life to their childhood years at home can they accumulate enough hours of practice. Little Pablo Picasso could barely read, he claimed, because he hardly went to school but did almost nothing but art since he was a toddler.

Classical composers, like other forms of genius, are most frequently the first-born child in the family. Professor Dean Simonton at the University of California has spent many years investigating creative genius, and found that in greatness there is little which is the product of chance and self-direction. The proto-musical baby is more likely to be born near the centre of musical activity for his day, where he would receive the best training and be exposed to the best role models. He would begin a music apprenticeship at a very early age, but also progress through his training much more rapidly than normal. Mozart started young and ended young. Young composers tend to be highly prolific, producing a large number of compositions, even though not all of them are masterworks. So prolific are the great composers in their lifetimes that a mere handful of them account for most of the works that make up the classical repertoire.

Werner von Braun, who developed the principles of rocket propulsion, failed in school algebra, it is said. Charles Darwin's parents and teachers held out little hope for him. His school reports complained unendingly that he wasn't interested in studying, only in shooting, riding and beetle-collecting. 'You care for nothing but shooting, dogs and rat-catching,' his father once told him, 'and you will be a disgrace to yourself and all your family!' Winston Churchill, a genius in war-time leadership, was an abysmal failure at school.

Marie Curie's schooling, as a basis for her two Nobel Prizes in science, could never have predicted the start of her rocky road to scientific genius. She was brilliant at school, yet no girl in the Poland of her day was permitted by the education authorities even to study science. Without family money, for years Maria worked as a lowly provincial governess, saving her pittance for a few science books and dreaming of Paris University, where the French would allow her to set her feminine foot in a laboratory and begin her studies.

Is there any way of making a genius?

There are parents who would like their child to be a world leader in something – anything. The world is not short of efforts, some of them rather strange. There was, for example, the Repository for Germinal Choice in Pasadena, California, otherwise known as the Nobel Sperm Bank. There, a woman could buy frozen sperm of the finest quality, donated by men with the finest minds. Her required abilities were limited to being able to pay for and bear the child. Her own genes were not seen as part of the equation by the man who set it up. Between 1980 and 1999, women flocked to the powerful freezers. It was a bit (um) seedy, the selection of the sperm donors being partly aimed at stopping the 'wrong' kind of people reproducing. But even Einstein couldn't manage to reproduce his genius in his children. Nobody knows how many of these 'Nobel Bank' babies were born, and as the records were haphazard, hundreds were unknowingly related to each other because some men donated a great deal of sperm. Of the thousands born, the only child measured with an extremely high IQ, rejected everything that his mother had striven so hard for. Instead, he spent his life playing his guitar in the Californian sun while trying to be spiritually a better person. The sperm bank folded.

For all the parents who set out to make their child superior in some way, some will succeed – but an infinitely greater number will fail. The burden on both the children and the rest of the family of being a 'failed' genius is terrible. Roughly, it seems that fathers are dominant in pushing their children into the world of rule-directed subjects like science and chess, and mothers, like Noël Coward's, into the world of the arts.

Lazlo Polgar of Budapest, had three lovely daughters: Judit, Zsuzsa and Zsofia. They spent their childhoods under their father's stern direction, training hard in chess. There was no let-up and little leisure, other than relaxing after international chess matches. By the age of 15, Judit had become the youngest Grandmaster ever, beating Bobby Fischer's record by a month. Zsuzsa became the second-highest ranked female player in the world and Zsofia the sixth. The sisters are the only family in which three siblings have the title of either Grandmaster or International Master.

Zsofia went on to shock the world in 1989, when at 14 she defeated a string of Soviet Grandmasters in Rome and achieved the highest performance rating of any chess player, male or female, in any open tournament in chess history, though she never pulled it off again. Judit became by far the strongest female chess player in history. Father Lazlo was only mediocre, and Klara, their mother, couldn't play at all. Lazlo wrote *How to Raise a Genius*, in which he claimed to be able to make a chess-champion of any child, and attempted to set up an institute for this purpose. Alas, the book was never published and the institute failed. The daughters, after all, shared their father's genes. Like Mozart, the Polgar girls too 'stood on the shoulders' of their father.

Ruth Lawrence was a little girl with a huge capacity for mathematics. She also had a dominant father. He tutored her at home by giving up his job when she was five. Little Ruth rarely played with other children. She came first out of 530 candidates for Oxford University entrance and entered aged 11 to read mathematics. Her father went with her, and the pair became a familiar sight around town, as he directed their tandem bike to lectures which they attended side by side. The other students joked that it was a metaphor for Ruth's lack of freedom. But if the academic pressure on her was intense, so was the media scrutiny. Her starred first-class honours degree at 13 was followed by a swift degree in physics, then a doctorate in mathematics at 17. Research posts at Harvard University, Paris and

Michigan followed – as did her father. In 1997 Ruth split from him and moved to Jerusalem to teach and to research at the Einstein Institute of Mathematics at the Hebrew University. As a Jew, she became Orthodox, married a mathematician and had two children. She is happy and has made it up with her father.

Sufiah Yusof started her maths degree at Oxford, in 2000, at the age of 13. She too had been dominated and taught by her father. But she ran away the day after her final exam. She was found by police but refused to go home, demanding of her father in an e-mail: 'Has it ever crossed your mind that the reason I left home was because I've finally had enough of 15 years of physical and emotional abuse?' Her father claimed she'd been abducted and brain-washed. She refuses to communicate with him. She is now a very happy high-class, high-earning prostitute.

Most universities in the UK have become wary of accepting highly advanced young teenagers as full-time students. Nowadays, every member of staff who comes into contact with a youngster has to be vetted, at some financial cost. Then there is the question of maturity in the subject studied, as well as social maturity. University is not only for learning a subject, but also to enjoy becoming fully adult. Most 18 year olds starting at university do not want to hang around with a 13 year old. Those who manage to be accepted young at university inevitably lose out on the wider education of university experience. A 13 year old can never be a normal university student.

There are so many other things in life that could add to the quality and richness of a youngster's life. Maybe a different high-level school or a day college to continue specialisation, or maybe a school in another country to experience a different kind of life and learning style. There is the Open University, as well as a whole world out there in which to gain experience and learn.

Some grab opportunity

Chance is as much a part of genius as it is of all life. Michael Faraday, for instance, the discoverer of electromagnetic induction, was a poor boy. In about 1804, he was apprenticed to a book-binder, but unlike all the other apprentices, took swift advantage of the literature he was handling to feed his curiosity. He was a genius in the making, and after seven years he was able to move on. He became secretary to Humphry Davy, a famous scientist; chance again opened the way for him to take his learning further, until he became a world famous genius with his own discoveries.

Albert Einstein's boyhood home was cultured, but not more so than thousands of others in Zurich of that time. A gifted child, he had a normal Swiss basic education. Myths about little Albert's school problems are widespread. Yet the truth is very different. His mother, Pauline, wrote in a letter to Albert's grandmother on 1 August 1886, 'Yesterday, Albert received his grades, he was again number one, his report card was brilliant.' He had also been accelerated at school and entered the Zurich Polytechnic a year early. It is strange that so many rumours about Albert's school days refer to him as poor at his school work and some even say he was dyslexic, even with Asperger syndrome. In my considerable reading on his life, which quotes the original sources, there is not a whisper of any scholastic or emotional problems, only political and emotional problems from his teachers.

In spite of Einstein's continually outstanding achievements, no teacher in the Luitpold Gymnasium would mentor him personally in the rigid system of that time. He faced authoritarian teachers who would brook no argument, fellow pupils who passively wrote down what their teachers told them, and years of mind-numbing rote learning. That negative atmosphere could have been exacerbated by his perky self-confidence in his own ideas, and also his being Jewish. But his spirit was strong. It was Einstein himself who turned his humble clerking job at the patent office to his own advantage – by using it to think. With that intellectual freedom, by his early twenties he was on the brink of world leadership in theoretical physics. Thousands of others had experienced the same barriers and opportunities as he had, but Albert Einstein, the genius, overcame his negative environment to change the world.

William Sidis was famous in 1930s America for being the most intelligent child who ever lived, but amounted to very little in the end. He had a distressed childhood under his father's insensitive control, constantly being presented as a media performer. Yet Norbert Wiener, of an equally extraordinary intelligence, and with a similar upbringing, became a genius in mathematics, notably as the founder of cybernetics.

If there is a gap in the hierarchy between giftedness and genius, it could well be filled by what some see as a new brand of child called Indigo, named after the colour of their psychic 'auras'. The children were almost all born in the USA around the time of the 2000 millennium. Lee Carroll and Jan Tober, in *The Indigo Children*, wrote about them as being super-gifted and talented, 'system buster' children. If you are sensitive, they write, their identification is relatively simple: just look into their eyes and see what 'old souls' they have.

The authors recommend the Montessori method of education for the children's needs. This is a child-centred system for young children devised by the Italian doctor, Maria Montessori, around the end of the nineteenth century. It emphasises self-directed activities by the children, and aims to keep the learning environment appropriate to the ability of the child. But I imagine that Maria Montessori, that down-to-earth doctor, would be a stout opponent of the idea that the little ones enjoying her system would be taught to think of themselves as having 'a divine origin and mission'. They are presented as being the next stage in human evolution, possessing paranormal abilities such as telepathy. Fortunately, they have direct contact with heavenly angels for guidance! Strangely, in the ten years since the millennium, none of the Indigo children has been seen to be outstanding in earthly terms.

Intelligence

An exceptionally high intelligence is by far the most popular criterion among teachers, parents, pupils and researchers for defining children as gifted. In its broadest sense, everyday intelligence is an individual's power to cope with his or her personal world. This might be the immediate objective of getting enough to eat, or a more distant one such as passing exams for a far-off future career. A person's intelligence is used to assess the choices available and then work out the most likely effective action in the circumstances.

Intelligence plays a big and very varied part in human life. Prejudices aside, it is a reliable indicator of an individual's life and provides a good indicator of how it will develop further. It has a major role in researching large groups of people and their epidemiology. Long-term studies of big populations show that intelligence is closely correlated with health, both physical and mental, education and crime rate.

Like most things in life, everyday intelligence can be improved with practice. The more frequently you do something, the better you will become at doing it. To a limited extent, measurable intelligence can also be increased by training in the kind of learning that is tapped by intelligence tests, that is, by the study of almost any subject. It may be why the intelligence level of Japanese school children is steadily going up more than that of other nations. They stay at school longer and work harder while they are there. Most people's intelligence could doubtless be used more efficiently and effectively. No-one, though, has yet discovered how to increase intelligence to the extent that slow learners could function even at an average level.

The differences between people's abilities are due to the interaction of heredity (the capacity they are born with) and environment (circumstances before and after birth). Give or take 10 per cent, the currently accepted figure is that about 70 per cent of the difference between people's intelligence is due to what they are born with and the rest to environmental effects. About 50 per cent of personality is inherited. Such information comes from comparing identical twins who have been separated at birth and brought up in different families without any contact with each other.

The proportional effects of heredity and environment, though, are likely to be different for the intellectually gifted. The environment plays a more powerful role for them. If your mind is open to learning, more of it will filter in and be registered in memory. An intelligence test will show up the learning from the environment. So the environmental influence is relatively greater when a child has extra mental power to absorb and make more effective use of information and ideas. It follows that, as brighter children can absorb more and at a higher level, they need nourishment with high-level educational provision if their potential is to be fully developed.

No child prodigies have ever, as children, managed to change the area of their advancement, and by the same token, the geniuses who did change the world were rarely child prodigies. It is rare to find in a child the spark, the psazz, that turns the humdrum writer into a Charles Dickens or the back-row violinist into an Anne-Sophie Mutter, who at 13 played with the Berlin Philharmonic Orchestra. No amount of diligent practice can make the heart of the listener leap. No writing about Shakespeare has ever approached his genius. How dry scholars and critics seem, compared with Shakespeare's own words, such as, 'Shall I compare thee to a summer's day?'

Although potential is present at birth, it will not 'automatically' emerge over the course of time unless the conditions are right. No-one can perform better than their personal genetic inheritance will allow, so there is no such thing as 'overachievement' brought about by 'hot-housing' or pushy parents. A performance can, though, be more polished. Alas, performing at a lower level than one's full potential is all too common. The diminishing of a child's feelings of worth, stereotyping of the gender-role or negative social attitudes can all place limitations on a child's development.

The Flynn effect

A strange new phenomenon has been growing since about 1950, called the 'Flynn Effect' after Professor James Flynn of the University of Otago, New Zealand. In his book *What is Intelligence?*, Flynn describes a year-on-year rise in measured intelligence, about three IQ points a decade. Yet while advanced countries may even be reaching a plateau by now, developing countries have yet to see it at all. Flynn says it's due to modern changes – such as more intellectually demanding work, greater use of information technology and smaller families so that each child gets more attention. For at least a century, youngsters have become much better at manipulating abstract concepts such as hypotheses and categories. Something major is happening in children's heads. It's not so much that natural intelligence is simply going up; the big changes are in the way it is developing and being used.

Certain intelligence tests are best designed to measure this new way of thinking – those which ask testees to match abstract, non-verbal patterns, like the Raven's Progressive Matrices. Yet the old-style IQ test which asks for memorised information is still the most popular, tying in with the school-style learning required for examinations. It's not that our ancestors were more stupid, but that they thought differently. Flynn provides an illuminating example – What do a dog and a rabbit have in common? A century ago, a bright child would have said that you catch rabbits with dogs – a concrete answer. Today, a bright modern child would say they are both mammals – an abstract answer.

This new style of abstract thinking offers a greatly superior capability to think through both theoretical and practical problems. Computers for education and even games can boost the curious child's knowledge and intellectual agility. Just using everyday appliances, such as VCRs, iPods and mobile communications equipment, demands a more abstract type of perception and reasoning, which older generations can find extremely difficult. The outcome is likely to be proportionally more children at the level that we would now call gifted.

This change could even alter the bell-shaped curve which social scientists use to see what is normal and what is unusual – see Figure 1. Most people's intelligence, about 60 per cent of the population, falls into the shaded part contained by the central bulk of the curve. The gifted come

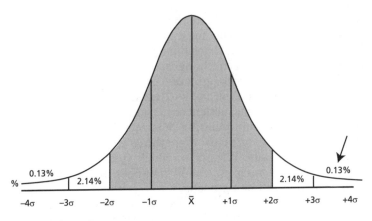

Figure 1 **The bell curve**

in at the right-hand end at the tip of the slow downward curve, indicating relatively fewer of them. Possibly that part will not diminish so gradually from now on.

In my psychology practice of many years, I am seeing increasing numbers of very young and unquestionably highly gifted children. Parents occasionally ask me to see them from about a year old, though I do not accept them until they reach two. The little ones behave naturally in their responses to test questions. This includes drawing with a pencil, spotting similarities and differences in pictures, word games, lining-up geometrical shapes, spotting a missing bit of a picture, and so on. I use the pattern tests which Professor Flynn sees as identifying the new kind of intelligence, but also the older-style intelligence tests which are valuable in assessing different ways of mental working.

I am probably the only person in Britain who tests such young children for gifts and talents, certainly in the numbers I see. It seems to me that since I have seen so many of them, there must be thousands of tiny children, just as capable and eager to learn. The importance of my work with these little ones is to bring attention to them. It is important for education authorities to recognise and make some provision for their learning before they start proper school. I've heard two year olds read fluently and seen them calculate double numbers in their heads. Yet they have three more years or so to wait for proper school, where the teacher will be faced with a child who has been reading fluently for years in a class where others have not.

Brains

Some neurologists claim that the potential for extreme giftedness leading to genius is inborn in the brain's organisation. Budding Einsteins or Beethovens typically have highly dominant right-brain hemispheres. For mathematicians, it's especially correlated with left-handedness. Whereas about 10 per cent of people are left-handed, for the mathematically gifted it's double, at about 20 to 25 per cent. It's the same for engineering. Michelangelo was left-handed and so were Leonardo da Vinci and many other artists and mathematically outstanding people.

There also seems to be a highly significant connection between mathematical gifts and a highly developed ability to make use of visualisation. This means being able to create images in the mind's eye and systematically manipulating them to solve problems. The gifted can make an image of a problem and imagine what it looks like twisted around in space among other images, to judge the best fit to solve a problem.

But nobody is totally dominated by either side of the brain. We use both all the time to a greater or lesser extent, depending on the job in hand. In fact, too much hemispheric dominance can be troublesome because any breakdown in brain connectivity can result in mental deficits. Dyslexia, for example, is thought to come from too much right-hemisphere dominance, which disrupts the connections between the hemispheres.

Each person's brain architecture biases the way things are seen and interpreted. For example, one person may code information about their world on the basis of its appearance and another code it verbally by name. This toing and froing between the dominance of different parts of the brain goes on throughout life.

The curtains close

After all these years, I am certain that to take just one aspect of a child's life, giftedness, as a basis for making decisions which will affect them for the rest of their lives, is to risk their emotional balance, and even their success in life. What are seen as gifts and talents are not only part of the whole person but also part of the society they live in. Quite a few in my study, now approaching middle-age, are still paying for decisions taken wrongly on their behalves in childhood because of that label. Being gifted, whatever the stereotype might be, was so often taken as the youngster's fundamental nature. It informed the world who they were.

'Youth's a stuff will not endure,' as Shakespeare said, and adulthood and responsibility built on childhood foundations last a long time. Too many of my study were hurried along in the school system faster than their natural emotional development, and it showed in their adult insecurity and sense of loss. No other study that I know of has taken such an intimate look at the long-term effects of school acceleration, which is why there is still such a (largely American) push for it for the gifted. We pride ourselves on giving our children the freedom to explore and think and develop at their own pace. Yet some would take that away from young people just because they are gifted.

Journalists and some psychologists cry out constantly about how today's children have no time to stand and stare or be creative, but are ferried daily to out-of-school learning, swimming, tennis, Mandarin, extra homework, chess and so on and so on. It is fashionable scaremongering (at least in the richer parts of the world), exemplified by the journalist Carl Honoré in his book, *Under Pressure: Rescuing Childhood from the Culture of Hyper-parenting*, to be balanced by prescriptions for Ritalin. But then, too much pressure afflicts anyone, child or adult. It is not only the gifted who suffer from it.

There are children who are hot-housed, of course, as they always have been throughout history. In my television series for Channel 4, *Child Genius*, the researchers found some seriously pressured children for me to investigate. One little boy, whom I call Tim, had never managed to find a friend at his primary school. His parents said other children had shunned him because he was too clever, and anyway, school was a waste of his precious time. Instead, they educated him at home, almost entirely via his computer screen for many hours every day. He was under great pressure to please his parents, and he accepted what they said – that he was not interested in other children. As he was an only child, Tim's total friends were his parents and grandparents. He was a sad little fellow, as so many viewers pointed out to me. Where there is such pressure, the loser is the child who fails to learn social skills and the ability to play – the roots of creativity. This is both because there is no time left for leisure and because play is considered a waste of time. Tim's primary play was kicking a football around the garden with his dad and his grandad. I strongly encouraged the family to either get him back into school or to some other place where there were children. They eventually compromised by allowing him to join the Scouts, where he has made some friends and seems happier.

Another of the children in the programmes was Annie, another only child who had almost no time to talk. It took months of negotiation to find the hours needed for filming. Apart from her schoolwork, at which she was doing extremely well, she had her piano lessons and practised for many hours each day. Her concert schedule was heavy. But by her early teenage years, her thoughts were beginning to turn to other ways of being. She considered taking a course in making film, for instance. Both parents of this only child were shocked by her attitude. Their minds were set on her being a concert pianist. Annie has audacity. For the time being, she is contradicting her parents in her teenage slamming-doors way, but will doubtless surprise the world when she is ready.

Poor mental health is part of the popular stereotype of the gifted and talented. When I tell people of my life-long study of the gifted, they often pull long faces to commiserate and tell me that I must have found a lot of distress among them. In fact, the gifted people in this 35-year study had experienced pretty much every aspect of normal life, on a par with the rest of the UK. Only Jeremy (Chapter 2) had suffered from mental illness so severe that it had disrupted his life.

Many others, though, told me of their depression and how as young adults their doctors had put them on anti-depressants, which had been of great help to them. Lewis Wolpert in his popular book *Malignant Sadness*, has talked about his own illness which many have found very helpful. The 2009 figures for clinical depression in the UK show that about one-third of all people have experienced it and taken medication to alleviate the symptoms. It is seen as a growing problem, in that depression is more frequently diagnosed and treated. Suicide is the second cause of death in young people in the United Kingdom, Canada and the USA. But only three of the young people in my study have considered it seriously: one had made an attempt without success, two of their parents had in fact taken their own lives.

I cannot provide a statistical figure of how the mental health of the people in my study compared with the general population because this group was too small. It is evident, though, from much research around the world that the gifted and talented do not suffer from mental health problems any more frequently than the rest of the population. On the contrary, they are usually much better equipped to weather the 'slings and arrows of outrageous fortune', as Hamlet put it. The exceptional strength of the gifted and talented in this study saw them through the effects of sometimes problematic parenting, sudden changes in life, physical disability, constant put-downs, false expectations, not enough money, being made use of for others' advantage, and so on. It was so often their gifts which gave them the extra power to get through. In Andy's case (Chapter 3) his life has actually depended on his extraordinarily high level of intelligence and creativity. Gifts and talents are good for you.

Not one person in my study was diagnosed with autism or Asperger syndrome, though the term was not as popular when they were children as it is now – the diagnosis was not available to them. A few of the solitary boys might have been afflicted, but only one of them had no friends at all. Some parents were concerned that their children did not seem happy in their teens, but others took comfort from that because they saw it as a typical 'sign' of giftedness.

King Soloman's biblical great law of education was to educate each child in accordance with its own way (Proverbs 22: 6). It has yet to be taken up entirely. The education for these gifted youngsters was rarely organised in respect of their special potentials in any field, other than academic learning. Vocational guidance has remained poor. The difficulties of providing for exceptionally high potential, whether unitary or broad-spread, are often too much for an individual school to cope with, despite their best intentions. And so, parents may have to take the promotion of their children's gifts and talents into their own hands. If the parents could not manage it, as I found from time to time, the outcome for the gifted children depended on their own initiatives. Out-of-school education can be valuable when it helps the youngster to focus and experiment with different kinds of learning. But general summer-schools for the gifted can all too often provide no more than extra school in congenial company. Hugely expensive attempts in the UK to provide these have floundered, with no lasting spin-off of new ideas or materials for the gifted.

The idea of what it is to be gifted and talented is so often defined by popular mythology and misunderstood. Being labelled gifted brings different reactions, both from the people around and from those who were labelled, and they are too often down-putting. The excitement of gifted-level discovery is viewed as excessive, their high energy as hyperactivity, their persistence as nagging, their imagination as not paying attention, their passion as being disruptive, their strong emotions and sensitivity as immaturity, and their creativity and self-directedness as oppositional. Because of such interpretations and expectations, some of those labelled gifted resented being categorised in that way, while others gloried in it. Most paid it little attention and got on with their lives.

Mark Twain said, with his usual succinctness, that 'It is differences of opinion that make horse races.' In my view, no amount of practice would make just any child into a world-winner, no more than any horse in the stables would triumph at the Derby. Being born with high-level potential is a privilege and indeed a gift. This does not imply that the recipient will use it well, for either themselves or society. Everyone in this book was born with the potential to be a genius. Alas, too many had to invest energy into emotional problems which put a brake on the intense focus and dedicated labour required to make great strides in any area. Others rose far above their social origins and expectations and reached exceptionally high standards, whether spiritual, like Rachel, the saint, or secular, like Gary who made it big in the financial world.

The depth and insights which have come from this long study have revealed the complexities in the lives of the gifted and talented in their everyday worlds. These individual worlds are as real and important for geniuses as they are for the rest of us. But also, by comparing the gifted growing up with the more average, I have been able to shine light on how the gifted, each in their different ways, faced challenges which only they were likely to encounter. I have interpreted the variety of influences the parents had in their attitudes and actions towards their gifted children. Because of the study's length, I've been able to show how individual reactions to even very early experiences can endure into the lives of these gifted men and women as they enter middle-age.

None of us has the ability to turn the clock back, as much as we would like to edit the past, but I hope that by seeing how others have handled their experiences, this book will demolish some detrimental myths about the gifted and provide understanding of ways to bring about the greatest success and happiness in gifted lives.

Bibliography

Most of the publications by Joan Freeman are on her website: www.joanfreeman.com

Alexander, P. (ed.) (2006) *Collins Complete Works of Shakespeare*, third edition, London: HarperCollins.

Bellow, S. (1976) *Humboldt's Gift*, New York: Viking.

Carroll, L. and Tober, J. (eds) (1999) *The Indigo Children: The New Kids Have Arrived*, Carlsbad, CA: Hay House.

Cornell, D. G. and Grossberg, I. N. (1989) 'Parent use of the term gifted correlates with family environment and child adjustment', *Journal for the Education of the Gifted* 12: 218–230.

Csíkszentmihályi, M. (1990) *Flow: The Psychology of Optimal Experience*, New York: Harper & Row.

Deary, I. J., Whalley, L. J. and Starr, J. M. (2009) *A Lifetime of Intelligence: Follow-up Studies of the Scottish Mental Surveys of 1932 and 1947*, Washington, DC: American Psychological Association.

Dunn, J. and Plomin, R. (1990) *Separate Lives: Why Siblings are so Different*, New York: Basic Books.

Eliot, T. S. (1945/2001) *Four Quartets*, London: Faber.

Ericsson, K. A. (1996) *The Road to Excellence: The Acquisition of Expert Performance in the Arts and Sciences, Sports and Games*, New York: Lawrence Erlbaum.

Eysenck, H. J. (1995) *Genius: The Natural History of Creativity*, Hove: Psychology Press.

Feinstein, J. S. (2006) *The Nature of Creative Development*, Stanford, CA: Stanford University Press.

Flynn, J. R. (2007) *What is Intelligence? Beyond the Flynn Effect*, Cambridge: Cambridge University Press.

Freeman, J. (ed.) (1985) *The Psychology of Gifted Children: Perspectives on Development and Education*, Chichester: Wiley.

Freeman, J. (1991) *Gifted Children Growing Up*, London: Cassell and Portsmouth, NH: Heinemann.

Freeman, J. (1996) *How to Raise a Bright Child: Practical Ways to Encourage Your Child's Talents from 0–5 Years*, London: Vermilion.

Freeman, J. (1998) 'Inborn talent exists', *Behavioral and Brain Sciences* 21 (3): 415.

Freeman, J. (1998) *Educating the Very Able: Current International Research*, London: The Stationery Office.

Freeman, J. (2000) 'Families, the essential context for gifts and talents', in K. A. Heller, F. J. Monks, R. Sternberg and R. Subotnik (eds) *International Handbook of Research and Development of Giftedness and Talent*, Oxford: Pergamon Press, pp. 669–83.

Freeman, J. (2001) *Gifted Children Grown Up*, London: David Fulton Publications and Philadelphia, PA: Taylor & Francis.

Freeman, J. (2002) *Out of School Educational Provision for the Gifted and Talented around the World*, Report for the Department for Education and Skills (UK Government).

Freeman, J. (2003) 'Scientific thinking in gifted children', in P. Csermely and L. Lederman (eds) *Science Education: Talent Recruitment and Public Understanding*, Amsterdam: NATO Scientific Affairs Division, pp. 17–30.

Freeman, J. (2003) 'Gender differences in gifted achievement in Britain and the USA', *Gifted Child Quarterly* 47: 202–11.

Freeman, J. (2004) 'Giftedness and mild neurological disorders', *ECHA News* 18: 6–8.

Freeman, J. (2005) 'Permission to be gifted: how conceptions of giftedness can change lives', in R. Sternberg and J. Davidson (eds) *Conceptions of Giftedness*, second edition, Cambridge: Cambridge University Press, pp. 80–97.

Freeman, J. (2008) 'Morality and giftedness', in T. Balchin, B. Hymer and D. Mathews (eds) *The Routledge International Companion to Gifted Education*, London and New York: Routledge, pp. 141–48.

Freeman, J. (2009) 'Literacy, flexible thinking and underachievement', in D. Montgomery (ed.) *Able, Gifted and Talented Underachievers*, Chichester: Wiley-Blackwell.

Freud, S. (1929) *Civilization and its Discontents*, New York: W.W. Norton.

Frith, U. (2008) *Autism: A Very Short Introduction*, Oxford: Oxford University Press.

Galton, F. (1869) *Hereditary Genius*, London: Macmillan.

Gardner, H. (1983) *Frames of Mind: The Theory of Multiple Intelligence*, New York: Basic Books.

Geake, J. G. (2009) *The Brain at School: Applications of Neuroscience in the Classroom*, London: McGraw-Hill.

Golding, W. (1954) *Lord of the Flies*, London: Faber.

Goleman, D. (1996) *Emotional Intelligence: Why It Can Matter More Than IQ*, New York: Bantam Books.

Goodall, E. (2005) *School's Out: Truancy and Exclusion*, London: New Philanthropy Capital.

Gross, M. U. M. (2004) *Exceptionally Gifted Children*, London: RoutledgeFalmer.

Hartwell, C. (2004) *Chetham's School and Library*, New Haven, CT and London: Yale University Press.

Hedges, L. V. and Nowell, A. (1995) 'Sex differences in mental test scores, variability, and numbers of high-scoring individuals', *Science* 269: 41–45.

Herrnstein, R. J. and Murray, C. (1994) *The Bell Curve: Intelligence and Class Structure in American Life*, New York: Free Press.

Hibbett, A. and Fogelman, K. (1990) 'Future lives of truants: family formation and health related behaviour', *British Journal of Educational Psychology* 60: 171–79.

Holahan, C. K. and Sears, R. R. (1995) *The Gifted Group in Later Maturing*, Stanford, CA: Stanford University Press.

Honoré, C. (2008) *Under Pressure: Rescuing Childhood from the Culture of Hyper-parenting*, Toronto: Knopf Canada.

Horowitz, F., Subotnik, R. and Matthews, D. (eds) (2009) *The Development of Giftedness and Talent across the Lifespan*, Washington, DC: American Psychological Association.

Jensen, A. R. (1969) 'How much can we boost IQ and scholastic attainment?', *Harvard Educational Review* 39: 1–123.

Jensen, A. R., (1973) *Educability and Group Differences*, London: Methuen.

Kafka, F. (1912) www.scribd.com/doc/2223563/eBooktxt-Franz-Kafka-Diaries-1912.

Kushner, D. (2005) *Jonny Magic and the Card Shark Kids: How a Gang of Geeks Beat the Odds and Stormed Las Vegas*, New York: Random House.

Landau, E. (1990) *The Courage to Be Gifted*, Unionville, NY: Trillium Press.

Lee, H. (1996) *Virginia Woolf*, London: Chatto & Windus.

Lewin, K. (1951) *Field Theory in Social Science*, New York: Harper and Row.

Maddox, B. (2003) *Rosalind Franklin: The Dark Lady of DNA*, London: HarperCollins.

McClelland, D. C. (1961) *The Achieving Society*, Princeton, NJ: Van Nostrand.

Meyers, J. (2005) *Married to Genius: A Fascinating Insight into* the Married Lives of Nine Modern Writers, London: Southbank Publishing and North Pomfret, VT: Trafalgar Square Publishing.

Milstein, N. and Volkov, S. (1991) From Russia to the West, London: Barrie and Jenkins.

Montgomery, D. (ed.) (2009) Able, Gifted and Talented Underachievers, second edition, Chichester: Wiley-Blackwell.

Neihart, M. (2002) 'Risk and resilience in gifted children: a conceptual framework', in M. Neihart, S. M. Reis, N. M. Robinson and S. M. Moon (eds) The Social and Emotional Development of Gifted Children: What Do We Know?, Washington, DC: Prufrock Press.

Plomin, R., DeFries, J. C., McClearn, G. E. and McGuff, N. F. (2001) Behavioral Genetics, fourth edition, New York: W. H. Freeman.

Plotz, D. (2005) The Genius Factory: Unraveling the Mysteries of the Nobel Prize Sperm Bank, New York: Simon and Schuster.

Quinn, S. (1995) Marie Curie: A Life, New York: Simon and Schuster.

Radford, J. (1990) Child Prodigies and Exceptional Early Achievers, London: Harvester Wheatsheaf.

Redfield Jamison, K. (1995) An Unquiet Mind: A Memoir of Moods and Madness, New York: Picador.

Richardson, J. (1991) A Life of Picasso. Volume 1: 1881–1906, London: Jonathan Cape.

Rossetti, C. (1862) Goblin Market and Other Poems, London and Cambridge: Macmillan.

Rotter, J. B. (1966) 'Generalised expectancies for internal versus external control of reinforcement', Psychological Monographs, 609.

Rutter, M. (1983) 'School effects on pupil progress: research findings and policy implications', Child Development 54: 1–29.

Simonton, D. K. (1994) Greatness: Who Makes History and Why?, New York: Guilford Press.

Smith, P. D. (2003) Einstein (Life & Times), London: Haus Publishing.

Sontag, S. (1978) Illness as Metaphor, New York: Farrar, Straus & Giroux.

Sternberg, R. J. (1997) Successful Intelligence: How Practical and Creative Intelligence Determine Success in Life, New York: Plume.

Subotnik, R. F. (1993) 'Talent developed: conversations with masters of the arts and sciences', Journal for the Education of the Gifted 16: 3.

Watson, J. (2007) Avoid Boring People, Oxford: Oxford University Press.

Watson, J. D. (1969) *The Double Helix: A Personal Account of the Discovery of the Structure of DNA*, London: Signet.

Winner, E. (1996) *Gifted Children: Myths and Realities*, New York: Basic Books.

Wolpert, L. (2003) *Malignant Sadness: The Anatomy of Depression*, London: Free Press.

Woolf, V. (1929) *A Room of One's Own*, London: Hogarth Press.

Zagorsky, J. L. (2007) 'Do you have to be smart to be rich? The impact of IQ on wealth, income and financial distress', *Intelligence* 35: 489–501.

Zilmer, E. A., Harrower, M., Rizler, B. A. and Archer, R. P. (1995) *The Quest for the Nazi Personality: A Psychological Investigation of Nazi War Criminals*, Hillsdale, NJ: Lawrence Erlbaum.

Zuckerman, H. (1983) 'The scientific elite: Nobel laureates' mutual influences', in R. S. Alec (ed.) *Genius and Eminence: The Social Psychology of Creativity and Exceptional Achievement*, Oxford: Oxford University Press.

Index